Author Unknown

Author Unknown

ON THE TRAIL OF ANONYMOUS

DON FOSTER

HENRY HOLT AND COMPANY | NEW YORK

Henry Holt and Company, LLC
Publishers since 1866
115 West 18th Street
New York, New York 10011

Grateful acknowledgment is made to the following for
permission to reprint previously published material:

"The Boy Who Laughed at Santa Claus" by Ogden Nash. Copyright © 1942
by Little, Brown. Reprinted with permission of Curtis Brown, Ltd.

How the Grinch Stole Christmas by Dr. Seuss. TM and copyright © 1957, renewed
1985 by Dr. Seuss Enterprises, L.P. Reprinted by permission of Random House
Children's Books, a division of Random House, Inc., and by arrangement with
International Creative Management.

Library of Congress Cataloging-in-Publication Data

Foster, Donald W., 1950–
    Author unknown : on the trail of Anonymous / Don Foster.—1st ed.
      p.   cm.
    Includes index.
    ISBN 0-8050-6357-9 (hb)
    1. English language—Style—Research—Methodology. 2. English language—Discourse
analysis—Methodology. 3. Anonymous writings—Research—Methodology. 4. Style,
Literary—Research—Methodology. 5. Authorship—Research—Methodology.
    6. Literary forgeries and mystifications. I. Title.

PE1421 .F59 2000
808'.007'2—dc21   00-063471

Henry Holt books are available for special promotions and
premiums. For details contact: Director, Special Markets.

First Edition 2000

Designed by Kelly S. Too

Printed in the United States of America

10 9 8 7 6 5 4 3 2 1

For my father,
David C. Foster

CONTENTS

Author Unknown

Prologue: On the Trail

JUST LEARNING

> O this learning, what a thing it is!
> —WILLIAM SHAKESPEARE, *THE TAMING OF THE SHREW* 1.2.159

My office is what you would imagine an English professor's office to be, piled high with student papers, and with writings I have studied by poets and playwrights, some still unknown. But intermixed with the literary texts are others by felons, zealots, or nameless resentniks whose identity or actions were of sufficient interest to the press, police, attorneys, or my fellow academics for someone to ask, "Who wrote this thing?" Two locked file cabinets, four drawers deep, are crammed with literary hoaxes, Internet libels, corporate shenanigans, terrorist threats, bogus wills, extortion letters, and anonymous harassments—and that's just the stuff I have had to save.

Some of the texts are well known: *Primary Colors,* the Unabom manifesto and Kaczynski papers, the Lewinsky-Tripp "Talking Points," the Atlanta-Birmingham "Army of God" letters, the JonBenét Ramsey ransom note. Somewhere under all of that is my own work of comparing and analyzing great literature, of teasing out the identifiers that let us know with confidence that a found composition is, indeed, say, a lost Beethoven or, in my case, a lost work of Shakespeare.

The story I have to tell is least of all my own. It is the fulfillment of what most of us would recognize, at first, as clichés. But those clichés have turned out, to my surprise, to be powerful and prophetic, which may account for their endurance: *They can run but not hide. The devil is in the details. We reveal ourselves most when we try to disguise ourselves. We make our destiny. Murder will out.* It is the story of how my work in dusty libraries and forgotten stacks of manuscripts drew me into headline battles I might have done well to avoid—but I have had, at least, the consolation of a front-row seat. It is not about me, but of all the mysteries we will explore, the most preposterous is how I ever came to be involved in the often grim work of police detectives, the FBI, federal prosecutors, and public defenders. If the story I have to tell were fiction, where the truth does not greatly matter and where the blood is not real, the incongruity would be comical: What is this Shakespeare scholar doing at a desk in a police situation room or at a podium at the FBI Academy?

It is a story of how the study of the textual nuances of Shakespearean language propelled me onto the stage of public dramas, some tawdry, others ghastly and brutal. Events of the past few years have called me away from the eloquent lands of Dunsinane and Elsinore, where there prevails a sort of poetic quasi-justice, to investigate texts of terrorism, political intrigue, and murder, and anonymous writings having no other purpose than to obstruct justice—and back again, safely, to the two-dimensional world of literary study. It has been said that Shakespeare soars on poetry and litters the stage with carnage. But this carnage—stabbings, bombings, slander, murder—was real.

WHAT AM I DOING HERE?

Raised on the Good Book, I discovered the Great Books while wandering the globe as a young adult. They came alive to me not in the classroom but in the world itself, where they were written. When my wife, Gwen, and I returned to California in 1977, Gwen enrolled at UC Santa Cruz while I took a teaching post that required no credential and paid $400 a month. It was where I learned about writing, though I was supposed to be teaching it. As director of the Soquel High School Writing Center, I trained the best students (volunteers who received academic credit) to assist the less capable. To visit the Center for help, students had to request a pass from their English teacher. Some came to better their writing skills, others to get out of English class. I did not really know each student by personality, but came to recognize them by their writing, in their problems, or in their brilliance: Brian—smart but can't spell. Ellen—bound to use passive voice. Justin—pronoun reference, parallel construction. Some, like Shakespeare's comic constables, Elbow and Dogberry, made fritters of the English tongue, though native-born. I remember one sophomore who could think of nowhere to go with his book report after his first sentence, which nonetheless sang and resonated with echoes of the ancient Anglo-Saxon: "This book is fuct."

One must eat. I enrolled in San Jose State University for the simple purpose of getting a teaching certificate. Looking through the 1978 catalog's fall offerings, my eye was caught by a graduate course in Shakespeare taught by Professor Scott Hymas. He was a genial, pipe-smoking scholar of the old school, who neither published nor perished but was a damned good teacher, a master, one of the best I've known. Since returning to the States I had spent my days with the expository prose of earnest, hardworking adolescents. My evenings and weekends were now spent with Shakespeare, who gave me back not just the Globe, but the world, in majestic verse and iambic pentameter. I put the real world on a back burner and forgot about it.

KNOCK, KNOCK

I was not looking for Shakespeare in 1984 when I found "A Funeral Elegy" by "W.S.," nor even looking for a good murder mystery—the poem is about a 1612 homicide victim—nor did I immediately recognize the verse as creditable to the greatest writer in the history of the English language. Twelve years later, having connected "W.S." with Shakespeare, I found myself on the front page of the *New York Times,* and hooked by my pants suspenders to a fast-moving train. I had to run fast to keep up. The arcane world of dusty archival libraries suddenly melted into a blur of political intrigue and criminal mayhem. This was not entirely un-Shakespearean in itself, but I was unprepared for the transition from academic discussions of fictional violence and cupidity to being a principal in cases involving corporate fraud or political scandal or homicidal violence.

The methodology I had used to ascertain the provenance of the "Funeral Elegy"—which is academic for Why I Pinned It on Shakespeare—was immediately understood by prosecutors and other probers to be a useful tool for unmasking the identities and hidden hands behind terrorist tracts, blackmail letters, and the like. The scientific analysis of a text—how mind and a hand conspire to commit acts of writing—can reveal features as sharp and telling as anything this side of fingerprints and DNA. Although we disguise our writing voice, it can never be fully masked. After the crime, the words remain. Like fingerprints and DNA.

I should add that another cliché soon to be proved to me was *No good deed goes unpunished.* Early in 1996 when I analyzed the text and concluded that reporter Joe Klein was the "Anonymous" author of *Primary Colors,* his colleagues forgave him for lying to their faces faster than he has me for telling the truth in *New York* magazine. But on the basis of that highly visible display of what was an arcane scholarly method, I have for the past several years been called into service, by press or police, as a gumshoe.

Not even after *Primary Colors* did it occur to me that my field of critical expertise might have application and usefulness outside academia—not until November 1996, when I was asked to examine the writings of a former university professor, Theodore J. Kaczynski. Two months later, with the known writings of the Unabomber sitting on my desk beside known writings by the defendant, I stepped backward through the looking glass and found myself in the real world again for the first time in years. Having entered literary studies in 1978, the same year in which Ted Kaczynski began his bombing crusade, I was now presented with a fresh challenge: to develop a science of literary forensics, to adapt for the courts and, later, for criminal investigations a methodology that was originally intended for the study of anonymous poems, plays, and novels.

DISARMING DEVICES

With unattributed texts—say, an e-mail from a Hotmail.com address, or a pseudonymous letter to the editor, or even a lyric poem—it is often impossible to connect the voice (the persona, the internal "I" of the text) with the name of whoever actually wrote the document. But with most anonymous texts, from Anglo-Saxon lays, to Elizabethan playscripts, to Internet libels, stylistic evidence can take us a lot further than many scholars and detectives have realized. Drawing on the success of my precursors in attributional research, and learning from their mistakes, I have sought to develop reliable methods by which to distinguish one writer's language from another's.

Though it would be interesting to examine the language of identical twins for possible exceptions, I venture to say that no two individuals write exactly the same way, using the same words in the same combinations, or with the same patterns of spelling and punctuation. No two adults in the same family (or corporation or motorcycle gang) have read the same books. No one writes consistently fluent sentences. It is that pattern of difference in each writer's use of language, and the repetition of distinguishing traits, that make it possible for a text analyst to discover the authorship of anonymous, pseudonymous, or forged documents.

Police detectives and literary scholars study different but analogous kinds of evidence. There is the "external" evidence, including personal testimony. External evidence on a bomb or murder weapon may include blood type, fingerprints, or traces of DNA. The corresponding evidence to be gleaned from anonymous writing may include such indicators as place of publication, or postmarks and mailing address. If there is an abundance of external evidence, text analysis may not be required at all. But most homicides and many anonymous documents are the work of people who do not wish to be recognized and who have, in fact, taken pains to efface or to falsify the external evidence.

"Internal evidence" is more difficult for the unknown felon or poet to expunge or conceal, often because the culprit is unable to perceive the difference between his own and someone else's work product. Even when leaving no fingerprints or an explicit signature, bomb builders leave traces of their identity on every device, not just identifiable tool marks, but the type and arrangement of initiator, trigger, fuel, oxidizer, wiring, shrapnel, or packaging, all of which may distinguish one pipe bomb from another, one builder from another—just as the evidence of watermarked paper or typewriter font in an anonymous document may be augmented by matters of page-formatting, punctuation, or vocabulary. In a bomb investigation, the study of component materials may establish where the offender acquired his physical materials. Corresponding study may lead the textual investigator to the sources from which an unknown writer has gathered ideas and phraseology. More broadly, there is the matter of "style," the distinctive way in which individuals select and assemble materials to construct either bombs or pieces of writing.

The police or media investigations for which my assistance is sought typically involve one or more Questioned Documents (QDs), texts of unknown provenance or authorship. I look at language, not penmanship. Too often I've seen myself mentioned as a "handwriting" expert, which I'm not, or as a "computer expert," which is a joke. It has also been reported that I have a crystal-ball computer program: you just feed an anonymous, pseudonymous, or forged text into Don Foster's amazing computer, along with some known writing samples by identified authors, and the software spits out a name: "William Shakespeare," "Ted Kaczynski," "Joe Klein." I wish it were that easy. I don't miss much, but the work is time-consuming, and the time spent is sometimes wasted, producing no more than a "maybe," or no attribution at all.

I have learned a lot in the past few years about criminological applications for linguistic analysis and how to present the evidence to investigative agencies or to the courts. While forensic experts like Henry Lee or Roy Hazelwood look at weapons and bodies, I consider words and punctuation. They do the bullet wounds and bite marks, I do indentation and split infinitives. They do body parts and DNA, I handle the ABC's and parts of speech. Text analysis, whether performed for professional literary studies or for the FBI, is a labor-intensive and stressful business. Apprehensive, I sometimes feel as if the work I've done bears comparison with that of an agent whose job it is to dismantle explosives: if I should get it right, my reward is a sigh of relief. If I make a mistake, however slight, I'd better duck, fast.

WORDS, WORDS, WORDS

When asked, *Who wrote this document?*, I usually begin the inquiry by asking of text databases, *Where else can I find similar language and writing habits?* That question may not lead me to the author, but it's usually good for information about the author's age, religion, education, job, motivation, or ideology. Study of an anonymous text does not always produce a decisive attribution, but I can usually narrow the field of suspects by isolating the geographic, ethnic, socioeconomic, corporate, or professional milieu to which the unknown writer belongs.

Whether for literary or criminal investigation, words are my stock-in-trade. A criminal offender hoping to avoid detection may change his appearance, his job, his place of residence. When questioned, he may change his story. Writers, too, may lie, denying their responsibility for a controversial or profitable or incriminating text. But none of us can easily change our basic vocabulary, our personal store of available words. Human beings, in that respect, are the prisoners of their own language. We write from within a repertoire in which certain thoughts and words and spellings are available to us while others are not.

Some words, of course, are content-specific. Two documents about making salad from "dandelion greens" may have been written by the same person (in this example, Ted Kaczynski), or one writer may have borrowed from another; but if two documents about gardening mention the words "dandelion," "hoe," and "trellis," that may indicate not common authorship or indebtedness but only a shared topic.

Familiar words misused can be helpful indicators as well. If an anonymous document advises its readers, "If at first you don't succeed, *preserve!* because you can't win without *preservance,*" possible authors would include George W. Bush. If another anonymous document speaks of "changing the *unforeseen* and *irreversible* events that may not occur," or applauds "the *bondage* between a mother and child," possible authors would include Dan Quayle. It is not just the words that a writer uses but the way in which those words are used or abused that makes it possible to distinguish one writer from another.

ORTHOGRAPHY AND PUNCTUATION

Whether for literary study or a criminal investigation, I consider the manner in which quotation marks, carets, cross-outs, dashes, and ellipses are written or typed. I look at handwritten symbols, dollar signs, ampersands; at the use or omission of periods with abbreviations and acronyms; at the writer's use of hyphens, commas, periods, colons, semicolons, slashes, spacing, capitalization. No two writers have identical skills and preferences. Shakespeare, writing with a goose quill, punctuated his texts lightly and, by modern standards, incorrectly. Ted Kaczynski, working usually on a manual typewriter, punctuated scrupulously but heavily, often placing unneeded commas before "because" and semicolons before "but." The Atlanta-Birmingham bomber writes "E.T.C." for "etc.," with extra periods. One suspect in the JonBenét Ramsey homicide wrote "etc." in all known writings except in a police exemplar, where "etcetera" was used instead. Solitary offenders who stretch their imaginations to make themselves sound like an "Army of God," or a Luddite "Freedom Club," or a "small foreign faction" typically forget that they may be betrayed not only by their fingerprints but even, sometimes, by their exclamation points!!!!

SPELLING

In the first paragraph of the handwritten "O.J. suicide note," Mr. Simpson writes "recitly" and "promblem," fairly accurate phonological spellings of the way in which he pronounces *recently* and *problem*. In the same paragraph, Simpson attempts to write that it was tough *splitting up* with Nicole, yet they *mutually agreed* that the separation was necessary. Distraught, he actually wrote that it was "tough spitting" with Nicole, and that their breakup was "murtually agresd." Such observations, at the investigative level, can sometimes supply a line of questioning for police detectives or FBI agents working a homicide case, but they have no have value as evidence in court.

Significant spellings in a critical document may include acceptable variants that indicate personal preference (*traveled* or *travelled, email* or *e-mail, ensure* or *insure, skilful* or *skillful*) or regional convention (*catalog* or *catalogue, color* or *colour, sceptic* or *skeptic, theater* or *theatre*). Misspellings may indicate dyslexia, or simple ignorance, or deliberate error.

Scrupulously correct spelling may indicate the author's level of skill, or only that the text has been mediated by an editor or an electronic spell-checker. It's usually easy to spot work that has been proofread by a machine and not by the writer. One of my earliest encounters with an electronic spell-checker came years ago with a student essay on Shakespeare's *Merchant of Venice*. Every time one expected to find mention of Shylock, a "Skylark" appeared, as if Antonio's bond or Portia's famed "mercy" speech were delivered to a bird, or to a Buick. Spell-checked documents may sometimes complicate my work, but the use of such tools can also work to the anonymous writer's disadvantage: uncorrected misspellings and mistaken corrections can help establish which brand of word processor it was that the writer employed to generate the document.

It is not uncommon for the author of a questioned document in a criminal or civil suit to misspell words on purpose. An offender may even mention and misspell his own name as an attempted diversion. It is less easy, except by using a spell-checker, for the writer to catch errors that are not deliberate. The first homicide investigation I ever assisted involved the death of a young woman and her mother-in-law. Scarcely any forensic evidence survived, but there was plenty of textual evidence, anonymous letters posted to police and media. Addressing a newspaper reporter named Rhonda, the unknown offender spelled her name "Rondha," by way of analogy with such Indian names as "Sandhya" or "Purandhri." (American students often make a similar error in reverse, writing "Ghandi" where Mahatma *Gandhi* is intended.)

In another of those anonymous messages, the professed killer wrote, "my friend and i are living the country [*sic*] so you will never find us." The writer of that sentence either omitted a preposition or misspelled the verb. It's either, "my friend and i are living [in] the country so you will never find us" (here in this rural community); or else, "my friend and i are [leaving] the country so you will never find us" (because we'll soon be gone from the U.S.A.). Where should the police look for the fugitive? The manner in which the writing error is emended may influence the entire course of the investigation. In this instance, my attention was already drawn to one Asian suspect, a native of India for whom "will" and "we'll," "living" and "leaving," were near homophones. In this instance, "leaving" was probably intended; in which case, the letter-writer's intended destination might well be India. That's not to say the author was in fact leaving the country, only that he hoped to fool the police detectives into thinking so, and to call off their investigation. Puzzled, the police called me instead.

GRAMMAR

Though I'm an English teacher, as a text analyst I don't care about so-called good grammar. In fact, bad grammar usually makes my job easier. Spelling and punctuation are useful to me only in original writings, but a subject's grammatical slips are useful even in orally transmitted form, such as police or press transcripts of a live interview or polygraph examination. Grammatical evidence may include pronoun errors (case, number, agreement), or consistency and correctness of verb tenses and auxiliary verbs, or the manner of using comparatives and superlatives, almost any repeated and characteristic lapse—or even scrupulously correct grammar, as in the known writings of Ted Kaczynski.

Grammatical as well as spelling and usage errors in the critical documents for my first homicide case indicated that the killer was probably someone for whom American English was a second language. My suspect, like the author of the anonymous letters, had chronic difficulty with the English present perfect (he has gone) and pluperfect (he had gone). The writer's many errors pointed toward a native speaker of Gujarati, a language spoken by more than 100 million people worldwide. In this Sanskrit-based tongue, the pastness of an action is indicated by a word placed at the end of a sentence, e.g., "[Dish broken] *tha*" (Gujarati syntax) for "The dish [has been, had been, was] broken" (English syntax), making it difficult for native speakers of Gujarati to master the English tenses. My prime suspect, like the author of the anonymous documents, had trouble as well with what grammarians call future perfect and conditional mode, and exhibited a mutual uncertainty about when to use the definite article, e.g., "to burn house." The professed killer, I inferred, was influenced by Gujarati, and perhaps even thinking in it, translating as he wrote.

Language and culture may be interrelated. In this case, the victims' house had been burned down with the slain women inside—their bodies immolated, as in the traditional Indian manner of disposing of the dead. Here was one more reason to believe that the writer of the post-offense letters was Indian-born and a speaker of Gujarati. The evidence that I presented with respect to spelling, grammar, diction, and the like is factual material and fully admissible in court. My opinion about what that evidence means, like my opinion of the interrelatedness of the language and the house fire, may not be.

PUTTING WORDS TOGETHER

No two people assemble words or sentences in precisely the same way. Most writers, including professional writers—even, I think, most professors of English or linguistics—are largely oblivious to their own stylistic preferences, giving no conscious thought to the position of their adverbs or to the frequency of their use of passive voice ("he shall be killed" for "we shall kill him"). Few give thought to whether they prefer *shall* or *will* for the future auxiliary, or *that* or *which* or *who* as a personal relative pronoun, or when, or why.

Ted Kaczynski likes to begin sentences with "Anyhow, . . ."; he loves a parenthetical "then": "She ran, then, to open the door. . . ." The author of *Primary Colors* inserts, frequently, a parenthetical adverb where a Valley Girl might, like, y'know, interpolate mall-speak, or a longshoreman, an obscenity. Sentence construction in the anonymous document may be conditioned by such factors as the age, gender, education, or community of the writer, but the writer's syntax will usually remain fairly constant from one type of writing to another, whether it's a college essay, a letter to Mom, or a threat to kill the president. When writing fiction, a journalist cannot suddenly abandon his manner of connecting clauses. A criminal suspect when telling a lie must still use the language that he or she knows, arranged in sentences that he or she is able to construct from within the prisonhouse of his own words. Not even a clever fellow like Ted Kaczynski can escape the cabin of his mind's linguistic system. Give anonymous offenders enough verbal rope and column inches, and they will hang themselves for you, every time.

THE ROAD TO XANADU

It was as a beginning graduate student years ago that I first read *The Road to Xanadu* (1927) by John Livingston Lowes. In this classic study, Lowes investigates writing as a cognitive process in which "hooked atoms" of phrasing and images, acquired through reading, combine to shape a writer's new composition (though without plagiarism or conscious borrowing). Some words and images simply cling like burrs to the reader's brain. Just as a dreamer may pull an object, a phrase, an incident from the day's activities for use in a nocturnal reverie, so may a poet, felon, or other writer pull words, phrases, and images—sometimes by the bucketful—from prior contact with other texts, other writers, other speakers. By Lowes's model, writing (speech, too, for that matter) is not so much *created* as *prompted*. Composition arises from a neurological network of verbal associations in the brain, some transient, some deeply rooted, each and all conditioned by some prior utterance that has been heard or read, and remembered. It is from a range of finite possibilities in the brain's symbolic store that writers assemble their own words and phrasing.

If I have made one important contribution to attributional research, whether in literary studies or criminal investigation, it is the perception that the mind of a writer (poet or felon, no matter which) cannot be understood without first inquiring after the texts, including television, film, and even music CDs, by which that mind has been conditioned. *You are what you read.* When you write, your reading leaves its imprint on the page. By isolating those "hooked atoms" of borrowed material, I am sometimes able, first, to identify the writer's recent (or early but influential) reading, then to identify the anonymous writer himself. If an unknown author has read texts *X, Y,* and *Z,* and a known author in the suspect pool has read those same texts, then that may be useful and admissible evidence, especially if those shared texts are not widely available.

One of my first chores when confronted with a questioned document in a literary or criminal investigation is to take notes on the known or probable sources for those "hooked atoms" of language— words, phrases, metaphors. I then assemble and electronically search large text archives to discover where else that language may appear. From what sources has the unknown author derived ideas, phrasing, slang, or ideology? From an Internet site? from *Soldier of Fortune* magazine? a Clint Eastwood film? Shakespeare? the Bible? If a suspect in a criminal case should happen to remark, "That's when the worm turned," a literary scholar may think, "Aha! An allusion to Shakespeare: 'The smallest worm will turn, being trodden on' "(3 *King Henry VI* 2.2.17). But the suspect may instead be recalling a Chicago Bulls basketball broadcast ("*The Worm turns, he shoots, he scores!*"), or he may be making conscious use of an old proverb, doubly prompted by unconscious recall of the dozens of Dennis Rodman newspaper stories of the past decade headlined *As the Worm Turns* (a title that owes as much to the soap opera *As the World Turns* as to Shakespeare).

Primary Colors contains one instance of the compound "tarmac-hopping," which, during my search for "Anonymous," turned up elsewhere only in the journalism of Joe Klein. The compound "melanin-deprived," in the same novel, showed up elsewhere only in "The Politically Correct 12 Days of Christmas," by "A. Nony Mouse," though *not* in known writings of Joe Klein. In this 1995 Christmas parody, which still circulates on the Internet, my true love on the tenth day sends "Ten *melanin-deprived* testosterone-poisoned scions of the patriarchal ruling class system leaping."[1] I have not been able to identify "A. Nony Mouse"; it may be that "melanin-deprived" is just one of those verbal atoms hooked by Joe Klein for use in *Primary Colors*, from a poem that he did not write but only read. It takes more than one atom to constitute "evidence."

In the search for words, images, and ideas that may have influenced a questioned document, the computer can be a helpful tool, searching billions of words in the time it takes you to read this sentence. The next step for the investigator/scholar is to read those books that were read by the unknown author, to study his magazines, to watch her films. The texts familiar to an unknown author are worth study, not only to locate borrowed phrasing and ideas but to develop an understanding of how the poet or felon *thinks*. Life does imitate art, often in the most perverse and ghastly manner. John Wilkes Booth drew inspiration to shoot Lincoln from Shakespeare's *Julius Caesar*, John W. Hinckley Jr. saw Scorsese's *Taxi Driver* and shot Reagan, and Mark David Chapman, reading Salinger's *Catcher in the Rye*, somehow found cause to kill John Lennon.

What first interested me in Theodore J. Kaczynski was not his manifesto or his bombs but his literary study of the Polish-born author Józef Teodor Konrad Korzeniowski, better known to English and American readers as Joseph Conrad. The Unabomber of the 1980s and 1990s was influenced by the Mad Bomber of the 1950s, and both were influenced (Kaczynski especially) by Joseph Conrad's *Secret Agent,* a novel that features a bomb-building "Professor," the leader of "FP," a hapless band of anarchists. Following Kaczynski's 1996 arrest, Edwin Yoder, in an op-ed piece called "Absurd Links in Unabomber Case," scorned the idea that the Unabom suspect was "inspired" by Conrad's novel.[2] But "inspired" is not far wrong. Unknown to Mr. Yoder, a worn copy of *The Secret Agent* was found in Ted Kaczynski's Montana residence. It was the Unabomber's all-time favorite novel, read more than a dozen times, and the only book, in thirty years of extant correspondence, that Ted Kaczynski ever recommended to his mother.

CASELOAD

In choosing file material for *Author Unknown* that will exemplify my techniques and make good reading, I have had a full dossier to draw on. Generally, it has seemed sensible to select stories that have intrinsic interest. Over the past four years I have worked on criminal as well as civil cases, some of them in the public eye. Most have involved documents—disputed wills, Internet libels, anonymous harassment in the workplace—that must remain confidential. I have excluded authorship problems that are well known but too easily solved, along with complex chronicles with a large cast of characters and pseudonyms that may be too hard to follow. Some famous attributional problems, such as the identity of Bernstein and Woodward's "Deep Throat," are ones that I have left alone because they seem insoluble on the available evidence. Others, such as the Atlanta-Birmingham bombings, have not yet been tried and so I cannot divulge evidence. In *Author Unknown* I will not discuss evidence or reveal undisclosed information about pending cases, not even to correct misinformation published in the press or on the Internet.

The JonBenét Ramsey homicide investigation, a difficult and painful business for everyone associated with it, produced an early bump in my learning curve. In 1997, when moving from tragic denouements to actual homicides, and from Stratford-upon-Avon to Quantico, it was perhaps inevitable that I should make a mistake, and I did. In June 1997, seven months before I was retained by the Boulder Police Department, before any case documents were available to me, I privately speculated with other observers concerning the Ramsey homicide, and actually took an uninvited and (as I would learn) unwelcome initiative to assist John and Patsy Ramsey, by private letter. At the time I knew virtually nothing about "true crime forums" and "online chatrooms," but was directed by others to despicable activity on the Internet by "jameson," an individual whose months-long obsession with the details of the killing of JonBenét—ascribed by jameson to a Colorado University friend of the older Ramsey boy—was too vile in its voyeuristic description to be a prank, too well informed to be madness, too full of seeming relevance to be ignored.

Competent and dedicated detectives, though much maligned in the press, were investigating the slaying of a child. As I later learned, the police had already investigated and dismissed jameson as a "code six wingnut," a phrase I had not heard before but one that I would soon come to appreciate. I regret the mistakes of intruding so quickly. That beginner's mistake impressed upon me a sense of limit when venturing from the safe world of academic debate into the minefield of criminal investigation. In January 1997, when brought onboard by the Boulder police, I took the lesson to heart, started over, and did the best I could, for justice and for JonBenét. Though I am bound by a confidentiality agreement not to discuss the investigation or court proceedings, I do stand by the statements that I have made for the record regarding that case and believe that the truth will eventually prevail.

The stories recounted in my first chapters—of W.S.'s 1612 "Funeral Elegy" and of the bestselling anonymous novel *Primary Colors*—are essentially literary. Notwithstanding the pained outcries of a few Shakespeareans and the pre-confession Joe Klein, no one got hurt. The big question for me was whether the methodology used on Renaissance poems and plays would also work on popular fiction. More specifically, would it work on *Primary Colors*? I believed it would. But when I announced that "Joe Klein wrote *Primary Colors*," Joe Klein, who ought to know, said that he hadn't. Clearly, one advantage of attributing anonymous texts to dead poets is that the dead poet cannot stand up and say, "It's not me, I didn't do it, this is silly."

A second consideration dominating my selection of cases has been a desire to illustrate the curve of my own learning as I moved beyond the sphere of academics to criminal investigation and forensic linguistics. Earlier I mentioned the Unabom case as a wakeup call. To assist Unabom prosecutors, I had to learn the difference between material that was useful at the investigative level and material that was actually admissible in court. I was obliged, for instance, to suppress my own interest in Joseph Conrad, Horacio Quiroga, and sundry other writers in whom Kaczynski and the Unabomber displayed mutual interest because literary texts were not at issue (except those expressly cited in the Unabom manifesto). Returning now to the Unabom documents four years after Ted's arrest, I retrace the Unabomber's steps, following the trail of words that led from Northwestern University to a remote cabin in the Northwest. If that invaluable tip had not come from the Kaczynski family, could the crimes have been solved?

Philip Weiss of the *New York Observer* called the "Talking

Points" author "the Anonymous of 1998," Washington's hottest attributional guessing game. As with *Primary Colors,* "Did you write it?" prompted denials all around. This time, however, more depended on the answer than an author's book royalties. The Independent Prosecutor, Kenneth Starr, took the document headed "points to make in affidavit" as evidence of a White House conspiracy to suborn perjury in the Paula Jones lawsuit. After a seven-month investigation that led to shocking revelations about President Clinton's sexual behavior, Starr quietly settled for the confession of Monica Lewinsky that it was she who wrote the "Talking Points." But she didn't.

In the final two chapters I return to the literary, and to my own town of Poughkeepsie, by way of redwood country and the North Pole. The enigmatic novelist Thomas Pynchon has been suspected of writing under the pseudonym of the West Coast bag lady "Wanda Tinasky." In my search for the true Wanda, I found myself looking, unwillingly, at another murder case, my journey taking me from the wacky to the ghastly. The scene that ends this strange, eventful history is a return to childhood and to the conception of Saint Nicholas, sans sleigh full of toys, sans reindeer, sans pipe, sans twinkling eyes, sans cherry nose. Santa Claus has been coming to town ever since "The Night Before Christmas" transfigured a dour European saint with a birchen rod into a jolly fat man in a red suit. But when Santa comes to my town this year, he'll be coming home.

CHAPTER ONE

Looking into Shakespeare

SHAKESPEARE'S SOILED FISH

What have we here? a man, or a fish? . . .
A fish: he smells like a fish; a very ancient and fish-like smell . . .
— WILLIAM SHAKESPEARE, *THE TEMPEST* 2.2.25

Mark Twain once remarked of Christopher Columbus that "it was wonderful to find America—but it would have been more wonderful to miss it."[1] I sometimes feel that way about "A Funeral Elegy for Master William Peter." When I first stumbled on this unfamiliar poem "by W.S." I was not looking for a lost work by William Shakespeare; I had no thought of sparking a heated literary debate, nor any wish to exasperate old-guard Shakespeareans. My project that afternoon in January 1984 was a modest one. As a graduate student of English literature at the University of California, Santa Barbara, I was investigating a typographical error.

In April 1609, the London stationer Thomas Thorpe published a paperback quarto entitled *Shake-speare's Sonnets*. He included, just inside the front cover, a cryptic salutation printed in all caps and ornamentally punctuated to resemble a lapidary inscription. Describing himself as a "WELL-WISHING ADVENTURER" and signing himself "T.T.," Thorpe wished

TO. THE. ONLIE. BEGETTER. OF.
THESE. INSUING. SONNETS.
Mr. W.H. ALL. HAPPINESSE.
AND. THAT. ETERNITIE.
PROMISED.
BY.
OUR. EVER-LIVING. POET.

Shake-speare's Sonnets, which competed in the marketplace with prose romances, comical ballads, and ribald satires, and even with news stories about convicted witches and congenitally joined twins, did not sell. Marketed for five pence, the seventy-eight-page first edition generated little interest. That was not true of Shakespeare's other publications. *Venus and Adonis,* a long, erotic poem, passed through ten printings in the poet's lifetime, and *The Rape of Lucrece* six, but Shakespeare's Sonnets were rarely reprinted, read, or admired until long after the author of *Hamlet* and *King Lear* had come to be viewed as England's national poet. When Shakespeare's neglected Sonnets were at last resurrected for English readers in the late eighteenth century, the poems were greeted with disdain. Editor George Steevens remarked of the Sonnets in 1793 that "the strongest act of Parliament that could be framed, would fail to compel readers into their service."[2]

Shakespeare's Sonnets seem to have improved with age ("Shall I compare thee to a summer's day? / Thou art more lovely and more temperate . . ."), but few of the poems have inspired as much commentary as that brief preface by their publisher, Thomas Thorpe. Many readers suspect that the all-caps greeting to Mr. W.H. may contain a secret message. This is especially true of "anti-Stratfordians"—individuals who believe that "Shakespeare" is not really Shakespeare but a conspiracy (and a pseudonym for Edward de Vere or Francis

Bacon or Christoper Marlowe or even Queen Elizabeth I). As decoded by amateur sleuths, Thorpe's prefatory wish has been discovered to contain such attributional secrets as "THESE SONNETS ALL BY E. VER." (*These sonnets all by E[dward] Ver[e]*), and "TO VERE HIS EPIGRAM," and "NIL VERO VERIUS" (*Nothing more true than Vere!*). One cryptographer of the Sir Francis Bacon party, by way of a secret decoding formula that I do not fully understand, has uncovered here an anagrammatic message that the Sonnets of Shakespeare are actually the "CYPPHRS" of "BEEKAAN."

The cryptographic approach to this ancient literary conundrum usually entails a minor reshuffling of the letters, or a reliance on unusual spellings like "cypphrs"—gambits that would not be allowed in a Scrabble game much less in Shakespeare scholarship. But, not to put too fine a point on it, professional Shakespeareans have obsessed over Thorpe's message as well. Around the world, library shelves sag beneath the weight of books and articles focused on the literary problem: Who was "W.H."? Was he the beautiful young man to whom most of the Sonnets are addressed? Was he the person from whom Thomas Thorpe obtained manuscript copy? Could W.H. be Shakespeare's literary patron?

Hyder Rollins, one of the great Shakespeare scholars of the twentieth century, observed wearily that Master W.H. "has caused the spilling of more ink, the utterance of more futile words, than almost any other personage or problem . . . and there is not the slightest likelihood that the mystery surrounding his initials will ever be dispelled in a fashion satisfactory to a majority of critics, editors, and commentators."[3] That was in 1944, but it was no easy matter to call off the troops. In 1965 the Canadian scholar Leslie Hotson confessed, "I cannot let the mystery of W.H. alone. In emulation of Sherlock Holmes, I find my thoughts irresistibly drawn to it . . . Since we have nothing to chew upon, small wonder that scepticism pours in its gas of doubt." Hotson imagines his readers "hot for certainties," but he was no more able to provide that certainty than were others.[4]

In the winter of 1983–1984, contemplating a doctoral dissertation on the Sonnets, I had no thought of identifying the elusive Mr. W.H., but I did think I should learn something about the conventions of the age with respect to Renaissance book dedications, epigraphs, and prefatory epistles, about which I knew very little. So I parked myself at a microfilm reader and began to explore what was then a brand-new research tool called "Early English Books, 1475–1640," a microfilm collection of every surviving English book, pamphlet, and single-page broadside printed during this historical period, a resource costing $350,000, available at UCLA. Taking the intercampus shuttle bus, I began making day trips to the UCLA library, to examine microfilm copies of early English books that were not yet available at the Santa Barbara campus.

Inching through reel after reel of book prefaces and dedicatory epistles and title-page blurbs, I had a few surprises. The one point on which all scholars and amateur sleuths had agreed was that William Shakespeare is the "EVER-LIVING POET" who promises us or Mr. W.H. "ETERNITIE." I was not so sure about that. In the sixteenth and seventeenth centuries, the term "ever-living" was applied sometimes to deceased Christians (once, to Chaucer, a dead poet), but reserved usually for God. When poetry was attacked by Puritans as an idle pursuit, its defenders typically replied that the word *poet* (from the Latin *poeta*) means "maker," and that God is himself a poet. This God-is-our-Poet trope appears in at least three books already known to Shakespeare by 1609 if not to Thorpe, including a book published by Shakespeare's fellow playwright Thomas Heywood only four months before *Shake-speare's Sonnets*.[5]

Nor could a human begetter like William Shakespeare deliver on a promise of ETERNITIE, a blessing mentioned in hundreds of Renaissance book prefaces and dedications but referring always to eternal life in heaven, not literary fame, and promised, according to the convention, in Holy Scripture, not in the sugared sonnets of a London playmaker. For English readers of Thorpe's generation, God in heaven was our EVER-LIVING POET ("Author," "Creator"), as opposed to a talented mortal like Mr. Shakespeare, and God was also the only Maker who can truly promise us ETERNITIE.

Who, then, was Mr. W.H., the only begetter of those ensuing 154 Sonnets? According to past scholarship, "W.H." was either the young man eulogized by Shakespeare as "beauty's rose," or he was the person who supplied Thorpe with manuscript copy. Looking around, I found that those two inferences were probably mistaken as well. The "BEGETTER" in Renaissance texts was an absolutely commonplace metaphor referring always to the author. According to this popular convention, translators did not qualify as "begetters" of the literary text—nor did commentators, publishers, patrons, paramours, scribes, inspirers, or suppliers of manuscript copy. Unless Thomas Thorpe was introducing a new twist to seventeenth-century convention, the "ONLIE BEGETTER" of the Sonnets had to be the mortal poet who wrote them.

When I viewed the 1609 epigraph in the light of these historical conventions, Thorpe's wish to the only begetter of Shakespeare's Sonnets seemed no more original or mysterious than the greeting on a Hallmark card: "To Mr. W. H., the sole author of this text, I wish happiness in this life and eternity hereafter, as promised in Holy Scripture by our Maker, the *ever*-living Poet."

But that second initial is wrong. One might suppose, from this front-page salutation, that Shakespeare's Sonnets were actually written by a Mr. William *H.*—fuel for new anti-Stratfordian conspiracy theories—were it not for the fact that Elizabethan printers often made mistakes when reproducing personal initials from manuscript copy. Such misprints occurred most often when the stationer of copyright did not have his own printing press, and paid someone else to do the printing—as Thomas Thorpe did the printer George Eld. Eld's typesetter may have made a mistake, misreading a majuscule *S* for an *H* (letters that can look very much alike in the standard "secretary hand" of the seventeenth century). More probably, he just omitted a letter from Thomas Thorpe's "Mr. W. SH." (Shakespeare's name during his own lifetime was abbreviated "W. SH." on other publications; and Thorpe himself elsewhere signs himself "TH. TH.")

If George Eld had printed "Mr. W. SH.," as was probably intended, Thorpe's meaning would have been obvious from day one. Forests might have been spared. But misprints have been causing trouble for literary scholarship ever since the invention of the printing press. Take F. O. Matthiessen, one of the great scholars and teachers of the twentieth century and a founder of American literary studies. Professor Matthiessen discovered the hard way that early American texts are no more reliable than early English ones. An expert on the fiction of Herman Melville, he once rhapsodized on the oxymoronic qualities of Herman Melville's image of the "soiled fish" in *White Jacket:* "Hardly anyone but Melville could have created the . . . 'soiled fish of the sea.' The *discordia concors,* the unexpected linking of the medium of cleanliness with filth, could only have sprung from an imagination that had apprehended the terrors of the deep, of the immaterial deep as well as the physical. . . ." Matthiessen thought the twisted image of the soiled fish to be "peculiarly Melville's," inimitable.[6]

But Matthiessen was unaware that the author actually wrote "coiled," not "soiled." Far from speaking in oxymorons, Melville was talking about a dead eel. It was not Melville, but the printer of Matthiessen's inaccurate edition of *White Jacket,* who "soiled" that dead, inert fish of the sea—producing a phrase that was aesthetically improved, perhaps, but mistaken—a printshop accident. If the printer had only made it a "boiled fish of the sea," Matthiessen would doubtless have spotted the misprint and saved himself a world of embarrassment.

BY W[ILLIAM] S[HAKESPEARE]

When all shall turn to dust from whence we came
And we low-leveled in a narrow grave,
What can we leave behind us but a name?

                    —W.S., "A FUNERAL ELEGY," LINES 193–95

One puzzle often leads to another. In the course of researching the article on "Master W.H." I encountered "A Funeral Elegy." I have no romantic tale to tell of finding a lost literary Shakespeare poem in the mildewed cellar of a Tudor mansion or in a locked chest sold at auction, nor even of calling up the original printed text from the rare-book archive at the Bodleian Library in Oxford. I first encountered W.S.'s "Funeral Elegy" in Los Angeles while sitting at a microfilm reader.

I had taken the shuttle bus to UCLA to spend yet another day reading early English books. Late in the afternoon, I came to a pamphlet called *A Funerall Elegye,* printed in 1612 by George Eld for Thomas Thorpe, the same duo that had published *Shake-speare's Sonnets* three years before. The publication contained what looked like a typical funeral poem, written for a Devonshire gentleman named William Peter and dedicated to his elder brother John, names that meant nothing to me. The author's initials, W.S., were not unusual. What first startled me was the poet's dedicatory epistle. Signed "W.S.," the 135-word salutation is closely modeled, in structure, length, and phrasing, on Shakespeare's dedication letter in *The Rape of Lucrece,* modeled in turn on the one in *Venus and Adonis.* Having already looked at thousands of book dedications and prefatory epistles, I had not seen another so closely resembling Shakespeare's.

Cranking my way through W.S.'s microfilmed "Funeral Elegy" one frame at a time, I was puzzled further by the poet's frequent echoing of Shakespeare. There was no explicit quotation, but W.S. obviously knew Shakespeare's late plays, and even a few earlier ones, such as *Richard II* (1596), which was revived in the winter of 1611–1612. W.S. predicts, for example, that Peter's death will be sadly lamented:

> such as do **recount that tale of woe,**
> Told by remembrance of the wisest heads,
> Will in the end conclude the matter so,
> As they **will all go weeping to their beds.**
> (*Elegy,* lines 167–70)

—which sounds a lot like Richard II's final speech to his wife just before his assassination:

> let them **tell thee tales**
> **Of woeful** ages long ago betid;
> And ere thou bid good night, to quit their griefs,
> Tell thou **the lamentable tale of me**
> **And send the hearers weeping to their beds.**
> (*Richard II* 5.1.41–45)

W.S. borrowed much of Shakespeare's rare diction, had many of Shakespeare's idiosyncrasies down pat, and had arranged for the poem to be printed by Shakespeare's stationer.

Granted that W.S.'s "Funeral Elegy" was not widely available until 1984 (the year in which I first encountered it on microfilm), I nevertheless thought it odd that the poem had never been discussed, nor even once noted, by Shakespeare scholars. There was a possibility, of course, that "W.S." was a forgery, a hoax, a serious imitation by a Shakespeare wannabe, or just one more "soiled fish," a misprint for some other set of initials. But the "W.S." appeared twice, first on the title page, again as the signatory for the letter of dedication to John Peter. "W.S." was not likely to be a misprint.

It was late in the afternoon. If I didn't hurry, I'd miss the shuttle bus, my only ride home to Santa Barbara. Without reading past line 200, I rewound the film, fed the reel into a microfilm copier, and began printing W.S.'s "Funeral Elegy."

A UCLA student stood beside me, waiting to use the machine. Quickly running out of pocket change, I gave him a dollar, explained that I had a bus to catch, and asked if he would fetch me some dimes from the circulation desk. He was quick, but it was a long poem—ten more coins didn't do it. I gave him another dollar; he brought another ten dimes. Struck by the archaic typeface, he asked me what it was. "An old poem," I replied. " 'A Funeral Elegy.' " Having now a copy of the text, I rewound the film, boxed it, and sprinted for the door. When I reached the parking lot, the punctual bus driver was already pulling away. I chased her down with arms flailing.

I didn't know what I had in my bag, but it looked pretty interesting. On the way home, I read the elegy in snatches, then put it down, then picked it up again, my opinion of its Shakespearean qualities ranging from "Maybe," to "Yes," to "Never in a million years," and back again.

The original 1612 text of the elegy was made difficult to read by erratic punctuation and dozens of typographical errors, the result of George Eld's careless or hasty printing, and by the poet's own difficult, often convoluted, sentence construction. Back home, after transcribing and editing the text from start to finish, I shared it with two of my graduate advisors at UCSB. One thought the elegy was Shakespeare, the other was noncommittal but interested. With their blessing I dropped my proposed dissertation on Shakespeare's Sonnets and chose to write instead about "A Funeral Elegy" by W.S. My goal was not to prove that Shakespeare wrote the poem, but to find out who did. No matter what, it seemed like a good story.

In March 1984 I approached William Sisler, then humanities editor at Oxford University Press, with a book proposal: Here was W.S.'s 1612 "Funeral Elegy," a hitherto unknown poem possibly by Shakespeare. My UCSB advisors assured Mr. Sisler that, in their opinion, this was an important project, and that Donald Foster, though a graduate student, was not daft.

I worried, more than was truly necessary, that other scholars might become interested in W.S.'s elegy before my own investigation was complete. Fearing disclosure, I asked Sisler to sign a contract affirming that the publisher's expert readers would keep this matter top secret, and that there would be no mention of the elegy in any Oxford University Press publication prior to the release of my book, whether or not O.U.P. decided to publish it. Upon receiving that signed contract in April 1984, I submitted my edited text of "A Funeral Elegy" along with a book proposal, a synopsis of some thirty pages.

As always happens with academic submissions, the manuscript was farmed out to a press reader, a scholarly referee and expert reviewer whose task it was to prepare for the editors an anonymous report concerning the merits of publication. Only two weeks after submitting my proposal, I received the anticipated reader's report, a two-page review that was neither enthusiastic nor gentle. I knew from the opening sentence that I was in trouble: "Donald W. Foster is an unfamiliar name to me, but I dare say we'll be hearing more from him. I gather too that he is young; no doubt a plus . . ."

My bemused reader turned thumbs down on my book proposal and urged me to rest up in a convalescent home for overwrought graduate students before writing another word. The author of the report said that the elegy couldn't be taken seriously as a Shakespeare poem (1) because there was insufficient *external* evidence that Shakespeare wrote it, such as a full name on the title page; (2) because authorship cannot be determined by *internal* evidence, such as diction, grammar, and syntax; and (3) because the poem was dull. (" 'W.S.' does not a Shakespeare prove, as Foster has enough wit to realize. . . .")

My anonymous reviewer was an established Shakespeare scholar, no doubt a plus. Had he signed his editorial report, his name would doubtless have been familiar to me. But I was puzzled. If the elegy is not certainly by Shakespeare, this reader seemed to say, why should anyone care who wrote it? The "W.S." problem had seemed to me quite interesting in itself. Why should it have produced so little curiosity in my expert reader? Faced now with rejection of my book proposal, another question arose: Who *was* my anonymous reader?

I thought I knew. While waiting to hear back from Oxford, I had been reading the work of Samuel Schoenbaum, a distinguished Shakespearean whose theoretical position was that you can't tell who wrote what on the basis of internal evidence, and whose work—that opinion, of course, excepted—I admired. The reviewer's criticism and language fell on my boxed ears like a drubbing from Samuel Schoenbaum. Closer study confirmed it. The linguistic habits in my anonymous report, and in Schoenbaum's published scholarship, were indistinguishable one from the other.

Hoping for a second chance, I wrote to Schoenbaum at the University of Maryland. Introducing myself, I said that I disagreed with him concerning the value of internal evidence in the determination of authorship. I mentioned, too, that I had just received a two-page reader's report in which the anonymous author took issue with my interest in a 1612 funeral poem. This anonymous report, I said, might have been done by a *very* good Schoenbaum imitator but was it not possibly written by Mr. Schoenbaum himself? I asked if we might yet discuss this matter of "A Funeral Elegy," as its authorship was not, for me, an unimportant or uninteresting question.

Having his hands full at the time with other matters, Professor Schoenbaum arranged for an English Department secretary at the University of Maryland to reply to my note, confirming my guess that he was indeed my reader while adding that he had nothing further to say on this subject. But there was life in it: Bill Sisler at Oxford University Press offered me the second chance I had hoped for, inviting me to resubmit when the dissertation was finished. If I could turn my interest in W.S.'s elegy into a sensible book, O.U.P. would still be interested.

Having now committed myself to a dissertation on "A Funeral Elegy," I had to learn something about W.S.'s dead friend, William Peter, about whom I knew nothing. Speaking of his friend's untimely death, W.S. laments that "such a man was sadly overthrown / By a hand guided by a cruel heart" (163–64). That sounded like a murder. Scouring library shelves for mention of John or William Peter, I found a confirmation that William Peter, son of Otho Peter of Bowhay, near Exeter, was slain on January 25, 1612 (just nineteen days before "A Funeral Elegy" was registered to be printed in London), by a kinsman named Edward Drew, also of Exeter.

W.S.'s elegy was shaping up as a topic for a criminal as well as an attributional investigation. With funding from the University of California, I packed my bags and flew to England with Gwen and our year-old baby. For three months in the summer of 1984—while lodging in youth hostels, boardinghouses, and campgrounds—I looked under every stone, behind every bush, in search of information about the victim William Peter, his killer Edward Drew, and his elegist W.S. Only two copies survive of the original paperbound quarto of "A Funeral Elegy." Both are at Oxford and each one is sandwiched between other printed pamphlets of the seventeenth century; both are bound in ancient leather volumes. Inspecting the two copies, I found no sign that either copy had ever been examined except by a bookworm, long deceased, that had eaten its way through the Bodleian text. I found no handwritten marginal notations, no "Yours truly, Shakespeare," no smoking gun.

William Peter, I learned, had studied at Exeter College, Oxford, for nine years off and on. Visiting the archives at Exeter College, I was admitted by the college librarian to a musty basement cell without windows, where I examined four-centuries-old registration books containing a record of matriculation, fellowships, disputations, and graduation. To learn when Peter was in residence at the college and when he was absent, I examined the college "Buttery Books," which recorded his charges for food. Five times in those years Peter remained absent for four months or longer, his disappearance coinciding on at least three occasions with visits to Oxford by Shakespeare's dramatic company; but that could easily be coincidental. I found no records directly linking Peter to the London theater.

It was in the Devon Record Office that I found the most interesting material. Until World War II, Exeter had one of the richest archives of testamentary and municipal records in all of England. During the German Blitz thousands of historical documents were destroyed by fire, but many survived, including a fascinating account of the Peter homicide compiled by Exeter's city recorder William Martyn.[7] In a detailed inquest postmortem, begun within hours of Peter's death, Martyn recorded testimony from those who saw and conversed with

Peter on the day he died. It was from the depositions taken by Martyn that I was able to assemble the story of what happened to W.S.'s friend on January 25, 1612.

Yᵉ MURDER OF WILL PETER

> Edward said vnto this Examinant: Brother, be advised, & discover
> by no meanes yoʳ knowledge in this busines . . .
> —WILLIAM MARTYN, DEPOSITION OF JOHN DREW (31 JANUARY 1612)[8]

On January 25, 1612, about ten in the morning, John and Edward Drew of Broadclyst rode forth from their Killerton estate for an afternoon of midwinter revels. John was dressed all in black, his elder brother Edward in a white cloak and white hat. Both men carried swords at their sides. Both were excellent riders. An Irish footman brought up the rear, to watch after the Drews' horses once they reached town.

At the Oxford Inn the Drews alighted for a drink. As they lingered, the host, Giles Geal, offered to sell the elder Drew "a fine-looking pony." Edward, who had a passion for horse-trading, asked to take her for a ride. As he mounted, his brother John asked him where he would ride. Edward answered that he would ride to Will Peter's and "make a quarrel with him about the buying of a horse." Drew, who had been excommunicated from Oxford University for having defrauded a local merchant, had borrowed money for a horse from "old Mr. Halse" when he returned home, and defaulted on that loan as well. Peter had mentioned the problem to Drew's mother, and would pay for the indiscretion.

Edward galloped up the broad road toward the Peter residence, Whipton House, some two miles to the east. When he arrived, a servant opened the gate and let him in. The Peters were seated for lunch. Upon learning that he had a visitor, Master Peter arose and went to the door to greet his wealthy kinsman, Edward Drew, who urged him to ride into Exeter. When Peter and Edward Drew came again to Geal's house, John Drew was gone, but he soon returned to the Oxford Inn, where he found his brother and Will Peter waiting for him over a pot of beer. An hour later, the three companions rode into town to Peter Chapman's place, where they ordered yet another round of drinks. Edward, who admired Will Peter's horse, suggested they make an exchange, but Peter refused to sell. Paying their bill, they rode next to the Bear Inn and proceeded to the cellar, where they called for a quart of canary wine. Alice Drake, the hostess, brought fresh biscuit cakes along with the wine and was about to serve them when Edward Drew "swore a great oath" and said that if she put those two cakes on the table he would throw them to the floor. Peter, evidently embarrassed by his friend's behavior, said, "I will eat a piece of biscuit, for I love it."

Mrs. Drake served one cake, broke it for Peter, and took the other away. But when she returned some few minutes later, Edward Drew began to "talk very wantonly" with her, wherewith, as she said later, she was "not well pleased." Peter again intervened, saying, "Take you no unkindness, for he is an idle gentleman"—at which point Edward arose from his seat and stormed out the door. John rose to follow but returned and sat down when Will Peter asked if they should not first drink up the wine.

The three friends, reuniting, rode next to the Dolphin. Peter stopped in at the Mermaid, across the way, to ask one of the servants there to walk his horse. He then followed the Drews into the Dolphin for another round of drinks. After greeting the host, he went upstairs to one of the large rooms reserved for "persons of quality," where he found Sir Edward Seymour engaged at cards. The three men drank another pot or two of beer and shared some wine with Sir Edward. They stayed at the Dolphin for almost an hour.

It was now well past sunset. As Peter and his two companions rose to leave, Edward Drew noticed a servant building a house of cards. Drew walked up, took a last swig of beer, and spewed it onto the table, knocking down the cards, then left the room laughing. This, apparently, prompted another rebuke from Will Peter.

On their way out, the two men were seen jostling each other on the staircase.

Peter crossed the street to the Mermaid to retrieve his horse while the Drews retrieved theirs. Tipping the servant for walking his horse, Peter mounted and was about to leave when he met an acquaintance, also on horseback. As they chatted by lamplight in the yard of the inn, they were joined by the Drews—who called out for two more pots of beer. When the beer was brought, they drank the first pot together, all four men remaining on horseback. Meanwhile, Edward Drew and Will Peter without speaking crossed their horses a dozen times or more, to prevent each other from leaving—which caused those standing about to suppose there was some "discontentment" between them. At last, Peter turned to go. Leaving the second pot of beer untouched, Edward Drew spurred his horse and followed, and was followed in turn by his brother John.

It was almost seven o'clock and pitch-dark, but the trio galloped through the city at a furious pace, Will Peter in the lead, up High Street, out the East Gate, and past the Oxford Inn, where the afternoon's revels had begun. Witnesses heard Edward call out, "He rideth fast, but I will ride faster, and will give him a nick before he gets home."

Alarmed, John shouted, "No, brother, do not hurt him!" Edward spurred his horse the faster. John quickened his pace but could not keep up. There was just enough light, as Edward caught up with Will Peter near St. Anne's Chapel, for John to see the glint of his brother's drawn sword. Moments later, John heard a crash as Peter and his horse tumbled, Peter being thrown off the causeway into the ditch.

Up the road a stretch, Edward stopped his horse, waited for John to catch up, and said, disingenuously, "I think Will Peter is fallen." Since it was too dark to see, they called Peter's name. No one answered. Not far back, though, near St. Anne's Chapel, a few persons were gathered in the dark by a doorway, one of them holding a lighted candle. John rode near them to investigate while Edward lurked in the shadows.

As bystanders later told the story, neither John nor his brother

Edward did "desire the said candle to look what was become of Will Peter." Instead they rode on toward Peter's residence. Along the way, just before the turning on the causeway near Whipton House, they came upon Peter's horse standing in the road. John suggested that they go back again, to look for their friend. "Did you not see Will Peter," asked Edward, "lying on the ground as you passed by?" John had not. "I did," said Edward. John asked whether they should not help him. Edward replied, "Let him alone!"

Arriving at Whipton House, Edward Drew knocked at the gate with his boot without dismounting. When a servant answered, he saw his master's riderless horse, and Edward Drew alongside. The servant asked where his master was. Drew replied, "He will come by and by." He then turned, spurred his horse, and rode away.

When Edward caught up with his younger brother, the two men rode home in silence to their Killerton estate. In bed after the light was put out, Edward said he wished that Will Peter were not dead, and that if he were not dead, he was perhaps gone back to Sir Edward Seymour at the Dolphin. John asked why he had struck Peter down. Edward snapped, "What is that to you?"—but added, some minutes later, "I pray God Master Peter be well."

Meanwhile, Will Peter's body had been found alongside the causeway and brought into a neighboring house. The commotion lasted most of the night. Peter had been stabbed with such force that the sword's point had been driven through his skull and deeply into his brain. The floor was awash in blood.

In the morning a constable came round to Killerton and arrested Edward Drew. John Drew, thinking it best to accompany the constable, fetched his horse as well. In the orchard before they came away, Edward said to his brother, as if by way of belated revelation, "Methought I saw Will Peter lying on the ground!" John held his peace.

The twenty men who sat on the coroner's jury returned an indictment of "willful murder" against Edward Drew, a hanging crime for which justice was usually swift and severe. Convicted killers were summarily sentenced, then hanged and disemboweled for carnivorous dogs. But gentleman and nobility were often spared these indignities. If wealthy and well connected, a felon could sometimes avoid even the inconvenience of a trial and conviction. That seems to have been the case with Edward Drew. The court of assizes, at which Drew should have been tried, convened quarterly, meeting next in the first week of February (while W.S. was still penning his "Funeral Elegy" for Drew's victim). His trial, however, was deferred until May, by which time he had broken out of jail. According to a Drew family tradition, he fled to Virginia (a popular refuge for English gentlemen in trouble with creditors or the law). The local authorities lacked the budget and manpower to track him down.

So that was the story of William Peter—which left the important questions about the elegy still unanswered. Before leaving Exeter, I visited the family tombs of the Peter and Drew families, inspected their wills and estate records, tracked down the current whereabouts of descendants. One sunny day I traced the steps that William Peter and Edward Drew took on January 25, 1612. Starting from Killerton, with a 1984 tourist map of Exeter in one hand and a 1600 street map in the other, I visited the sites of the Oxford, the Dolphin, and the Mermaid frequented by William Peter and his irascible, bar-hopping kinsman. Taking the afternoon, I stopped for scones and Devonshire clotted cream on the site of the Bear Inn, where Alice Drake fed Will Peter his last biscuit, and ended the day's exploration at the approximate spot where William Peter was stabbed and fell from his horse. The hospitable vicar of Exminster and Mrs. Webber of Bowhay (Peter's ancestral home) treated me to tea and had much information to share about local history. Those social visits were a highlight of the trip, but I had not yet identified "W.S.," and there was still work to be done in other counties.

A search for historical documents took me to the Public Record Office in London, to the British Museum, and eventually to seven county record offices and to more than a dozen university and cathedral libraries. In the course of my research I learned that Drew, Peter, and Shakespeare knew many of the same individuals. Edward Drew had grown up with Shakespeare's colleague Francis Beaumont. A Devonshire friend and neighbor of William Peter, John Ford, wrote for Shakespeare's theater company as early as 1613. Peter's family relations included Thomas Russell, one of Shakespeare's closest friends and the overseer of his will, and Henry Willoughby, another Oxford student associated with Shakespeare.

By the end of the summer, I felt I had garnered all that could be learned of the life of William Peter—none of which proved his association with William Shakespeare, nor, for that matter, with any other known poet whose initials were "W.S." After three months in England I returned to Santa Barbara with reams of notes and photocopied documents—genealogies, postmortems, wills, business dealings, college records, correspondence, circles of acquaintance—but I was no closer than when I left to knowing who wrote "A Funeral Elegy," and I was certainly not so hardy a soul as to ascribe a funeral poem to Shakespeare without hard evidence. Feeling burdened by the amount of work it was taking to investigate who wrote "A Funeral Elegy," I started to wish I had written that dissertation on the Sonnets instead.

WHAT DREADFUL DOLE IS HERE?

> This is a very scurvy tune to sing at a man's funeral . . .
> —WILLIAM SHAKESPEARE, *THE TEMPEST* 2.2.44

The case for Shakespeare's authorship of the elegy would have to depend on evidence more substantial than a web of mutual acquaintance. If the elegy was not by some other W.S., then there should be a unique stylistic match between W.S. and Shakespeare. Back home now, turning to the internal evidence, I found that the language of W.S., though spare in its use of metaphor and wit, registered a close match with Shakespeare's by all accepted measures of attributional evidence. There were routinely quantifiable matters—the frequency of common "function words" (and, but, not, that) and the rate of feminine endings and of enjambment (verse lines that run over into the next without an end-stop or syntactical break). W.S. employed words and usages rarely found outside Shakespeare, and exhibited syntactical idiosyncrasies known to be distinctive to Shakespeare, such as Shakespeare's odd tendency to use *who* with inanimate objects ("book who," "leg who," "bushes through whom"). W.S. evidently knew Shakespeare plays not yet published in 1612, and Shakespeare when writing *Henry VIII* in 1612–1613 seemed to recall W.S.'s "Funeral Elegy." W.S. and Shakespeare shared the same source material, including unpublished manuscripts in the possession of Shakespeare's theatrical company and Ben Jonson's *Sejanus,* one of only two plays *not* by Shakespeare in which Shakespeare is known to have acted. There was far more here than could be explained away by coincidence.

To investigate which of these features might yet be found elsewhere in the literature of the period, I compiled comparative text archives, something never systematically attempted before in this line of work. One cross-sample included all known prose and poetry by all writers with the initials "W.S." active from 1570 to 1630 (Shakespeare lived from 1564 to 1616). A second cross-sample comprised all English memorial verse published during the same period. I read all of it, including some 82,000 lines of forgotten and eminently forgettable poetry, much of it from what might be called the "Dainty Duck" school of seventeenth-century funeral verse, a mode of poetry lampooned in *A Midsummer Night's Dream:* "What dreadful dole is here? / Eyes, do you see? / How can it be? / O dainty duck! O dear." Woebegone poets of Shakespeare's day, writing without satirical intent, typically produced such lines as these by Henry Burton: "What doleful noise is this? What shrieks? What cries? / Listen, mine ears! Look out, my wakeful spies!"[9] Testing contemporaneous funeral poems by time-tested attributional methodologies, I found no poet but one, William Peter's friend W.S., whose vocabulary and sources and prosody exhibited a singularly high correlation with Shakespeare's.

When all was said and done, the internal evidence for Shakespeare's authorship of the Peter elegy looked strong though not incontestable. The text accurately represented Shakespeare's characteristic language and linguistic habits. One big sticking point, however, remained: the poetry. W.S.'s "Funeral Elegy" is a somber affair, undramatic even in its best moments:

> For when the world lies wintered in the storms
> Of fearful consummation, and lays down
> Th' unsteady change of his fantastic forms,
> Expecting ever to be overthrown;
> When the proud height of much affected sin
> Shall ripen to a head, and in that pride
> End in the miseries it did begin
> And fall amidst the glory of his tide;
> Then in a book where every work is writ
> Shall this man's actions be revealed, . . . [10]

A funereal performance, no match for *As You Like It* or *Venus and Adonis,* W.S.'s elegy is longer and much less imaginative than the funeral verses and epitaphs scattered throughout Shakespeare's plays.

Having no axe to grind, I mustered arguments against an attribution to Shakespeare and laid them out in a chapter called "Contrary Evidence." (Years later, more than one academic rascal, hoping to refute Shakespeare's authorship of the elegy, would select material from my "Contrary Evidence" and preface their borrowed objections with the remark, "Even Foster admits that . . .") By August 1985 my dissertation was finished and defended, my Ph.D. complete. I submitted a copy of the book to Oxford University Press, confident that I had set forth a balanced argument, and fully expected a positive review. A month later I received an anonymous reader's report, my second. Thumbs down! Though based now on a book-length typescript, this new review was otherwise much like the first. The elegy couldn't be Shakespeare's, it said, because there was insufficient external evidence; because authorship cannot be determined by internal linguistic evidence; and because the elegy was dull. And if Shakespeare didn't write the elegy, what difference does it make?

I had no inkling who wrote this second report, but by now I had developed some skill in attributional methodology. I thought I could find out. And I needed to try: in a tight academic job market, a nixed book proposal can be a kiss of death. There were a few obvious clues: the use of quotation marks in the five-page document was in the English style, with single quotation marks where an American scholar would use double quotes. The spelling, too, pointed to an English author: "Shakespearian," "skilfully," "scepticism," "analysing," "defence," "rancour." The diction and prose style of my anonymous reader's report were in the comfortable style of an Oxbridge scholar ("an elegy of close on 600 lines"). My reader was fond of adverbs ("emptily pious," "engagingly fluent," "absolutely prove . . ."). Choices in hyphenation included "over-long," "non-dramatic" "title-page." He or she was fussy with semicolons, yet prone to faulty parallel construction.

With a few hours' research in the UCSB library—beginning with English Shakespeare scholars whose work had been published by Oxford University Press—I determined that my author was Stanley Wells, then senior editor of *The New Complete Oxford Shakespeare* (an ongoing project undertaken a decade earlier and scheduled for completion in 1986). Having my academic future at stake and nothing to lose, I wrote to Dr. Wells. I thanked him (a little disingenuously, I confess) for his thoughtful review of "Elegy by W.S."; genuinely praised his extensive contribution to Shakespeare studies; and requested a bibliographic citation: I had been chided in his report for neglecting to mention a study that was not yet published, and I inquired where I might obtain a copy.

A few weeks later I found a letter from Stanley Wells in my UCSB mailbox. Not wishing to be late for my section of freshman English (I was still, at this time, a graduate teaching assistant), I proceeded to my classroom and began my lecture but could not focus on the text at hand. Halfway through the hour, I interrupted myself with the story of my letter to Stanley Wells, and said that the unopened reply was with me at that very moment. I begged the class's indulgence while I paused to open it. My academic future, I said, might depend on its content.

A wag sitting in the back of the classroom provided me with a drumroll on his desktop. With a pounding heart and an audience of nineteen beagle-eyed freshmen, I opened my letter from Dr. Wells, dated 1 October, which began: "Dear Mr. Foster, Thank you for your kind letter—I am surprised that Bill Sisler revealed my identity, but I hope you found the report in some ways helpful. . . ."

I wrote back, explaining to Dr. Wells with imperfectly concealed glee that Mr. Sisler had not been so unprofessional as to reveal anyone's identity. It was by relying on methods employed in "Elegy by W.S.: A Study in Attribution" that I had established Dr. Wells's authorship of that anonymous reader's report. Dr. Wells was not amused. If Mr. Sisler was amused, he did not say so. I was advised to try another press.

Rebuffed by Oxford, I submitted the identical book-length typescript to Harvard University Press. A month later, I received a wonderfully detailed and helpful report, anonymous as always, thirteen pages long, single-spaced, full of useful suggestions. This third referee's report strongly recommended publication. I fell to work at once on the suggested revisions, jubilant that my dissertation would appear under Harvard's imprint. But it was not to be.

SHALL I DIE?

> Shall I die? Shall I fly
> Lovers' baits and deceits, sorrow breeding?
> Shall I fend? Shall I send?
> Shall I shew, and not rue my proceeding?/ . . . /
> To delay, some say,
> In such a case causeth repenting.
>
> —"WILLIAM SHAKESPEARE," FROM AN OXFORD MANUSCRIPT[11]

In November, again on my way to teach a freshman English class at UCSB, I was met in the hallway by Professor Richard Helgerson, who motioned me into his office. My faculty advisors were gathered in a huddle: the editors of the *Oxford Shakespeare*, they said, had issued a press release the day before, to announce their discovery of a lost Shakespeare poem. It was all over the morning news. What did I know about that?

I was confused. Had Wells said something about "A Funeral Elegy"? No, early reports said nothing of the elegy. It was evidently a jingle beginning, "Shall I die? Shall I fly/Lovers' baits and deceits," a seventeenth-century poem preserved in an Oxford manuscript and subscribed "William Shakespeare" (though not in Shakespeare's own hand). The Shakespeare attribution for "Shall I die?" had been endorsed by Samuel Schoenbaum. ("It's a brilliant discovery," said Schoenbaum to the *New York Times*. "I like it.")[12] Other Shakespeareans were following suit.

"Oh, that," I said. The "Shakespeare" attribution for "Shall I die?" had been documented long ago in standard reference works. Curious nonetheless, I had examined and transcribed the text of "Shall I die?" while in Oxford back in 1984 and had used the lyric in my classes at UCSB as an example of bogus Shakespeare. This poem, I said, is not news.

My advisors breathed a sigh of relief, assuring me that I had nothing to worry about, but their optimism was premature. Within twenty-four hours, after a stunned silence in which the entire world absorbed the news of a new "Shakespeare" poem, the academic establishment exploded into raucous laughter. In the weeks that followed, "Shall I die?" was made fodder for jokes from London to Bombay to the Johnny Carson show. "Did you hear that the Oxford editors discovered a new poem by Shakespeare? But now they think they might be wrong. The poem begins, *There once was a man from Nantucket . . .*"

The "Shall I die?" episode illustrates the surprising degree to which scholarship gravitates toward the media rather than vice versa. Shakespeareans generally take interest in the Shakespeare dubia (uncertainly attributed texts) only in brief flashes, on those rare occasions when a debatable attribution appears in the news. There is a tendency to respond more directly to the publicity than to the evidentiary case and to lose interest as soon as the academic community has moved toward evident consensus one way or the other. "Shall I die?" and its Shakespearean attribution, though new to Stanley Wells and Gary Taylor, had long been known to other scholars without generating widespread interest. Neither good nor bad, probably a stage jig, "Shall I die?" was just one of several lyrics ascribed on doubtful grounds to William Shakespeare during the course of the seventeenth century.

Once "Shall I die?" made headlines, it was a different story. Scholarly interest, formerly nonexistent, turned into a feeding frenzy by academic barracuda. Most readers when confronted with "Shall I die? Shall I fly" had the same response to the poem's opening line: "Yes, *please!*" Everyone, it seemed, was eager for this bad "Shakespeare" poem to be buried its full 135 lamely anapestic feet deep, the sooner, the better, and by any means possible. Tainted by its brush with greatness, "Shall I die?" was described, far and wide, as the most ridiculous piece of rubbish produced in the seventeenth century.

With cheeks stung red by this icy blast, Stanley Wells did an about-face, directing all queries to his junior associate, Gary Taylor, the American. Taylor stood his ground, insisting that the attribution should be credited: "I found the literary equivalent of Sleeping Beauty," he quipped, "a nameless, naked poem, awakening from the ancient sheets in which it had lain undisturbed for centuries."[13] But it was Taylor himself who was forced to eat the poisoned apple. English newspaper editors, quickly repenting of their earlier congratulatory headlines, took the lead in dismissing the new lost Shakespeare poem as the product of an American scholar's gullibility. Journalists in the U.K. mocked Taylor's acquired Oxford accent, his taste in poetry, his earring, his well-worn pink sports coat—none of which, of course, had any bearing on the rightness or wrongness of the attribution.

Scholars were even less gracious. Never was a Shakespeare scholar so bethumped, in the public press and at academic cocktail parties, as Gary Taylor. The *Times Literary Supplement* kept the frenzy going with mirthful letters to the editor, but no one presented concrete evidence that the attribution was wrong. Taylor was simply shouted down by a chorus of voices saying that "Shall I die? Shall I fly" was not good enough to have been written by the Bard of Avon.

Knowing that I was about to place myself in Taylor's position—announcing as possibly Shakespeare's a long poem that folks wouldn't like very much—my faculty advisors petitioned UCSB's chancellor for special funding, obtained it, and put me on a plane for Oxford to cobble together an authoritative reply to the claims that Stanley Wells and Gary Taylor had made for "Shall I die?" Unless I could establish for scholars that there are dependable grounds on which to test doubtful Shakespeare attributions, my own dainty duck, which had not yet taken flight, was as good as dead.

On December 12, after checking into a bed-and-breakfast, I walked to the editorial office of *The New Complete Oxford Shakespeare,* intent upon meeting Stanley Wells and Gary Taylor. But Taylor by this time was in seclusion and Dr. Wells was in an Oxford hospital, having surgery on his nose, which inspired his colleagues to make irreverent jokes concerning the perils of sniffing out bad Shakespeare.

Taking copious notes on the "Shall I die?" manuscript, I returned home and wrote a spirited rebuttal to the Wells-Taylor attribution for "Shall I die?" sharpening my points somewhat more than was required for the occasion. The *Times Literary Supplement* and the *New York Times Book Review* jointly published my commentary, *TLS* including my Santa Barbara address on "Cinderella Lane," a spot sounding so full of enchantment that folks could not resist writing me with their good wishes. My mailbox was soon crammed with congratulatory letters and thank-you notes.[14] Many came from persons outside the academy, addressing me as if I had just saved the president. I grew uneasy with the cultural phenomenon to which I had lent myself.

In the meantime, I was left with a still-unpublished, perhaps unpublishable, book-length manuscript on "A Funeral Elegy." Witnessing the mortification at O.U.P. over "Shall I die?" Harvard's editorial board decided it was best to let sleeping doggerel lie. Despite the recommendation of their expert reader, Harvard's editors now returned my typescript to me with their regrets, explaining that Harvard could not risk the prestige and reputation of its University Press by seeming to endorse a doubtful Shakespeare attribution.

This time, it was do or die. Returning with weary steps to the UCSB library, I weeded out suspects one by one and concluded after a few days' study that my anonymous and sympathetic reader for Harvard University Press had to be Gwynne Blakemore Evans, editor of *The Riverside Shakespeare*. Once I was sure of it, I telephoned his office in Cambridge, Massachusetts. When he answered the telephone, I said, "Hello, Professor Evans? My name is Donald Foster—"

"Oh, yes," said Professor Evans.

I said that I believed him to be the anonymous reader of my typescript, "Elegy by W.S.: A Study in Attribution," submitted recently to Harvard University Press. He said, yes, indeed he was. Professor Evans was unaware that the editors at Harvard had overruled him, but he wished me luck with another press. Nothing else could be done. I thanked him for his efforts and hung up, resolved to publish my tiresome dissertation and then to bail on literary attribution.

Submitting my typescript to the University of Delaware Press, I was awarded a contract and, a year later, the Delaware Shakespeare Prize. But the wheels of academic presses turn slowly. While my book was still in production, a bumper crop of new "Shakespeare" discoveries came down the corn chute. Eric Sams published *Shakespeare's Lost Play,* crediting Shakespeare with an anonymous chronicle called *Edmund Ironside.* Mark Dominik believed Shakespeare wrote Thomas Middleton and William Rowley's *The Birth of Merlin.* Peter Levi credited him with a lyric poem beginning, "As this is endless," by William Skipwith.[15] And when Wells and Taylor's *New Complete Oxford Shakespeare* finally appeared in 1986, the volume included not only "Shall I die?" but a dozen additional verses of seemingly undecidable authorship. Most amazingly, when these additional "Shakespeare" poems were gathered and published, they were met with virtual silence, even among the *Oxford Shakespeare*'s most vigorous critics. *Moral:* if you value tranquillity and your own whippable hide, keep your name and your attributions out of the headlines.

SHAKESPEARE'S AMAZING NEW BAD POEM

> The alleged "Shakespeare" elegy: Shall it die or shall it fly? . . . re-
> lentlessly sententious, mind-numbingly mediocre, destabilizingly
> dull-witted . . . a poem that I believe will eventually end up in the
> dust heap of literary history. . . .
>
> —RON ROSENBAUM, *NEW YORK OBSERVER* (24 FEBRUARY 1997)

By this time I had taken up residence in New York and was teaching at Vassar, but I was not sanguine about the prospects for my "Elegy by W.S." Coming on the heels of so many attributional controversies, I was bound to appear like the broom-and-wheelbarrow man at the tail end of a messy parade. Busy with teaching duties, I paid no attention to the publication of Stanley Wells's *New Complete Oxford Shakespeare* until receiving a note from a UCSB friend, who told me to check out page 137 of the editorial commentary, where I would find a paragraph about W.S.'s "Funeral Elegy" under the heading "Works *Excluded* from This Edition" (italics mine):

> *A Funeral Elegy:* An elegy, almost 600 lines long, "In memory of the late Vertuous Maister William Peter of Whipton neere Excester," attributed on the title page to "W.S." . . . It begins "Since Time, and his predestinated end, / Abridg'd the circuit of his hope-full dayes." It seems not to have attracted critical attention, perhaps because it survives in only two copies (both at Oxford); but its style does not encourage us to believe that it could represent a product of Shakespeare's maturity. . . .[16]

This is what is known by Pentagon strategists as "a preemptive strike," and in Anglo-American literary studies as "business as usual." But as a newcomer to the profession I was stunned to see my work being used in this way. The Oxford editors went on to paraphrase an argument I had set out in the 1985 typescript, read by Wells, under my compilation of "Contrary Evidence"—that a literal reading of the elegist's reference to "days of youth" could rule out Shakespeare as the poem's author. When *Elegy by W.S.* finally rolled off a Delaware press, Shakespeareans would be entitled to say, "Oh yes, that poem that Stanley Wells considered and rejected." Having been promised by Bill Sisler's signed contract in 1984 that the elegy would not be mentioned in any O.U.P. text prior to the publication of my book, I had not looked to receive this bullet in the buttock.

"No point in getting upset," I told myself.

"You're too upset," said Gwen.

When I next saw Stanley Wells it was at the April convention of the Shakespeare Association of America. Having slipped out of a dull lecture, I rounded a corner and came upon Dr. Wells in the lobby, all alone, slightly frantic, lifting cushions one after the other from the hotel sofas and chairs, obviously searching for something he had misplaced. I watched this solitary spectacle for a moment, trying to think of the perfect thing to say. Spotting me, Wells stood bolt upright. If I had thought he would appreciate the joke, I'd have said, "Looking for lost Shakespeare poems?" or even, "Need some pocket change?"

By this time, the whole planet had come to view "Shakespeare discoveries" as a phenomenon not unlike Elvis sightings. I was less than optimistic about a congratulatory reception for *Elegy by W.S.: A Study in Attribution*.[17] And indeed, when the book appeared in 1989 it was reviewed without enthusiasm, one reviewer asking idly how such "exemplary methodology" should have led me to such an unsatisfactory conclusion. Shakespeare is a great author, the elegy not so great, and scholars are by nature a careful breed. No one wished to jump up and down on a limb for a text that wasn't certainly Shakespeare's and that added nothing to the poet's reputation, including me. Busy now with an edition of early women writers, I was glad to be done with literary attribution. I had gathered new evidence on the authorship of "A Funeral Elegy," tending to confirm an attribution to Shakespeare, but it could wait until my retirement.

At the April 1989 convention of the Shakespeare Association of

America, held that year in Austin, Texas, a representative of the Associated University Presses was on hand at the New Books exhibit,
with a banner announcing disposition of the Delaware Shakespeare
Prize. On display were copies of my *Elegy by W.S.*, hot off the press
and cooling fast. On the third day of the conference, over lunch, I
was introduced to Richard Abrams, an authority on Shakespeare's last
plays and late style. He expressed surprise at the lack of conference
buzz about the Peter elegy. As a hitherto uncommented trove of
Shakespeare allusion, wasn't the elegy an important text no matter
who wrote it? I shrugged off the apparent indifference with an indif-
ferent remark or two of my own about how the Shakespeare attribution for this undramatic poem was best tested by time and
published debate, not by newspaper headlines and shrill hysterics in
the Letters column of the *Times Literary Supplement*. Abrams had no
trouble with the restrained, unimaginative language throughout the
elegy. In his reading, W.S.'s funeral poem was not so much untheatrical as antitheatrical, further proof of Shakespeare's Prospero-like
turn, at the end of his career, against the conventions of his own art
and artfulness.[18]

It made sense to me that the elegy should be greeted with thoughtful caution—as, say, when volunteers are asked to open a door behind
which awaits either a lottery ticket or a case of leprosy. The recent
string of bruited "Shakespeare" discoveries had left Wells and Taylor,
Sams, Dominik, and Levi and their supporters feeling bruised, and
almost everyone else weary or suspicious. If there should be a vocal
response to an untheatrical or antitheatrical funeral poem by Shakespeare, it promised to be like that of a protective mother upon learning
that her son has kited a check: "My boy would never do something
like that!" But there was already plenty of evidence on the table suggesting that our boy not only would, but did.

LAMENTABLE NEWS

> O, whither tends the lamentable spite
> Of this world's teenful apprehension,
> Which understands all things amiss, . . .
> —WILLIAM SHAKESPEARE, "A FUNERAL ELEGY," LINES 269–71

The media snowball was first set into motion in Chicago, almost imperceptibly, at the December 1995 convention of the Modern Language Association. Every year between Christmas and New Year's, some American city is overrun with twelve to seventeen thousand professors of literature, members of the MLA, each wearing a little name tag and speaking in a lit-crit jargon that falls on the ears of the locals like a foreign tongue. It is at the annual MLA convention that much of the profession's business gets conducted—job interviews, marketing of manuscripts, textbook promotions, editorial board meetings, hobnobbing with old colleagues and classmates, cash bars, adultery, intellectual and political debate. The schedule is packed from dawn to dusk with edifying seminars and important lectures on topics of critical interest. (By "important," I mean "interesting to literary scholars." In my profession, whenever anyone has produced commendable commentary of any kind, we describe it as "important"— "this *important* book on Jacobean cross-dressing," "her *important* essay on alchemy," "his *important* talk on Q1 *Love's Labour's Lost.*")

The convention moves from city to city—but for me, Chicago has always been the most happening place for an MLA convention. It was as a new Ph.D. at the 1985 MLA at Chicago's Hyatt Regency that I first interviewed for teaching jobs (including the Vassar position) amid the swirl of controversy over "Shall I die? Shall I fly." At the 1990 MLA, same city, same hotel, I spent two hours stuck in an oxygen-free elevator with twenty-two other academics, most of whom had something to say (some of which was not grammatically fastidious) and only one emergency telephone on which to say it. At the 1995 convention (same city, same hotel), a correspondent for the *Chicago*

Tribune reported on the MLA's Special Session on "A Funeral Elegy," featuring Richard Abrams, Stephen Booth, Leo Daugherty, Lars Engle, and myself. One scholar in the audience grumbled about a conspiracy afoot to make a silk purse of a sow's ear by stitching Shakespeare's name to a dull funeral poem. But the reporter, who ordinarily wrote for the entertainment section, was sufficiently entertained to write a brief story for the *Trib* comparing "A Funeral Elegy" to a pigskin, and the five speakers to Northwestern's 1995 championship football team. Go, Wildcats! And way to go, you Shakespeare professors![19]

Sunday, January 14, 1996. Arising early as usual, Gwen and I read the Sunday *New York Times* over a cup of coffee. I winced a little at the front-page headline: "A Sleuth Gets His Suspect: Shakespeare."[20] To the man or woman on the street, "literary sleuth" sounds like a cool thing to be, but it's not how a college professor engaged in literary criticism and theory wishes to be identified. With a headline like that one, it was only a matter of time—about two days—before newspaper and magazine photographers started asking me to pose with a Sherlock Holmes hat and a magnifying glass. But the *Times* article, for all that, was well researched, balanced, and accurate, nothing to complain about. Bill Honan, a seasoned reporter, got it right.

The London *Times,* caught flat-footed, followed the next day with a story that described the 578-line elegy as a "sonnet" (which it isn't), written in rhymed "couplets" (which it isn't), found in a lost "manuscript" (which it wasn't), assigned to Shakespeare by computer (which it wasn't), and "homoerotic in tone" (which it isn't, though I wish it *were*—W.S.'s funeral verse is no more erotic than cold cabbage). Interviewed by the *Times,* Peter Levi ("As this is endless") remarked sourly of my methodology that "Such analysis is almost always complete rubbish."[21] Stanley Wells ("Shall I die?") remarked to the *Times,* and to the London *Observer,* and to the BBC and CBC, and to readers of the *Times Literary Supplement,* and to anyone who would listen, that the elegy is too "boring" to be Shakespeare's, and that he had a "gut instinct" that Peter Levi was right about the methodology.

Joseph Sobran, an American anti-Stratfordian, published an article stating that the "Funeral Elegy" was actually written by the Earl of Oxford, many years before William Peter died. An English Shakespearean (responding, perhaps, to the Levi-Wells assessment of my methodology) sent me the transcript of what he said was the fragment of an Elizabethan theatrical manuscript, purchased at auction and of scholarly interest. He hoped that I could examine the text and render an opinion. (I did: it was an elaborate but unconvincing hoax, ca. January 1996). While the first parodies of "A Funeral Elegy" appeared on the Internet, reporters from New York to Melbourne clamored for stories on the "new" Shakespeare poem. The circus parade had begun, not of my own making, but there was no stopping it.

DAMNATION

> Yet, as the devils led away the man, . . . being gone past, Hopeful looked after him, and espied on his back a paper with this inscription, "Wanton professor, and damnable apostate."
>
> —JOHN BUNYAN, *PILGRIM'S PROGRESS*

Of nearly forty new attributions ventured in my book *Elegy by W.S.*, most of them to minor poets, none had been contested. Only one would be contested now: the one getting attention from the press. To propose an addition to the Shakespeare canon is like announcing that you've found a lost Book of the Bible, due for inclusion in future editions. A challenge to the canon of an important writer like God or Shakespeare invites a trial by fire. And history shows that it is usually the attributor who gets burned.

After several years of quiet scholarly pursuits, I suddenly found myself surrounded by a small band of indignant Shakespeareans whooping for my scalp. Small, but fierce. A posse of scholars, mostly British, swore that this stinker would be admitted to the Shakespeare canon only over their dead bodies. Stanley Wells and Peter Levi were followed by Brian Vickers, Richard Proudfoot, and Katherine Duncan-Jones. Wells and Proudfoot identified W.S. as a country parson hired by the Peter family. Successive articles and letters identified him as Simon Wastell the younger, and then Simon Wastell the elder (Brian Vickers), Sir William Strode of Plympton Erle or a kinsman (Katherine Duncan-Jones), then John Ford (Vickers again). Worse, in the pages of *TLS* the attribution was seen as a symptom of moral decay. Vickers put "American" text analysis right up there with feminism, Derrida, and Lacan as a symptom of cultural decline. Duncan-Jones blasted the American professoriate as "irresponsible" in an article that cited scholarly interest in the "Shakespeare" elegy as an indication of all that's wrong with "America's politically correct universities."[22]

None of the alternative attributions turned out as well as the attributors had planned. In May 1997, Dr. Katherine Duncan-Jones announced the "true" author of the elegy: "Not only was it not Shakespeare, it was a man widely regarded as one of the era's worst authors . . . the Rev. William Sclater," a Puritan zealot and polemicist. Promising to the editors of *Shakespeare Studies* her proofs that Sclater-Did-It, Duncan-Jones lamented in a press interview that her discovery came too late for the elegy to be withdrawn from those new American editions of Shakespeare's Complete Works.[23]

In a surprise move a few months later, Dr. Duncan-Jones hauled me onto the deck with her, opining in a letter to *TLS* that I now *supported* her "identification of the true author" (Rev. Sclater). A month after that, as the Sclater ship foundered and sank, Duncan-Jones wrote still another letter to *TLS*, stating that, anyway, her attribution to Sclater was "a suggestion only, not a downright assertion."[24] Duncan-Jones has since taken the position that "A Funeral Elegy" is so tiresome that it doesn't really matter *who* wrote the damned thing, so long as it wasn't Shakespeare. But the discovery that Sclater was a mistake came too late for Duncan-Jones's Sclater-Did-It essay to be withdrawn from the 1997 volume of *Shakespeare Studies*.[25]

While the effort to Save Our Shakespeare occupied these few scholars, my attention was diverted. Only a few days after "A Sleuth Gets His Suspect" appeared in the *New York Times,* Random House released the smash bestseller *Primary Colors* by "Anonymous." The search for Anonymous created a storm that soon dragged me into its vortex as well, pulling me not just from Shakespeare but from the family dinner table. On February 15, 1996, as my two boys were walking home from school, they cut across Vassar's campus and saw an extraordinary sight—a helicopter, ascending like a small spacecraft from the college hockey field. They ran to find Gwen, shouting "Mom, Mom, you're not going to believe this! A *helicopter* just took off from Vassar!"

"I know," sighed Gwen. "Your dad is on it."

CHAPTER TWO

No, Really, He Is Anonymous

LIFE'S CALLING

> The man said, "I was once a fair and flourishing professor,
> ... I once was, as I thought, fair for the Celestial City."
>
> —JOHN BUNYAN'S "PROFESSOR," IN *PILGRIM'S PROGRESS*[1]

The first I ever heard of Poughkeepsie was in the movie *The French Connection,* a 1971 thriller about the heroin trade. The film opens with a street Santa Claus (detective Jimmy "Popeye" Doyle in disguise) chasing down a dope peddler named Willie. After collaring his man in a vacant lot, Doyle slams him against a fence and drills him with rapid-fire questions: "When's the last time you picked your feet, Willie? I've got a man in Poughkeepsie who wants to talk to you. You ever been to Poughkeepsie? Huh? ... You've been to Poughkeepsie, haven't ya! ... You sat on the edge of the bed, didn't ya! Ya took off your shoes, you put your finger between your toes, and ya picked your feet, didn't ya! Now, *say* it!"

Squirming in the detective's neck-hold, Willie squeals out, "Yes, yes!"—to which Doyle replies, "I'm gonna bust your ass for those three bags, and then I'm gonna nail you for pickin' your feet in Pough-keepsie!"[2]

January 28, 1986. Poughkeepsie (*puh-KIP-see*), New York, a Hudson River town seventy-five miles north of the Big Apple, is the home of Vassar College. I won't forget my first visit. Having completed my Ph.D. at the University of California, I was making the rounds of various East Coast universities and colleges at which I had been offered a job or been asked for an on-campus interview. On the morning of my flight, just before I left Santa Barbara, temperatures in the Northeast were in the 40s and raining, not bad. But by the time I landed in Newark, the mercury had plummeted to something-something below zero. The roads were sheeted over with ice.

Driving northward to Poughkeepsie after visits to Princeton and Rutgers, I turned on the radio of my little yellow rental car and was stunned by the first words over the air: "At 11:39 this morning, shortly after what looked like a perfect launch, the space shuttle *Challenger* exploded in midair. All seven persons on board are presumed dead." I reached for the volume control as if I had misheard the news. At that precise moment, with my attention still fixed on the radio dial, my right front wheel was jolted by a road hazard that flattened the tire and bent the rim. For a brief second, I had the weird sensation that I had just collided with a piece of the space shuttle.

Coasting noisily to the shoulder of I-87, I parked, dug out the tire iron, jack, and spare, and fell to work, having brought nothing warmer than a professorish-looking sports coat. No gloves, no hat, no sweater, no long underwear. It was a miserable business, changing that tire. By the time I reached Poughkeepsie, with grimy hands, chattering teeth, and a hacking cough, I wanted to go home. If I needed to pick my feet I would do it in Santa Barbara. But when I passed through the limestone arch of Vassar's main gate and saw the campus for the first time, I fell in love with its spacious lawns, ancient trees, ivy-covered halls, hiking and biking trails, environmental preserve, and nine-hole golf course. Twenty-two hundred students: doing the math, that came out to roughly two students per acre, with one instructor for every ten undergraduates. Vassar seemed like a good place to settle into the quiet, idyllic life of a Shakespeare professor. Seven months later, in August, I drove cross-continent with Gwen and our two boys, Blake (then aged three) and Eric (still a baby), to begin our new life in Poughkeepsie.

Vassar has a bustling-enough campus for eleven months of the year, but from late December through mid-January, with the students gone, it's a no-man's-land. Faculty members over break attend academic conferences, or conduct research in London or Paris or the Bahamas, or else just hunker down at home to prepare for the new semester. Deer wander the grounds undisturbed. A few late-traveling Canada geese hang out by Sunset Lake, ignoring joggers but taking wing when a fox draws near. Nothing much happens. Even the library shuts down.

January 13, 1996. One Saturday about halfway through my tenth year at Vassar, and three weeks into winter break, I puttered about the house doing I can't remember just what. About ten P.M., the telephone rang. My caller identified himself as David Reiter of ABC News.

"Professor Foster? Did you know that you are *front-page news* in tomorrow's *New York Times*?"

I knew there was to be an article, but no, I didn't expect it to be on page one—and the story wasn't about me, really, it was about "A Funeral Elegy."

"Yes, but it was you who found the poem. You researched the thing. It took what?—a dozen years for the poem to be authenticated as a lost work by William Shakespeare . . ."

"Well . . . ," I said.

". . . and we want to do an exclusive interview with you for ABC *World News Tonight.*"

I hesitated.

"We can send a film crew to Poughkeepsie first thing in the morning. An ABC correspondent, probably Catherine Crier, will conduct the interview. It shouldn't take you more than an hour or two, and you can be on your way."

The story as told by ABC News would last for a minute, and be well told. The attention would be good for Vassar, good for Shakespeare studies, and probably wouldn't hurt me, either.

But with only a week left in which to prepare for the new semester, I could see that the remainder of my break would not go as planned.

APPREHENDING ANONYMOUS

"Code yellow."
"I'll find him, hold on. He ain't doing anything that important."
—ANONYMOUS, *PRIMARY COLORS*

I had no inkling that media interest in "A Funeral Elegy" would lead me from poets to killers, or from Stratford-upon-Avon to Quantico, nor did I have time to think about it. As the elegy became news in New York, then in London and around the world, my home and office telephones rang more or less constantly for more than a month, making it difficult to type a complete sentence, tie both shoes, or brush my teeth. Flossing was out of the question. The telephone was like a colicky baby—every time I tried to put it down for a rest, it erupted again into noise. Most of the folks calling had not read the poem, but had heard that it was pretty homoerotic.

Two weeks after the *Times* story, phones were still ringing but a new query was interjected: it was not always "May we interview you about the Shakespeare poem?" (on Australian or Brazilian or Canadian or Danish or Zimbabwean television) nor even "Can you fax us a copy?" but rather, "Who wrote *Primary Colors*?" Having gone for days without reading a paper, without so much as eating a meal sitting down, I knew nothing of "Anonymous," or of *Primary Colors*, a moderately funny novel modeled on Robert Penn Warren's *All the King's Men* but satirizing Bill Clinton's 1992 presidential campaign.

The pseudonym "Anonymous" was a stroke of genius. Released on January 22 with a first printing of just 62,000 copies, *Primary Colors* rocketed to the top of bestseller lists and stayed there, promising not to come down again until someone could figure out who wrote it. Most Beltway journalists suspected that it was written by one of their own stripe. At cocktail parties and press conferences, reporters interrogated one another with suspicion. Challenged by the White House to find Anonymous and to blow the author's cover, the *New York Times* and the *Washington Post* pulled out all the stops, each paper assigning an investigative team to solve this semiliterary problem. Nominations from the press included Sidney Blumenthal and Michael Kelly, political writers for *The New Yorker;* humorist Christopher Buckley; Lisa Grunwald, novelist and sister of former Clinton aide Mandy Grunwald; the *Times's* Maureen Dowd; *New Republic* columnist Michael Lewis; Erik Tarloff, screenwriter and husband of Clinton advisor Laura Tyson; the *Doonesbury* cartoonist, Garry Trudeau; and some fifty others. Noting that the novel's fictional narrator is black, some commentators looked for a black author, with Christopher Buckley voting for Toni Morrison, and Princeton's Elaine Showalter nominating the Harvard scholar Henry Louis Gates.

Newsweek's Mark Miller observed that the author of *Primary Colors* "had both real inside knowledge and a dead-on eye. . . . Clinton ('Jack Stanton') is captured perfectly." White House senior aide George Stephanopoulos, Miller reported, was "obsessed with the book" and "startled by how his character's thoughts . . . mirror his own." Miller, who spent a year inside the Clinton camp and witnessed many of the same scenes that Anonymous presents as fiction, wondered aloud, "How did the author know?"[3] Of course, the real question, at least the one that was obsessing Stephanopoulos and his colleagues as well as every journalist who had ever written about the Clintons, was *How can we know the author*?

Someone got the idea, "Let's call that Vassar Shakespeare professor and see what he thinks!" Pretty soon, everyone was doing it. Prompted by the recent story in the *New York Times* called "A Sleuth Gets His Suspect: Shakespeare," reporters and editors wondered if literary scholarship could do the trick for *Primary Colors*. So, while still fielding calls about "A Funeral Elegy" from *L'Express* and *L'Espresso* magazines and the *Times of India* and the Shakespeare Society of Japan, and from one sweet little old lady from Massachusetts who called daily, I was invited to identify Anonymous for the press— a prospect that seemed, to me, about as appealing as prostate trouble. But Ariel Kaminer, a staff writer for *New York* magazine, was persistent.

"Sorry, Ms. Kaminer, I can't help you."

"Why not? This is a *really* big story."

"There's a good reason why not. I have classes to prepare."

"So you don't think you can identify Anonymous?"

"I didn't say that."

"Why can't you?"

"Maybe I can, I dunno."

"What would you need?"

"Well, first off, I'd need a machine-readable text of the novel so that I can do electronic searches for words, phrases, collocations."

Kaminer said: "No prob. I can get you that. What else?"

"There are millions of people in this country, most of whom know how to write. I would need someplace to begin, a list of suspects to investigate."

"Got it! The *Washington Post* has already published a list of thirty-five suspects."

"How many of those thirty-five have already denied writing the novel?"

"All of them. But—"

"Forget it."

"But we've got a few more names, and I thought you could add to the list as other names turn up."

"Look, I haven't even *read* this book. Sorry."

"We'll send you a copy. Tell us what you think."

It seemed like an interesting problem. If I failed to discover which of 270 million Americans wrote the novel, I'd be none the worse for having tried; on the other hand, a success would demonstrate that the methodology can be effective not only on Renaissance texts but for virtually any English text—and this, I thought, would have some academic value by providing a touchstone with respect to the new "Shakespeare" poem. Ever since that article in the London *Times,* when reporters called, the first question was usually "Does the elegy truly show that Shakespeare was a homosexual?" Something was needed to regain perspective and to focus interest on the methodology. Of course, if I named the author of *Primary Colors* and got it *wrong,* that would be not so good. I may as well put the "Shakespeare" elegy into a blender and eat it for breakfast, and tell Dr. Wells & Co. to save their bullets.

The next day, by FedEx, I received from *New York* a hard copy and electronic text of *Primary Colors,* with a list of the *Post*'s thirty-five nominees for Anonymous, all of whom had declined the nomination; together with blocks of electronic text from what were then the leading suspects; also, a ream of printed articles, interviews, and op-ed pieces; and a promise of more writing samples yet to come.

With a shortlist of only thirty-five suspects, finding Anonymous promised to be a pretty easy assignment, but there was no guarantee that the actual author was numbered among the *Post*'s prime suspects. To get started, I flipped through *Primary Colors,* flagging four hundred of Anonymous's least common words (*ablaze, abruptly, abyss . . . zipped up, zombie, zoned in*), then began searching the suspects' writing samples for an author whose vocabulary closely matched that of *Primary Colors.*

The results were discouraging: per ten thousand words of text, none of the candidates registered a singularly high usage of the flagged words. Having little else to go on, I asked *New York* for longer cross-samples, and for new candidates. The editors sent me Thomas Caplan, a novelist and a college roommate of Clinton's; *Newsweek* writers Peter Goldman and Mark Miller; syndicated columnist Molly Ivins, rumored to be former Clinton speechwriter Paul Begala's ghost; *Times* reporter Elizabeth Kolbert; and novelist

Marylouise Oates, conveniently married to Democratic consultant Bob Shrum. Scanning every file for a high concentration of *Primary Colors* vocabulary, my net remained empty. This computer-assisted search failed to deliver a single plausible suspect. It looked as if I would have to read the book.

Having scheduled a talk that Friday at UCLA, I had no time to read *Primary Colors,* but I dropped the novel into my carry-on bag, just in case. I read it on the plane.

When the announcement came to prepare for landing at LAX, seats upright, tray-tables stowed, all electronic devices turned off, our bags stored safely beneath the seat in front of us, I was on the last chapter. "So was it a good book?" asked the person sitting next to me, as I put it away. "Oh, I dunno," I said, truthfully. When reading a text of unknown or disputed authorship, I have developed an odd way of reading, by which my brain records ideas and words and punctuation from the printed page while the story goes zipping right past me, unattended. Having finished *Primary Colors,* I had a good fix on the text's orthography, diction, sentence construction, source material, political ideology, and points of anxiety; and I had inferred quite a bit about the author's psyche. I just didn't know the *story*—that would have to wait for a second read-through on the flight home.

Anonymous, like any anonymous writer, revealed a good deal about his way of viewing the world, and about himself, and about his purpose for writing. If the novel was an insider's story of the 1992 Clinton campaign, it was also a tale of disillusionment, of resentment. As depicted in *Primary Colors,* the Clinton/Stanton figure makes you mad. In fact, someone should punch him. Actually, someone does punch him: the Hillary/Susan figure smacks him right in the kisser on page 122. This from a woman who could "come after your scrawny little ding-a-ling with a pair of garden shears."[4] The Clinton/Stanton figure deserves it. Hillary/Susan then goes after the the novel's scrawny narrator, Henry Burton (not to be confused with the Renaissance elegist of that name), but this time it's for love, not for attempted emasculation, and for a sweet hour's passionate revenge on her philandering husband. Where, then, does the "inside story" of Clinton's marriage and political campaign veer off into a smear by innuendo? Posing as a "tell-all" exposé, the novel felt to me like an assault on the Clintons by someone who somehow felt betrayed.

The author also seemed to have some issues about blacks and women. In *Primary Colors* there are good blacks and bad blacks. Campaign aide Henry Burton, narrator of the story and a stand-in for both Stephanopoulos and the author, is a good black with deep ambivalence toward Jack Stanton, his admiration mixed with anger and disgust. The book opens with Henry's observation that Governor Stanton "was a big fellow, looking seriously pale on the streets of Harlem in deep summer. I am small and not so dark, not very threatening to Caucasians; I do not strut my stuff." One moral of *Primary Colors* is that liberal politicians are bad news for good blacks. In the final chapter, overcome with dyspepsia, Henry vomits, then rejects Stanton in a wave of moral disgust.

The two kinds of females in *Primary Colors* are bitches and bimbos. Jack Stanton is married to one kind while chasing the other. But here, too, Henry is ambivalent. Apart from his one-night stand with Susan, Henry has only a brief fling with the vaguely asexual Daisy. She pulls off her shirt and asks for sex: " 'I'm practically a guy . . . up top,' she said. She did have a nice—pert, sexy in a businesslike way— bottom. 'Okay,' " says Henry—though he finds most women unappetizing, or frightening. For example, there's Libby, a 250-pound women's libber, who points guns at men's crotches and threatens to blast away their genitals, just like Hillary/Susan with her garden shears.

Though Henry and his creator, Anonymous, both love to use the F-word whenever possible, they both have trouble imagining anyone actually performing it. The sexual liaisons between Henry and Susan and Henry and Daisy are so totally unconvincing that Henry himself can hardly believe they happened. Together with campaign director Richard Jemmons/James Carville (who "looks like he was sired during the love scene from *Deliverance*"), Henry finds candidate

Stanton's weakness for a "hairslut" utterly perplexing. The two men lie on Henry's hotel bed, chuckling over Stanton's weakness for Cashmere McLeod, who looks "hilarious: truck-stop pinups." Stanton's bimbo "had breasts, that was clear enough. But the rest of her body remained a mystery, as did the quality of her mind." The suggestion that *Primary Colors* was written by a woman—novelist Lisa Grunwald, *New York Times* columnist Maureen Dowd, or indeed any woman—was perhaps thinkable, but not likely.

Anonymous exhibits a lot of journalistic inside-baseball, and I noticed that the novelist seemed an avid fan of one side: in the world of *Primary Colors,* no one can get accurate and fast-breaking news except from the *Washington Post* and its affiliates. On the road, in piney-woods country, Henry must have the *Post* faxed to him or else settle for the "thin, unsatisfying" *New York Times*. Henry opines that the *Times*'s "speculative articles" seem "dense." One *Times* reporter is "better known for oenophilia than initiative"; another suffers from Ivy League envy; another "always tapped the purest—if not quite the freshest—vein of conventional wisdom. And the *Post*? "The *Post* was always a beat ahead of the others when it came to nuance and minutiae."

As represented by Anonymous in *Primary Colors,* no journalistic enterprise is more potent—or more to be feared by liberals—than those damned conservative pundits who write for *Newsweek* (which the Washington Post Company owns). At one point, Henry whines that *Newsweek* "buried us with a derisive piece called 'The Anatomy of a Flameout.' " Just two words from George Will are enough to sink Stanton in the opinion polls; one piercing question from Will leaves the Stanton team "badly damaged." Meanwhile, *Newsweek*'s rival, *Time,* harmlessly collects dust in Momma Stanton's "magazine rack, next to the La-Z-Boy," together with *The Smithsonian*.

Such observations as these are what literary scholars would call "internal biographical evidence." From such evidence one might have guessed that the author of *Primary Colors* was white, middle-aged, male, ambivalent about women; someone loyal to *Newsweek* or the

Post; someone who wished to tutor blacks in what's good for them. But the author's puffing for *Newsweek* could be a false lead planted to put canny readers off the scent. And Henry's persistent difficulties with heterosexual desire might be read as an anti-gay joke, or even an anti-black one: throughout *Primary Colors,* Henry's tamed blackness is the visible sign of defective manhood: " 'Where are you staying?' she whispered, her lips and a tiny hint of tongue on my ear. 'Uhhh . . . L'Afrique,' I said." (Pronounced aloud: *La Freak.*) " 'That's the faggot hotel,' she said, pulling back." Anonymous might share nothing of Henry's sexual ambivalence. He might be a heterosexual male suffering from deep homosexual panic. I noted that *Primary Colors* was dedicated to the author's anonymous partner ("For my spouse, living proof that flamboyance and discretion are not mutually exclusive"), which could point the reader away from—or toward—a gay author. But his political persuasions were clear enough.

PRIMARY CULPRIT

> I began to feel different when I—or rather, Anonymous, sat down to write. . . . Finally, I asked my agent: "Have I changed over the course of this? Am I becoming Anonymous? Am I different now?"
> —ANONYMOUS, *"NO, REALLY, I AM ANONYMOUS"* (19 MAY 1996)[5]

While I was at UCLA giving that guest lecture, *New York* delivered, by e-mail, a virtual library to my office computer—a greatly expanded electronic archive of writings by possible suspects. All of the *Post*'s thirty-five candidates were now represented in the *Primary Colors* text archive, plus a few others whose work I had added to the pool myself, political journalists and a few novelists. Returning to my office on Monday, not yet ready for Tuesday's classes, I thought I'd poke around in *New York*'s text archive, just for a few minutes, to see if any of the archived writers looked like plausible candidates, and spent the whole day on it. Every little while, a new batch of files came over the Internet. About 4 P.M. I called Kurt Andersen, *New York*'s editor. "Sorry, I'm getting nowhere. The best I can do is maybe supply some kind of sliding probability for the writers I've already considered, but I'd say it's about zero for all of them."

Andersen said, "Keep trying."

None of the suspects examined so far had a vocabulary closely resembling that of Anonymous. Nor could I find a candidate who *sounded* like Anonymous. Few of the *Post*'s suspects shared the in-your-face aggressiveness of *Primary Colors*. Marylouise Lisa Oates's writing was too sincere, indeed, too *chaste,* and Grunwald's too thoughtful. Christopher Buckley's prose is more fluid than that of Anonymous, with consecutive parenthetical phrases, branching syntax, fewer fragments. None of the candidates shared, in any notable way, the orthographical or syntactical habits of Anonymous, and none seemed to share his fixation on race and aggressive women.

There were a few false leads. Anonymous employed dozens of words and phrases that appeared also in Michael Kelly's work, a few of which were unusual though not rare (*reedy, rabbity, machine-gun nests*).[6] Like Kelly, Anonymous often coined words beginning with *un-* or *quasi-*. Again like Kelly, Anonymous habitually referred to buildings, walls, halls, as "cinder-block," without which term Anonymous was often at a loss for descriptive adjectives when speaking of architecture. The two authors often had a similar cadence: "standing up, standing over the table, hands on the shoulders of two of the students, leaning over the table" (Anon.); "leaning half out of windows, perched on roofs, standing on bumpers" (Kelly); "sycophancy frays the nerves, clogs the arteries" (Anon.); "surrounded by aides and sycophants. . . . One clogged and broken main" (Kelly). In addition, Michael Kelly and Maureen Dowd—friends who have written collaboratively—shared a few words or phrases with Anonymous, such as "Elvis sideburns," that did not appear in the other samples. But Kelly didn't pan out. His overall lexical correlation with Anonymous was not high, and there were many obstacles to a Kelly attribution, such as a terribly high frequency of *the,* a word appearing far more often in Kelly's work than in *Primary Colors* or in the work of the other candidates. Anonymous may have read *Martyrs' Day,* Kelly's book on the Gulf war, but it could not be shown that Kelly actually wrote *Primary Colors*.

Lisa Grunwald was among the last to be ruled out. She shared with Anonymous a few words not found in any of the other cross-samples—*cracker, firefly, misty, reflexively, underpants*—and there were a few possibly interesting collocations, such as "traces of light" (Anon.) and Grunwald's "the light traced." Like Anonymous, Grunwald often mentioned the touching of elbows and shoulders; like Anonymous, she often described clothing in lavish detail. But there were too few distinctive similarities to identify Grunwald with Anonymous.

At this point I nearly gave up. The problem wasn't that Anonymous was an especially tough nut to crack—the prominent features of his language and prose style were easily observed—but with only four candidates eliminated and twenty-one yet to go, there seemed little chance that I could identify Anonymous before he or she was exposed through other means. I still had classes to prepare, papers to grade.

Already late for dinner, I tried Joe Klein, whose recent columns for *Newsweek* seemed like the next-best place to search. The *Washington Post* had given 50-to-1 odds against Klein's authorship.

Bingo! Anonymous's vocabulary was all over Joe Klein's journalism, and vice versa. Here, at last, was a writer who set the lights flashing and the bells ringing. None of these adverbs is especially unusual—*entirely, fiercely, incredibly, mortally, particularly, precisely, profoundly, reflexively, relentlessly, seriously, subtly, surprisingly, ultimately, utterly, vaguely, wistfully*—but all of these were used repeatedly by Klein and Anonymous, while other familiar adverbs, even common adverbs, were avoided by these two writers. I found that Klein and Anonymous loved unusual adjectives ending in -*y* and -*inous*: thus *cartoony, chunky, cottony, crackly, dorky, snarly* (Anon); *loony, clunky, flunky, fluttery, lumpy, semi-dorky, slouchy, smarmy* (Klein); *giddy, jittery, mushy, scruffy, squishy, sleazy, slushy, talky* (both); *rectitudinous, oleaginous* (Klein); *slimetudinous, vertiginous* (Anon.); *gelatinous* (both)—to name a few.

Like Anonymous, Klein favors adverbs made from -*y* adjectives: *crazily, eerily, goofily, handily, huffily, juicily, scarily, spottily, uncannily,* etc. Both Klein and Anonymous added letters to their interjections: *ahh, aww, naww.* Both were into "modes": *listening mode, opaque mode, mega-explain mode, filial mode, mega-vulture mode* (Anon.); *uplift mode, crisis mode, campaign mode* (Klein). Likewise "styles": *outdoor-stadium style* (Klein), *hunting-lodge-style* (Anon.), *faux-plantation-style* (Anon.). There was chronological correspondence: Anonymous made repeated use of the same otherwise uncommon adjectives being used by Klein in his *Newsweek* column during the period in which *Primary Colors* was written (*elusive, flagrant, giddy, lugubrious, plaid, preemptive, reflexive, steaming, tribal*), and often in similar contexts, as when Anonymous, like Klein, described a primary campaign as "larval." Among more common words, Anonymous and Klein selected the same few for drumbeat repetition (*comfortable, uncomfortable, embarrassing, embarrassment, explosive*). Both Klein and Anonymous loved to coin words beginning in *hyper-, mega-, non-, post-, quasi-, and semi-.* (Klein, like Anonymous, coined more words using these prefixes than all the other authors combined.) So, too, for words ending in -*ish:* thus *hawkish, puckish, radicalish, smallish, wonkish* (Klein); *darkish, dullish, puckish, smallish, warmish* (Anon.); and many more—no one else in the sample came close. A few coinages (*unironic* and *tarmac-hopping*) appeared in both Klein and Anonymous but nowhere else, not even in my dictionary. So, too, for peculiar usage, such as *riffle,* which is used by Klein and Anonymous to mean "rifle" or "rustle" (a usage for which the *Oxford English Dictionary* supplies no instance in the past thousand years); and shared slang, like *gazillion,* used by Klein and Anonymous but appearing in no other cross-sample.

I found that Klein and Anonymous borrowed or invented similar compound adjectives. There's *melanin-deprived* (Anon.) and *gadfly-deprived* (Klein); *well-oiled* (Anon.) and *well-greased* (Klein); *not-very-convincing* (Anon.) and *not-so-funny* or *not-so-modest* (Klein). And while there were a number of compounds used by Anonymous that appeared elsewhere only in my Klein cross-sample (*glad-hand, nose-count, road-testing, tarmac-hopping*, et al.), one of the most distinctive features of the Klein-Anonymous manner was the sheer fecundity of compounds, the lengths to which words were playfully strung out: Klein liked to create such verbal constructions as *"triple-back-over-somersault-and-pander-pirouette"* and *"Scare-Seniors-to-Death strategy"*; so, too, did Anonymous, who would link as many as twelve or fourteen words into one long compound.

No single word or group of words could establish Klein's authorship of *Primary Colors,* but once the computer pointed me in the direction of Joe Klein and I began to compare his work with that of Anonymous, the affinities between *Primary Colors* and Klein's *Newsweek* column emerged across the spectrum. Anonymous, like Joe Klein, loves the colon, loves to play with it: thus. And: thus. For emphasis, in both writers: fragments galore. Like Klein, Anonymous loves dashes that bracket—usually—an adverb or adverbial phrase, or that stand on their own—precisely. Anonymous, like Klein, likes short sentences beginning "And then" or "And so," and short ones ending in "sort of": "This was, sort of" (Anon.). "Howard was legendary himself, sort of" (Anon.). "Well, sort of" (Klein). "Fort Green is booming, sort of" (Klein). Both Klein and Anonymous capitalize phrases for special emphasis: "World's Most Obscure Universities Tour" (Anon.); "Religious Right and Lifestyle Left," "Not a Politician" (Klein), etc. Both indulge themselves in the same ungrammaticisms: *kind of enjoyed, kind of chuckled* (Anon.); *kind of intrigued, kind of hoping* (Klein). Both run words together for cuteness: *mumblemumblemumble* (Klein); *okayokay* (Anon.). Both prefer *fella* over *fellow.* Both like the same pejorative epithets: *shitbucket, slimebucket* (Anon.); *gutbucket* (Klein).

I found Anonymous meditating, repeatedly, on the meaning of a nuanced handshake, beginning in the novel's second paragraph:

We shook hands. My inability to recall that particular moment more precisely is disappointing: the handshake is the threshold act, the beginning of politics. I've seen him do it two million times now, but I couldn't tell you how he does it, the right-handed part of it, the strength, quality, duration of it, the rudiments of pressing the flesh. I can, however, tell you a whole lot about what he does with his other hand. He is a genius with it. He might put it on your elbow, or up by your biceps.

And here's Klein, from his column of February 12, 1996 (which appeared as I was conducting my research for *New York* magazine):

Call me stupid, but I've just figured out how to shake hands with Bob Dole . . . Nixon was one of the few who knew, from the start, how to shake hands with him: left-handed. So I tried it. And it changed everything. For once, Dole and I were looking each other in the eye. His grip was strong (he worked for years to rebuild that strength). And he shot me a surprised, delighted look: you finally got it, kid. There is, of course, a metaphor here.

Surveying back issues of *Newsweek* I found that Klein shared Anonymous's pleasure in observing observation itself: "Listening [to Stanton] is an intense, disconcerting phenomenon" (Anon.); listening to Steve Forbes is "a painful, awkward, stultifying experience," while "watching [the Million Man March] was a moving, engrossing, depressing experience" (Klein).

Anonymous described Jack Stanton (his Bill Clinton figure) with irony that seemed to have been borrowed from Joe Klein's description of God, or vice versa. Klein, on God: "It's the Big Guy. . . . He loves you. You are bathed in His light." Anonymous, on Stanton: "He was a big fellow. . . . He is interested in you. He is honored to meet you." Anonymous even seemed to borrow clever plot ideas from the *Newsweek* columnist. Klein: "Inevitably, some rectitudinous soul will have to admit, 'Yes, I tried snorting cocaine. It was an incredibly stupid thing to do.' " In *Primary Colors,* the not quite rectitudinous—indeed, slimetudinous—candidate Freddy Picker does just that. Most important, Anonymous seemed to think like Joe Klein. In fact, he had read Klein's *Newsweek* commentaries on race and seemed to think it was pretty smart stuff. Good blacks are hardworking, middle-class, nonthreatening. Bad blacks need quotas, affirmative action, welfare, gerrymandering.

William Shakespeare in 1609 remarked on the difficulties of remaining anonymous once one's style has become a matter of public record: "Why write I still all one, ever the same, / And keep invention in a noted weed, / That every word doth almost tell my name?" So, too, for Joe Klein. In *Primary Colors,* every page, every sentence, whispered in my ear: "Joe Klein." Especially that opening sentence, chapter 1, page 1. Klein's roman à clef begins with what sounded to my ears like a private joke, one that Anonymous probably thought his readers, or at least those untutored in German, would overlook: "I am *small* and not so dark," he says. Read: "I am *klein*—and I'm not really black."

YELLOW, RED, AND BLUE

> And: Do you know how it happens at a moment like that, when you are embarrassed like that, you will look directly—reflexively—at the very person you don't want to see you?
>
> —ANONYMOUS, *PRIMARY COLORS*

I called Kurt Andersen. "I think I've got him."

"Who is it?"

"Who writes the article?"

"You give us the evidence, and we'll quote you."

"No, I want to write the piece myself, under my own byline." If this attribution was to serve as a touchstone for "A Funeral Elegy," I would have to stand or fall on my own. Andersen said I could have a thousand words.

"So who is it?"

"Joe Klein, a columnist for *Newsweek.*"

"Joe *Klein*?—Are you *sure*?"

"Just wait till you see the evidence."

Pulling an all-nighter, I delivered a one-thousand-word draft on Wednesday morning.

Andersen liked it. Perhaps he was expecting something more pedantic. "Give us another thousand," he said. "Today." I was weary, and time was short—Andersen hoped to run the piece in his next issue. Returning to the keyboard, I sent *New York* my paragraphs by e-mail, one or two at a time. Larry Doyle, my copy editor, checked facts, advised me on timing, tone, and organization, and kept me from falling asleep, facedown, on the keyboard. He was a huge help.

As I posted one paragraph after another, Doyle pared me down to a taut article that came in under four thousand words. By midnight Wednesday, I was finished. We had only one disagreement, at the last minute, arising from my scholarly equivocations. Professors of literature are rarely required to be "right" about anything. In my academic discipline, we don't usually produce *facts*—we produce incredibly clever interpretive commentary. Attribution is the one field within literary studies that requires one to state opinions, right or wrong, about matters of fact, and it is a wise attributor who peppers his statements with "perhaps." Scholars call this practice "due caution." The rest of the English-speaking world calls it "covering your ass." CYA is actually a time-honored literary convention, at least as old as Socrates and Aristotle. Aristotle covered his, and thrived. Socrates, who didn't, was forced to swallow hemlock.

But when I received from *New York* my copyedited text of "Primary Culprit," something was missing—"maybe" and "If not, then."[7] Larry Doyle had zero tolerance for academic toe-picking. He wanted me to say right out, "I *know* who wrote *Primary Colors*." This is what is known to magazine editors as "point-sharpening," and to scholars as suicide. My main point was that Joe Klein wrote *Primary Colors,* but when the article was returned to me it was filed so sharp that if I had a pratfall, I'd be skewered.

Midnight Wednesday. I had not slept in forty-two hours. Asking for time to think it over, I read and reread my text as copyedited. Seeking reassurance, I searched for, and found, that *Washington Post* article in which Joe Klein and various others were polled concerning their possible authorship of *Primary Colors*. Klein had denied that he was Anonymous—sort of. Interestingly, of the thirty-five candidates interviewed, Joe Klein was the most equivocal in his denial: "I am Spartacus," he said. "All of us who are accused of this should stand up and say, 'I am Spartacus.' And share the royalties."[8] Spartacus was a gladiator who led a successful revolt against the decadent Romans in 73 B.C. He became a legend in his own time, as well as the subject of a Stanley Kubrick movie. In the movie, Spartacus owns up to his identity lest his followers be killed. But then, in a surprising move, all the other slaves shield the real Spartacus by claiming, "I am Spartacus." Was Klein identifying himself as Spartacus no. 1, the Kirk Douglas character, or as one of the followers prepared to die for their leader? That was a nondenial-denial. I was struck as well by Klein's posture of indignation ("All of us who are accused . . .") and by that evasive demonstrative pronoun ("accused of *this*"—this what?). The entire statement seemed a little too performative, too planned.

I had arrived at a point at which I had to decide whether I was sure I was right. I thought that I was. I had the evidence to back me up. But what if I was wrong? I reread the point-sharpened text one more time, and my own uncut version. As a piece of writing, the article was better without my cowardly scholarly equivocations. I called Larry Doyle. "I can't afford to be wrong on this one," I said. "But I'm not wrong. Go for it."

WRONG!

> He was cool. He didn't seem at all perturbed. "It was all a big mistake."
>
> —ANONYMOUS, *PRIMARY COLORS*

Before proceeding to my Shakespeare class on Thursday morning I called *Newsweek* to give Joe Klein a heads-up. He was out, but I left him a voice-mail message, identified myself, and requested a return call, saying that it concerned the novel *Primary Colors*. I then headed off to class to spend the next ninety minutes with twenty-six undergrads on *Much Ado About Nothing,* not fully appreciating the irony that Anonymous, for the media, was a much hotter ado than William Shakespeare, and "A Funeral Elegy" nothing at all. By 11:15, when I emerged from class, the news was out of the bag: the editors of *New York* had issued an announcement that Anonymous was anonymous no longer, but Joe Klein. The college switchboard was already flooded with incoming calls, including one from Jim Houtrides, a producer for CBS News. Unable to reach me while I was in class, Houtridas had arranged with the college's Press and Information Office for me to do an exclusive interview with CBS concerning Klein's alleged authorship of *Primary Colors.*

"But Joe Klein *works* for CBS as a correspondent," I said upon learning of this development.

"Oh, c'mon, this will be great for Vassar. Joe Klein has no control over CBS News. Besides, Klein works with Dan Rather. These folks are from CBS *Sunday Morning,* one of the best news shows on television. No connection. You have nothing to worry about."

As we spoke, there was a knock on my office door. It was CBS News. While the crew unpacked their bags in my office, I continued to field phone calls. There was the *phut-phut-phut* of a helicopter. "There's Martha now," someone said.

During a momentary lull, a cameraman told me, "Sorry, but we may have to unplug your telephone during the interview." He unplugged my telephone. I sat down with Martha Teichner. There were questions. "Okay, B-roll" (no talk, just pictures of the Shakespeare professor tapping at his computer). "Okay, pack it up."

I returned the cord to my office phone. The phone rang. "Hello, Professor Foster? Your telephone seems to be out of order, we've been—"

"Sorry, can't talk. Call back tomorrow." (*Click*) I had to call Gwen. "Gwen, they're taking me to New York."

"Who? Why? When?"

"CBS News. Anonymous. Now. Can you grab me a sports coat, tie, and travel kit?"

"Are you kidding? *No*—I'm at *work*."

"Please?"

"No, this is crazy. I can't leave work right now. Oh, all right."

A cameraman hopped into the CBS News van, met Gwen at the house. Meanwhile, I took the opportunity to check my voice-mail—forty-seven messages, the first of which was from the man of the hour:

> Hello, Professor. This is Joe Klein. I know what you're going to say. You're going to say I wrote this thing. You know, when I read this book I noticed that whoever wrote it probably read my column, and borrowed some words and phrases. But what are you, a *time* expert? [*Chuckle*] I'd like you to tell me *when* I could have written this. I'm busy covering the presidential campaign. Bye now. [*Click*]

There was no time for messages 2 through 47. The cameraman had returned with my coat, tie, and travel kit. "Here's your stuff." A helicopter was waiting on the hockey field. I was whisked away. I was thinking, "That was another nondenial-denial." I was not thinking: "Foster, you're an idiot. There's money involved. What will you do if he lies?" Somewhere around West Point, with my head resting on the glass bubble of a CBS whirlybird, I dozed off and slept like a baby, all the way to Manhattan.

The right hand of a news organization doesn't always know what the left hand is doing. While I was conducting a rushed but entirely congenial interview with Martha Teichner in Poughkeepsie, a copy of "Primary Culprit: Who Is Anonymous?" was faxed to Joe Klein, who was in New Hampshire covering the presidential primary, and who blew his top when he read it. Klein called *New York* and blistered Kurt Andersen's phone-ear with a string of crimson expletives, then called Dan Rather, denied writing *Primary Colors,* and (in the words of a CBS colleague) demanded that Rather "piss on the story." Could Dan do that? Yes, Dan could. He was happy to oblige.

At 6:30 P.M. on February 15, 1996, I joined the staff of *New York* magazine before a television set to watch the *CBS Evening News*. There were no big stories that day. Still, the *Primary Colors* exclusive was slow to appear, deferred to the final sixty seconds of the broadcast. When the moment finally arrived, Dan Rather let me have it: "A scholar who recently used his computer to identify what *he* says is an undiscovered poem by Shakespeare and got some high-profile attention for himself has now unleashed his machine on author 'Anonymous.' " That struck me as a little unfair. I felt less like a self-promoter than like a draftee. To mock the absurdity of my conclusion that Joe Klein wrote *Primary Colors,* Rather did everything but roll his eyes and giggle. The CBS cameras then cut to a calm and smiling Joe Klein, who dismissed the attribution as ludicrous: "Now I know what it's like to be the Flavor of the Week. It is not me," he said. "I did not do it. This is silly." End of story.

DESPAIR

> I am now a man of despair, and am shut up in it, as in this iron cage.... I cannot get out, O, *now* I cannot.... I did then promise my self much delight; but now every one of those things also bite me and gnaw me like a burning worm ...
>
> —THE "PROFESSOR," *PILGRIM'S PROGRESS*[9]

Published in *New York* as a sidebar to my own article, "Primary Culprit," was Jacob Weisberg's "Revenge Fantasy: *Primary Colors* Is Quintessential Klein, Bitter About Clinton, Obsessive About Race"—nothing new there—but I learned a lot from Weisberg's piece that I didn't already know, such as the fact that Joe Klein and Anonymous had the same literary agent, Kathy Robbins (could that be a coincidence?), and that Joe Klein had covered the 1992 Clinton campaign for—guess which magazine—*New York*! "Why didn't you tell me about this when I was writing my article," I asked Andersen, "or give me those *New York* pieces as part of the Klein writing sample?" "Didn't think of it" was the polite reply. But the truth may be that Andersen did not want to influence my opinion. *New York*'s editors handled their list of suspects, and their expert witness, just as a police chief would do: no hints, suggestions, tips, nudges, or winks: you cannot afford to say or do anything that might influence the witness.

I also learned from Weisberg's sidebar that Joe Klein had been Clinton's leading media sympathizer in the early days of the campaign (almost, indeed, a protégé, as registered in his Clinton coverage for *New York*), but eventually turned from Clinton in disgust, not unlike Henry Burton does from Governor Jack Stanton in *Primary Colors*). And it was from Weisberg's sidebar that I learned why Joe Klein was not suspected sooner by his fellow journalists: Klein is himself satirized in *Primary Colors,* in the figure of Jerry "Asshole" Rosen, a yappy supporter of Governor Jack Stanton ("Rosen was the political writer at *Manhattan* magazine. He was a friendly-and-an-important-one. If he liked you . . ."). Intended as a diversion for canny readers, this piece of self-satire had led fellow journos to discount Klein as a suspect. While schmoozing with colleagues at the Iowa caucuses, Klein had fumed loudly, "red-faced and indignant," according to the *Post,* asking if his reputation matched that of the fictional Jerry Rosen's. In my own reading of *Primary Colors,* the Jerry Rosen diversion zipped right past me, unnoticed. Sometimes it's helpful not to be "in the know." But I took reassurance from Weisberg's sidebar that Klein's denial was, in fact, a lie.

In the morning, after an appearance on *Good Morning America* in which I looked tired, tense, and edgy (this, from my wife—I would not watch the videotape), I returned home to Poughkeepsie bearing a load of back issues of *New York,* each of which contained an article on the Clinton campaign written by Joe Klein; and many of which contained incidents dramatized in *Primary Colors* in much the same language used by Anonymous. Icing on the cake: it had to be Joe Klein who wrote *Primary Colors.*

But what if the author of *Primary Colors* had used Klein's *New York* articles on Clinton as his primary source? Might not that account for some of the Kleinisms in Anonymous's prose? What if, in fact, Anonymous was a Joe Klein wannabe who stole Klein's manner and then mocked him in the figure of Jerry Rosen? That did not seem to me a plausible explanation, but it was one I would have to consider before I could stand up and say: "Don't believe this man. He lies."

Then came another bombshell—and this time, my confidence in Joe Klein's sole authorship of the novel was truly shaken. Back home in Poughkeepsie, I flopped down on a sofa after dinner and picked up *Newsweek*, the latest issue, which had been sitting untouched on a coffee table. On the very first page of news was a special report called "Primary Suspect," a *Newsweek* "exclusive" identifying the author of *Primary Colors* as one Luciano Siracusano, a former speechwriter for Mario Cuomo. *Newsweek*, at least, had the good scholarly sense to equivocate, saying that the search for Anonymous "*may* finally be over" (my emphasis), though *Newsweek*'s position was pretty clear: Siracusano's smiling photograph was captioned "*The Author.*" When "surprised by a call from *Newsweek*, Siracusano said, 'I haven't confirmed it and I haven't denied it, but I am interested in having the book sell.' "[10]

Hoo-boy. Would Klein, a senior editor at *Newsweek*, allow his own news organization to run an "exclusive" naming Siracusano as the author if Klein knew that the story was absolutely untrue? Not possible. Come to think of it, would Dan Rather of CBS News, without having evidence that my attribution was, in fact, a mistake, use his bully pulpit to belittle a college professor? Siracusano's writing had not been included in my text samples. When I got to Joe Klein, I had told *New York* that no other writing samples were necessary—I had my man. But I must have gotten it wrong, all wrong, the biggest mistake of my professional life, and in a very public way. Klein must have given his collaborator, Siracusano, enough of a hand in the book to give himself plausible deniability. This was very, very bad news.

Reviewing my analysis, I thought it impossible that Joe Klein was telling the truth. But when I looked at Klein's statements and credentials, it did not seem possible he would lie. Most professional journalists do care about facts. It's their stock-in-trade. When it's a matter of record, a journalist may equivocate, but it makes him squirm to lie baldly. And when it came to "Truth" with a capital T, who was more rectitudinous than Joe Klein? Take that January 22 column in *Newsweek*, "Lawyering the Truth," in which Klein had damned Bill and Hillary Rodham Clinton as "congenital fudgers." "Their tendency to lawyer the truth," wrote Klein with disgust, "has been manifest since the very earliest stages of their public lives . . . lawyering, fudging, misdirection, obfuscation, and generally slouchy behavior. . . . Are they flat-out liars? It's not impossible. . . . The intensity of their denials is fascinating." That was the last Joe Klein column I had examined before putting the finishing touches on my article for *New York*.

As I was still digesting, with a foretaste of doom, the *Newsweek* scoop on Siracusano, the telephone rang. It was Mary Tabor, a reporter for the *New York Times*. She had listened to Joe Klein's side of the story. She was calling now to get mine. I should have asked her to call back later, when I was not feeling so . . . yellow.

"Hello, Professor Foster. So, did Joe Klein write *Primary Colors* or didn't he? He says he didn't."

"I believe he did, yes."

"You *believe* he did?"

"Yes."

"But it says right here, in your *New York* article, that you *know* he did."

"Well, *he* says that he *didn't*." A thought had just occurred to me, five minutes before, that maybe there was an accomplice, a collaborator who prepared the final draft, giving Klein plausible deniability. "I think it's quite possible," I said to Tabor, "that two people are involved in the book. I'm looking at someone else very closely." (And in fact, I was staring at his picture at that very moment, in *Newsweek*, which lay open before me on the kitchen countertop. Luciano Siracusano: "The Author.")

"No, wait. Listen to this: '*How can we know the author? We can. And I do.*' Did you write those words, or didn't you?"

"Well, actually, I—"

"Actually, what?"

"Nothing."

"Did you write that, or didn't you?"

"I wrote, 'How can we know the author?' The extra phrase, 'We can, and I do,' was—what d'ya call it—*point-sharpening*."

"What? They put *words* in your mouth?"

"Yes, but—no. It's not their fault. Scratch that. I signed off on it, agreed to the article as published."

"How about this: 'Joe Klein wrote *Primary Colors*.' "

"Yes, I wrote that."

"So then you *do* know that Joe Klein wrote *Primary Colors*!"

"Yes, but—"

"But what?"

"Well, I wrote, 'Joe Klein wrote *Primary Colors*. Or else it was an incredibly clever imitator of Joe Klein.' The editors thought I shouldn't be so equivocal. We discussed it. I said okay. I signed off on it."

"So which is it now, Joe Klein, or an imitator?"

"Joe Klein. In my opinion."

"But you're not *sure*!"

"Yes, I'm sure—I think—I don't know how to explain it. All of the evidence points to Joe Klein. It's uncanny. You can't just imitate another person's language that perfectly. It *has* to be Klein. But—"

"But before, you *knew* that Joe Klein wrote *Primary Colors*, and now you're not so sure. Now maybe Anonymous is *two* people."

It was horrible. Mary Tabor didn't just score points off me, she thumped me up one side and down the other and reduced me to a puddle of Jell-O. Hanging up the phone, I slid down against the kitchen wall and sat there on the floor with my head between my knees, hands over head, fingers locked, white-knuckled, the picture of misery. It was a posture that I first learned in the corridors of the Turner Grade School in West Chicago, Illinois, during civil defense drills, in preparation for the day when the Soviets might just drop the

Big One on us schoolkids. I recalled the old chestnut: "Heads down now, children, between your legs—*and kiss your ass good-bye.*"

My article on *Primary Colors,* having begun as a scoop, looked now like a bad career move. With a dozen years of academic work and my professional reputation at stake, I had pitted my judgment against the combined authority of CBS News, Dan Rather, and *Newsweek* magazine. I had made a horrible, terrible mistake, at the worst possible moment, just when my attribution of "A Funeral Elegy" was hanging in the balance.

Twenty minutes later the phone rang again. It was Kurt Andersen. "If Mary Tabor calls for the *New York Times,*" he said, "tell her to call back tomorrow. Don't talk to her tonight."

"It's too late," I said. "I already did." He groaned. "And I didn't handle it so well." Another groan. I summarized the interview. Groan. Andersen could just imagine how the story would play in the next day's paper. "Go to bed," he said. And I did.

TRUE COLORS

> *Boswell:* Supposing the person who wrote "Junius" were asked whether he was the authour, might he deny it?
>
> *Johnson:* . . . If you were sure that he wrote "Junius" would you, if he denied it, think as well of him afterwards? . . . But stay, Sir; here is another case. Supposing the authour had told me confidentially that he had written "Junius," and I were asked if he had, I should hold myself at liberty to deny it, as being under a previous promise, express or implied, to conceal it. Now what I ought to do for the authour, may I not do for myself?
>
> —BOSWELL, *LIFE OF JOHNSON* (13 JUNE 1750)[11]

On the evening that my *New York* article was released and all the next day, Joe Klein was pestered in New Hampshire by fellow journalists with inconvenient questions. Klein sulked and swore, denying that he had a hand in *Primary Colors,* finally shouting, over the din of the pressroom, for everyone's consumption, "FOR GOD'S SAKE, DEFINITELY, I DIDN'T WRITE IT!" Later, spotting Jacob Weisberg at the bar, Klein walked over to him and started screaming at him, not caring who overheard. He was fighting mad over that *New York* sidebar, "Revenge Fantasy." Who did Weisberg think he was?

Returning home to Pelham, New York, Klein assured his friends and neighbors that he did not know who wrote *Primary Colors,* did not write the book himself, and did not contribute to it in any way. David Von Drehle of the *Washington Post* asked his old pal if he'd stake his journalistic credibility on that denial. Joe said yes—according to Drehle, in the strongest possible terms. Drehle took Joe at his word.

While Klein was still fretting over my *New York* article, I was busy fretting over that *Newsweek* exclusive reporting that Luciano Siracusano was the true author of *Primary Colors.* After a fitful night's sleep, I knocked out a letter for *Newsweek*'s Letters column, and faxed it: "I cannot believe that Siracusano wrote the book without Joe Klein's involvement." I heard back from the Letters editor, George Hackett, by telephone. Speaking, I think, from conviction, Hackett advised me to withdraw: "You're *wrong,*" he said. "Joe Klein is a senior editor here at *Newsweek* and he did *not* write *Primary Colors.*"

Finding my letter rejected by *Newsweek,* assured by George Hackett that I was barking up the wrong tree, I tried to bark up Klein's: I called him on the telephone, returning his call of February 15. But Klein could not be reached. Anyone who called his office that week, and there must have been hundreds who tried, got the same recorded message: a long, overly chatty discourse in which Klein denied writing *Primary Colors*—sort of. I transcribed the text verbatim, calling his *Newsweek* phone a dozen times until I was sure I had it down, precisely, word for word:

> Hi, this is Joe Klein. For all (heh-heh) you people calling (heh-heh) about *Primary Colors,* let me just say *New York* magazine hired the *wrong* computer and the *wrong* expert (heh-heh). They probably

should have hired the one playing Garry *Kasparov* (heh-heh). Um, look, from the moment that I read this book I realized that whoever wrote it was a very close reader of my column, and probably watched me on TV a lot, and maybe even someone I've spoken to. Um, so like everyone else I'm really *curious* about it, but I've been too busy covering the pen—uh, the presidential campaign—to obsess on it.

Um, it might have been more, uh, profitable for *New York* magazine to have hired a *time study* expert, to figure out when I *could* have written it, uh, written this thing. But, but I *am* flattered, and—and the professor did get *one* thing right, "I *am* small and not so dark." And I hope, I hope you guys will give me space to write my column and live my life and go on as before. And for those of you still looking for the author of this thing, good luck, I hope you find him soon, and happy hunting. Take care. Bye. I'll talk to you.

There were things about this phone message—prepared for the media, not for my ears—that were of interest to me. Trying to distance himself from the text, Klein avoids saying "*Primary Colors*"—preferring "it," or "this book," or "this thing" (just as the perpetrator of a homicide will avoid saying "murder" or "victim"). Lawyering the truth, he implies but does not actually affirm that the manifest likeness between himself and "the author of this thing" can be discounted as slavish imitation—but by whom? By the work of a Joe Klein copycat, "a very close reader" of his *Newsweek* columns as well as someone who "probably watched me on TV a lot. . . ." Unlike his calm soundbite for CBS News, Klein sounded nervous—almost, at one point, demoralized, hoping yet to "live my life and go on as before." His twittery giggle ("heh-heh") was unconvincing. At a critical moment, he tripped over his own tongue: "I am busy covering the pen—uh, the presidential campaign." (Classic Freudian slip: *I can't allow my pen to be exposed—uh, no, scratch that.*) Klein had also faltered when letting the words "I *could* have written it" pass over his tongue and through his lips, prompting a reflexive clarification: "when I *could* have written it, uh, written this thing."

Even the most habitual prevaricator will speak true insofar as he or she is able, if only because one is less likely then to become entrapped in self-contradiction. But these gross evasions were palpable and self-defeating. Klein did not sound to me like a falsely accused innocent. It was not impossible that he was telling the truth, but that overlong, over-the-top telephone denial exhibited all the traits of a guilty suspect who hoped to deceive his callers without lying more than was absolutely necessary. In a criminal investigation, as much information can be gleaned from bad liars as from those who tell the whole truth and nothing but. Not many people, not even many criminals, lie well. The truth has a way of slipping out. Klein seemed to be letting it slip.

The one thing that I looked to find in this chatty phone message is the one thing that was missing: Klein never says "I did not write *Primary Colors*." Instead he zeroes in on the little kicker that I placed at the tail end of my essay, an explication of the novel's concealed joke, "I am *klein*—and I'm not really black." Identifying this as the "*one* thing" the professor got "right," Klein makes it *wrong*, displacing my gotcha! paraphrase with the original words as they appeared in the novel—as if I had identified Klein as Anonymous on the basis of his short physical stature ("the professor did get *one* thing right, 'I *am* small . . .' "). But the truth is that I never knew, until hearing this phone message, that Klein also happens to be *little*. In fact, the thought never entered my head.

IN THE LURCH

> It's so unfair. So goddamn unfair, don't you think? You work so hard. . . . You know, I had it figured. I knew what could be done, could be said, how far you could go—and then this . . . professor—.
>
> —ANONYMOUS, *PRIMARY COLORS*

Hoping still for a checkmate, I studied Klein's next moves as a writer. Not waiting for the February 19 issue of *Newsweek* to arrive in the mail, I picked up a copy at the Vassar College bookstore. *Newsweek* found no room to discuss *Primary Colors* in this issue except on its "Periscope" page, which highlighted remarks by Joe Klein suggesting that the professor from Vassar should use his computer to play chess.

I turned next to Klein's regular column. This week's offering, written and in production before my *New York* article appeared, was called "A Lurch Toward Love." The article described what Joe Klein took for a softer, gentler Pat Buchanan, a conservative you could almost love.

And there it was, in all its splendor: the prose style of Joe Klein a.k.a. Anonymous—the dashes, the invented compound words, the adjectives ending in *−y*, the capitalized phrases, the cutely spelled interjections. A *squishy*, a *nawww*, and sentence fragments galore. Once again—interestingly—I found the adverb pasted between dashes, Klein/Anonymous style, along with the same adverbs that I had said were preferred by Klein/Anonymous. The author's preoccupation with race was still on display as well, with Klein taking a slam at "the lifestyle liberals and racial panderers." *Newsweek*'s "Lurch Toward Love" was Anonymous from start to finish, signed "Joe Klein."

A week later, in his column of February 26 ("How Clinton Could Screw Up"), something drastic and sudden happened to Joe Klein's prose. "The professor" happened to it. One week after publication of my *New York* article, Joe Klein was a new man. Where were the hallmarks of the Anonymous/Klein style, as alleged by that professor writing for *New York* magazine? Gone! No *awww*s or *nawww*s or *slushy*s or *wishy-washy*s or *mode*s. Hardly any fragments or dashes or coined compound words. All of the words highlighted in "Primary Culprit" as vintage Anonymous/Klein were missing as well. Most notably, one week after praising Pat Buchanan, Klein now depicted himself as politically correct—sort of—by criticizing Jesse Helms. In a sudden lurch toward liberalism, a politically correct Joe Klein on February 26 denounced Helms's "disgraceful, race-baiting 1990 reelection campaign."

Taking "Primary Culprit" as a guide to the prose style of Anonymous/Klein, someone had slyly deleted from Klein's February

26 column the linguistic and stylistic and ideological evidence that might seem to validate my central thesis—that Joe Klein and Anonymous were one and the same. But within a few weeks, try as he might, those telltale Kleinisms crept back into his *Newsweek* prose, making Joe Klein sound once again like the author of *Primary Colors*.

Taking advantage of his sudden notoriety, Joe Klein went on the lecture circuit as the man who was not Anonymous. He delivered a speech to college students and business groups, the same speech that he had been giving on such occasions before his name was linked to *Primary Colors*—a lecture in which he called for America to return to traditional values. During Q&A, Klein dismissed the *New York* article as "silly," the work of an "Elizabethan professor" who "went off the deep end." While Anonymous cashed in, I was getting hammered in academia and on the Internet for having staked so much on the attribution of a popular novel, and for having blown it. (Reasoning: If Foster guessed wrong on *Primary Colors*, why believe that Shakespeare wrote "A Funeral Elegy"?) I had been invited to address the International Shakespeare Association in April, in a general session called "A New Shakespeare Discovery." By the time I got there, the ISA program committee had renamed its Foster session "A New 'Shakespeare' Discovery?" A few senior scholars who had endorsed the elegy attribution issued clarifications or ducked out of sight. My credibility, in the toilet since February, could not be restored unless it was proved that Joe Klein was lying; that *Newsweek* magazine was a purveyor of fiction; and that Dan Rather was a credulous gull. The odds were not in my favor.

Several of Klein's friends and colleagues spoke to me by telephone. Some were skeptical: "I *know* Joe Klein. Joe Klein is a *friend* of mine. And let me tell you, if Joe Klein wrote *Primary Colors*, it wouldn't just surprise me—it would change my view of the *world*. You can quote me on that" (Walter Shapiro). Others were less sure: "I thought it was Klein when I first read the book. When we confronted him, he denied it, and we accepted that. But now I'm thinking it's Klein. Anyway, it's not Siracusano" (George Stephanopoulos). I received tips. One national newsmagazine had information that Anonymous was the political novelist Garrett Epps—an attribution that I was able to disprove. A Manhattan reporter kept me on edge with almost daily phone calls concerning her theory, well researched, that the novel was written by Peter Grunwald, the brother of Lisa and Mandy—an attribution that I could not disprove because I had no writing sample for Peter Grunwald. That one made me sweat. Let's forget Luciano Siracusano. Given Klein's close friendship with sister Mandy, might not Peter Grunwald be a paid collaborator?—someone who would bear the lash for Klein if a public whipping seemed imminent over *Primary Colors*? What if Peter Grunwald should suddenly drop breeches for the sake of his friend and say, like Shakespeare's Launce the clown: "You do him the more wrong, . . . 'Twas *I* did the thing you wot of!"[12]

"NO, REALLY, I *AM* ANONYMOUS"

> I am free to live among you, unnoticed. . . . I am free to try my hand
> at this again. And believe me, I will.
> —ANONYMOUS, *NEW YORK TIMES BOOK REVIEW* (19 MAY 1996)[13]

For six nail-biting months, I searched for an alternative candidate or plausible collaborator, and came up empty-handed. I could never find another writer whose language habits matched those of Anonymous and Joe Klein. There must be some devil in the details that I had somehow overlooked that was known to CBS News, *Newsweek*, and Joe Klein. Studying the problem from every angle, I couldn't puzzle it out. Then, in May, the author of *Primary Colors* contributed a piece to the *New York Times Book Review*—an article called "No, Really, I *Am* Anonymous"—by Anonymous. This new writing sample was welcome, especially since the title sounded to my ears like a jokey, veiled confession, the admission of someone who had already said that he was *not* Anonymous. Someone, in short, like Joe Klein. The intensity of Klein's denials had peaked early, back in February, in the days immediately following the release of "Primary Culprit." By May, still speaking to student and business groups (same old speech about old-fashioned values), Klein no longer said, "I am not Anonymous"—period. He now began the old lecture by saying, "I am not Anonymous. But I do have a confession to make. I am *Ambiguous.*"

The line usually got a laugh—such a good laugh, evidently, that Anonymous in "No, Really, [etc.]" began his *NYTBR* piece in much the same way: "I have a confession to make," wrote Anonymous. "No, not *that* one. Don't be silly. It's this: I'm suffering from post-traumatic success disorder."

With a reported $6 million in royalties and another million-plus for the film, Anonymous was unlikely, at this point in his career, to garner much pity for his "suffering," but suffering he was. Not yet ready to make a clean breast of it, Anonymous half-acknowledges something else, something having to do with a character issue, half-revealing a fear that he's been "unfaithful" to himself and to others, well, not really, but: "I feel a little bit like Joanne Woodward in *The Three Faces of Eve,* minus a face. *Which is not to say that I consider myself two-faced*" (my emphasis). The addition of that seemingly unnecessary afterthought is a little like saying to your therapist, "Doc, tonight I feel a little bit like a tragic hero. Which is not to say that I feel an urge to kill my father and marry my mother." *Red flag!*

Shakespeare's Falstaff when caught in a monstrous lie reports altruistic motives and announces that "I shall think the better of myself, and thee, during my life" for having lied. Like Falstaff, Anonymous ascends on angel wings, soaring high above those "underemployed commentators" who "ruminated on the 'morality' of what [he's] done." It would have been a "moral breach" for him to disclose his identity. Come to think of it, writes Anonymous, he is, today, "a better person for having kept [his] mouth shut." Anonymous says he had to cultivate "a strict discipline . . . an almost religious humility," not to fess up.

Why so much fretting, the reader might well have asked, over mere *anonymity*? Books and articles are published anonymously every day of the week without causing the author any such grief. But it was not, surely, anonymity that raised a moral dilemma for Anonymous. There was something more fundamental that was troubling him, a question of character: What if your desire for anonymity leads you into deceit and mendacity? What if you have preserved your anonymity and book sales but injured colleagues and friends?

In "No, Really, I *Am* Anonymous," Anonymous registers his beef against—guess who—"the computer." The author of *Primary Colors* blames his troubles as Anonymous on electronic gadgetry, complaining that "the computer" kept defeating him as he wrote, which left him feeling demolished, in need of "reconstructing." But why should Anonymous be fretting in the *New York Times Book Review* over "the computer"? What did that have to do with anything, if Anonymous was not Joe Klein? Of the *Post*'s thirty-five candidates, none but Mr. Klein had notable cause to feel blue over what "the computer" may or may not have done to poor Anonymous.

The penultimate paragraph of "No, Really, I *Am* Anonymous" was a dead giveaway. Writing of a months-long media frenzy, wading now in tears of self-pity, Anonymous complained sourly that the press attention had been "perverse and occasionally nauseating." Growling at critics who misunderstood his intentions, Anonymous likened himself to his own fictional Governor Stanton when "the witless ravenous pack descended on him [i.e., Stanton] in New Hampshire [i.e., in *Primary Colors*]." I asked myself: Who could say that except Joe Klein? Who, among the *Post*'s thirty-five candidates—or among the rest of the nation, for that matter—was harassed by a horde of merciless journos, making Anonymous feel both nauseated and guilty? No one but Joe Klein. Come to think of it, it was in New Hampshire that the witless, ravenous pack first descended on him, beginning on that day when my "Primary Culprit" first appeared out of the blue like a thunderclap.

On the face of it, Joe Klein had no cause to complain that his name was mentioned as the author of *Primary Colors*. By almost anyone's account, Anonymous, at first, seemed like a terrific thing to be. During those first heady weeks, *Primary Colors* was selling faster than ice cubes in hell, making a ton of money; the Clinton camp was visibly discomfited; and the Washington and New York press corps were having one big hoot. When other journos, pundits, and novelists (besides Joe Klein) were asked if they were Anonymous, the typical response was "No—but I wish I were" (Sally Quinn). "*Primary Colors* is the best book I never wrote" (Mark Miller). "Words cannot describe how much I wish I had written it" (Walter Shapiro). And so on, for dozens of others. This nearly universal sentiment was perhaps best captured by a cartoon in *The New Yorker:* an ordinary schmo is lying in bed, grinning widely, hands folded behind his head, musing to his spouse, "I had a wonderful dream that Anonymous turned out to be *me.*" Being identified as Anonymous was not the problem—not for Joe Klein, not for anyone. Why, then, was Anonymous so *miserable*?

Defending his right to remain silent now and forever, Anonymous in "No, Really," complains: "I wanted the *book* to be reviewed, not the *author*" (emphasis added). And here, possibly, was the true crux, the main reason why the author felt lousy. Anonymous wished that he could turn back the clock and recover those innocent days when his books and articles were read as *journalism,* not as grist for psychoanalysis or literary deconstruction. Anonymous, too late, discovered the perils of writing fiction: people don't always read your stuff the way you think it should be read.

So, too, with Joe Klein. As reported to me secondhand by various of his friends and colleagues, Klein did not mind so much that the *New York* article had analyzed his punctuation, vocabulary, syntax, and characteristic phrasing. He didn't even mind that "the professor" seemed to poke a little fun. What made Klein crazy-mad was that I had found evidence of sexual and racial anxieties in his signed journalism and, just as transparently, in his fiction—anxieties that Klein protested were none of his own. Then others came along, like Weis-

berg, to say, "Oh, c'mon, Joe—you're *obsessed* with the race issue!"
To say nothing of his being obsessed with the masculinity issue, which
was worse, almost.

Journalists and literary scholars sometimes think differently about
the ways in which a text should be read. A news reporter may conceive
of reading as a consumer activity: the reporter supplies the facts, "stories" that are both true and accurate; the reader consumes them. A
political correspondent may at times be annoyed with readers who
take issue with his opinions, or a reporter with faultfinders who
charge that his story is incorrect, but it's rare that a journalistic text
is subjected to literary interpretation. Journalists do not and should
not expect their work to be read in the same way that a work of fiction
or a lyric poem will be read. The move from journalism to fiction
changes all that. It may not be *fair* to read novels as English teachers
read them—but that's a risk that any writer takes the moment his or
her text appears in print, especially when writing fiction.

I will confess now to one bit of harmless mischief. In my first
reading of *Primary Colors* I noted the many awkward sexual encounters, a few sneering remarks about homosexuality, the semi-impotent
black narrator. These and other clues pointed me toward an author
preoccupied with his own masculinity. Before closing my article for
New York, I made inquiry and learned that Joe Klein was indeed
married, as Anonymous professes to be in the book's dedication. Still,
I thought I'd tweak him a little for those homophobic jokes. I did not
believe, and did not say, that the author of *Primary Colors* is gay. I
wrote only that Anonymous *could* be gay—adding that we cannot
tell for sure when the internal evidence is so *inconclusive*. By poking
the author's evident sore spot, his masculine anxiety, I had hoped to
force Anonymous out of the closet. I thought that the question "Is
Anonymous gay?" might motivate the angst-ridden author to jump
up and say, "Here I am, and I'm *NOT*!" The strategy backfired. My
remarks had goosed the suspect harder than intended, driving Anonymous up the wall but not into the open.

Writing three months later for the *New York Times Book Review*,

Anonymous set the record straight in the opening paragraph. If anyone really wants to know, he is straight, and (trust him!) he has no trouble in bed. The *NYTBR* piece leads off with a news flash from Anonymous's bedroom, with the report of a sexy, "titillating" spouse (his adjective, not mine), a total woman, who nuzzles his ear and coos, and who says, "Can I, y'know, do it with—Anonymous tonight?" The concern in that first paragraph with bedroom politics and masculine virility was another tipoff that "No, Really, I *Am* Anonymous" was written by Joe Klein—and that he was writing against "Primary Culprit." (*See? The professor got me all wrong! Anonymous is wayyy hetero!*)

There were other issues. I was one of many readers and reviewers to have tasked the anonymous author of *Primary Colors* for tarring real-life people under the umbrella of fiction. In "No, Really," Anonymous defends himself against that charge as well, saying now ("with some vehemence") that his characters are merely "archetypal," "familiar political types." (Familiar indeed: the Indecisive Italian Governor of New York Type, the Little Rock's First Lady Ball-Cutter Type, the Decidedly Horny Governor of Arkansas Type....)

Having dramatized political "archetypes"—not Bill or Hillary Clinton or any other real-life individual—Anonymous says he was "sort of horrified" when "well-known public figures . . . began to *accuse* one another" (my emphasis) of writing *Primary Colors*. But having allowed this thought to surface—that he is, in fact, to *blame* for writing such a book, Anonymous suddenly disclaims responsibility for the entire narrative, blaming the story and its archetypal characters on his Muse: the truest thing about writing fiction, says Anonymous in "No, Really," is that a novel writes itself. The way it turns out is not really the author's fault. The characters really do take on lives of their own. The plot really does acquire its own inevitability. Don't blame Anonymous.

Despite his reputed $6 million in royalties, the *Primary Colors* mystery man by this time sounded grumpy, tired of the game, a fugitive ready to give himself up. In "No, Really," Anonymous made no effort to conceal his Kleinisms—the fragments, the adverbial pepper, the "schizzy twinges," the quirky capitals and parenthetical use of dashes—it was all there, laid out for anyone to see. He was ready to fold.

Trying to walk a mile in Klein's Armani shoes, it occurred to me that he couldn't just give himself up without being prompted or prodded. At this late juncture his identity would have to be discovered—probably, I thought, by a fellow journalist, possibly by *Newsweek* or by someone at the *Washington Post*. Klein could then say, "Okay, you got me at last," and we could all go home. I told my friends to watch for Joe Klein to cave, any day now.

OUTED

> And so I wanted you to have it—that's the only copy left. We destroyed the others. I wanted you to have it because it might help you to know what others are gonna be digging after, and maybe finding. . . .
>
> —ANONYMOUS, *PRIMARY COLORS*

A few weeks later, the drama ended as suddenly as it had begun. On July 17 the *Washington Post* published a story by David Streitfeld showing that handwritten notations on the original typescript of *Primary Colors* formed a perfect match with the handwriting of Joe Klein.[14] The author's typescript, dated April 1995 (the month in which Random House had acquired it), was *marked "CONFIDENTIAL! For your eyes only!! Do not distribute to booksellers!!"* A year later, in May 1996, about the time of Anonymous's world-weary encore in the *New York Times Book Review*, someone—Random House's Daniel Menaker or an assistant, or Klein's agent, or Klein himself—sold that original *"For your eyes only!!"* typescript anyway, to a Hudson Valley book dealer, who sold it in turn to David Streitfeld of the *Washington Post*. "From another source," Streitfeld luckily obtained "several pages of Joe Klein's own handwriting." A lucky match between the two was then confirmed by the handwriting expert Maureen Casey Owens.[15]

Responding at once to the *Post*'s story, Random House called a press conference to issue an announcement about *Primary Colors*. The media gathered, full of expectation. After a few preliminary remarks by Harry Evans, the president of Random House, out stepped Joe Klein, wearing a plastic nose and a fake mustache. Removing the disguise, he said, "My name is Joe Klein and I wrote *Primary Colors*."

It was all over but the tongue-clucking and the suing. In the days and weeks that followed, editorials from coast to coast hammered Joe Klein and his Marathon Lie with such eloquence and indignation that I saw no cause to interject myself into the discussion. Glad that the ordeal was over (and even, to tell the truth, feeling exhausted and a little angry), my only comment was "No comment"; but it was nice to have the noose removed from my vulnerable and rope-burned academic neck. A literacy teacher named Daria Carter-Clark sued Klein for libel, protesting that she most certainly did *not* have sex with Bill Clinton, as was strongly implied by Klein in his dramatization of the governor's 1991 visit to a Harlem literacy clinic. When various commentators opined that I should take action as well, the suggestion was not overlooked by libel attorneys, whose offers rained down on me like manna from heaven, promising a big settlement, $10 million minimum, if I'd sue Klein for defamation and *libel per se*, with Random House and *Newsweek* named as a co-defendants, the "deep pockets." I thought it over and said no. It had been a tough experience for me in many ways, but it was over. Most academics believe in free speech, including the freedom to lie. In the end, truth usually prevails (which is not always true with lawyers). But I confess to moments of wishing I had not squandered the opportunity.

As it turns out, it was not only Joe Klein but *Newsweek*'s editor, Maynard Parker, who knew that the magazine's February 12 exclusive about Luciano Siracusano was a load of hooey (along with the rest of *Newsweek*'s coverage, such as Mark Miller's January 29 inquiry, "Who Wrote the Book on Bill?"—but for Miller, at least, it was an honest question).[16] Maynard Parker announced that Joe Klein would take a "leave of absence" from his *Newsweek* post (a three-week vacation). But first, to be fair, Parker let Joe keep on dumping. In "A Brush with Anonymity" (July 29), his last column before the three-week vacation, Klein tells the lamentable tale of Joe and the Professor. "Here is what I thought was going to happen last January," he says:

> *Primary Colors,* my anonymous novel, would be a modest success. . . . I figured I would be a likely suspect and would have to deny authorship. I figured no one would believe me. Friends, colleagues, and pols would say, "Awww, c'mon Joe, it's you. No question. Don't hang noodles on our ears." And with that, it would be over: mystery solved. . . . A week before the New Hampshire primary, the roof caved in. *New York* magazine hired a Vassar professor with a computer program to analyze the styles of the various suspects. It was a pretty good program. But neither the professor nor the magazine called to ask my reaction until they'd already issued a press release. The things said about me in the release and the accompanying article were insulting, inaccurate, and ridiculous.[17]

Not much in this report was true. The text analysis was my own. I have no "computer program." The computer was useful to me as a search tool, a device by which to begin the search for Anonymous. As for the heads-up, neither I nor *New York*'s editors were obliged to call Joe Klein in advance—"Why should we have called him sooner?" Kurt Andersen asked. "So that he could start lying sooner?"—but Joe Klein *was* called, on the morning of February 15, only hours after the article was finished. He returned with a jocund message, amused, until he read "Primary Culprit" and bristled. Nor do I find, either in my own work or in *New York*'s press release, any ridiculous or insulting remark; nor can I discover any inaccuracies except, perhaps, my stated opinion that "journalists like Klein do care about facts," and that a professional newsman "may equivocate, but it makes him squirm to lie baldly." I believed those statements to be true. In fact, I still do. In most cases.

In his July 29 column, before taking three weeks off for bad behavior, Joe Klein admits having lied. But he ended his "Brush with Anonymity," and an episode in his life and mine, on a note of altruism, observing that his traumatic experience as Anonymous argues the need for political reform in America, and for Bill and Hillary Clinton to return to traditional values: "Sure. I've said some things I'll probably always regret. . . . It is very easy to screw up, and it is unrelenting. But *they* do it every day, and that is no way for a civilized nation to choose its leaders. Of course, this was one of the themes of *Primary Colors*."[18]

CHAPTER THREE

A Professor's Whodunit

TED'S STORY

> To quote from Joseph Conrad's *Heart of Darkness,* "I had to deal
> with a being to whom I could not appeal in the name of anything
> high or low. . . . There was nothing either above or below him. . . .
> He had kicked himself loose of the earth. . . . He was alone."
>
> —TED KACZYNSKI, "AUTOBIOGRAPHY" (1979)[1]

April 28, 1999. I had a fine view of the surrounding countryside from
my room on the seventh floor of the "Quantico Hilton," the poshest
of three dormitory buildings at the FBI Academy. Soon after I had
arrived, registered, been fitted with an ID tag, and was settled into my
room, I gave Gwen a call. "What's it like?" she asked.

"Clean as a whistle, no frills. Single bed with a mattress and a
folded stack of fresh linens. You don't worry about losing your key
because you don't have one—the guest rooms have no locks." Resting
on my mattress, which I had not yet sheeted, were my bag, a parcel
of sensitive documents, and a laptop computer. "Evidently," I joked,
"security here is not a problem."

The campus, which has the appearance of a small university, is situated in a quiet wooded area, the silence being broken only by the *rat-a-tat-tat* of gunfire from a nearby range and the sporadic report of high-powered rifles. Twenty-one buildings are linked at ground level by a maze of glass corridors. The sunny second-floor dining hall can be hard to find on a first visit, but the food is plentiful and good, and the facility is spotless. Next door to the cafeteria is a pub for after-hours socializing, and a small movie theater. The athletic facilities are first-rate, the classrooms well equipped, and the library, in its way, excellent.

Within jogging distance of the main complex, just across Hoover Road, is a small city called Hogan's Alley, used for training, with a bank, school, church, theater, hardware store, houses, courthouse, post office, motel, and casino. Behind the Hollywood facades are offices, classrooms, and audiovisual facilities. Hired actors perform the roles of hostage-taker, drug dealer, crazed gunman, cardsharp, trial court judge, hired assassin, mad bomber. No Shakespeare.

The Academy serves as a "new agent" training center for the FBI as well as for the Drug Enforcement Administration. The DEA recruits, who wear green shirts and khaki slacks, bark out a crisp "Good morning!" or "Good evening!" to everyone they pass in the halls, including me. The blue-shirted FBI recruits do not. I see no one in a trench coat and black wing tips.

Guest instructors like me are welcome to shop in the Academy store for FBI ballpoint pens or exercise gear, or for an FBI Academy T-shirt, but the racks are filled mostly with sizes XL and XXL. In this place there's no market for Large and Medium. I worked out with these barrel-chested guys one afternoon in the gym. They're big.

Regular teaching staff at the Academy includes about a hundred special agents, most of whom hold advanced degrees in criminology, forensic science, abnormal psychology. I was here by invitation of the National Center for the Analysis of Violent Crime, headed by Supervisory Special Agent (SSA) James Fitzgerald. Fitzgerald's office consolidates research into every kind of violent criminal activity while providing investigative support to local law enforcement agencies. To remain on the cutting edge of criminological study, Fitzgerald's unit has been tireless in developing new resources and testing new strategies for analyzing the behavior and language of violent offenders.

After making up the bed, reviewing my notes, and testing my PowerPoint slides for the next day's session, I opened a large envelope containing my evening's reading material. Inside was Ted Kaczynski's handwritten 1979 "Autobiography," a 200-page document I had not seen before, found in his Montana residence, a copy of which is stored at Quantico with the Unabom archive. Theodore John Kaczynski, now doing time in a Colorado supermax penitentiary, was no longer a threat to society, nor even much of a mystery to most Americans, but I found myself interested in the stories of his life, in the words and texts that helped to make him who he is. In April 1996, 22,000 pages of writing were pulled from Kaczynski's tiny home, papers crammed into mildewed boxes in the cabin's loft, and in notebooks on the suspect's desk, and stashed in heaps on shelves and under the bed. In the 1979 "Autobiography," penned in his parents' Lombard, Illinois, home, Ted writes frankly of his unhappy childhood, adolescent misery, adult disappointments, and sexual obsessions. He tells of his lifelong struggle to find words adequate to express his passion for freedom, his great rage, his almost inexpressible hatred. The manuscript closes with a scholar's coldly intellectual account of his decision to become a serial killer.

RECOGNITION

> In one of the Brothers movies, as Chico was entering, Groucho said: "Hello, you look similar to a man that I know and his name is Ravelli." Chico answered: "I am Ravelli." "Ha," responded Groucho: "that explains the similarity."
> —TED KACZYNSKI, IN A LETTER TO HIS BROTHER, DAVID (1989)[2]

From June 22, 1993, when a terrorist calling himself "FC" renewed his deadly crusade against college professors and businessmen after a five-year hiatus, until April 3, 1996, when the FBI arrested Theodore Kaczynski, I opened my mail gingerly, taking every advised precaution, but there was not much cause for concern. As the Unabomber explained in a 1995 letter to the *New York Times,* he intended to kill or maim university scientists and engineers, as many as possible, but he was loath to think that anyone would suspect him of wishing "to hurt professors who study archaeology, history, literature, or harmless stuff like that." Literature, according to Ted Kaczynski's "Autobiography," is one of the "bullshit subjects," an academic discipline whose few insights are so mixed up with harmless nonsense that no one, not even a genius in mathematics, can easily "extract the kernels of truth from amongst the garbage."[3]

But if we literary scholars were unimperiled by FC, neither was FC much threatened by us. Contrary to some media reports, I did not help solve the Unabom case. In May 1978, when FC's first mail bomb detonated at Northwestern University, injuring Terry Marker, I was teaching high school English in Santa Cruz. In April 1995, when the sixteenth device exploded in Sacramento, killing Gilbert Murray, I was teaching Shakespeare classes at Vassar College. The *New York Times* article about the Shakespeare elegy had not yet appeared and *Primary Colors* wouldn't be published for another nine months. In the interim, the thought never entered my head to assist the FBI in its search for a university bomber, nor was anyone likely to call. In fact, I was on the wrong end of the investigation altogether. In 1993, when Jim Freeman took over as Special Agent in Charge of the Unabom Task Force, he cast a wide net, trawling a computer-generated pool of more than 50,000 "possible" and some 600 "plausible" suspects. My own name remained in the bucket until the day of the arrest. As a sometime woodworker, and as a resident of the Chicago suburbs (till 1973), then of California (till 1986), I was one of hundreds who looked like a better bet than Theodore Kaczynski of Montana. Kaczynski's date of birth (1942) was much too early for the FBI profile of an offender born 1957–1962, and his address of record since 1981 (available from the Harvard alumni office) was "788 Banchat Pesh, Khadar Khel, Afghanistan." Until David Kaczynski's attorney, Anthony Bisceglie, led investigators to a resident of Montana, the name Ted Kaczynski was not one that rocketed to the surface.

The identity of the mysterious FC, the acronym by which Ted Kaczynski most often identified himself during his seventeen-year-long campaign of terror, was cracked in Paris, by Linda Patrik, a professor of philosophy (another of Ted's designated "bullshit subjects"). Reading about FC and his manifesto while vacationing in France, Professor Patrik was struck by evident points of similarity between the Unabomber and her brother-in-law, an angry Montana hermit whom she feared but had never actually met. The FBI was said to be looking for a native of Chicago with ties to Salt Lake City and Northern California, an angry loner with woodworking ability, experience with explosives, and a deep-seated resentment of modern technology. When Patrik was joined in Paris by her husband, David Kaczynski, she mentioned her unsettling intuition that his brother, Ted, could be the Unabomber. David at first found the suggestion unthinkable. Teddy was a resentnik, maybe crazy, but he would never really hurt anyone. Patrik gave it a rest.

In mid-October, back home but nagged by an irrepressible suspicion, Professor Patrik downloaded the Unabom manifesto, "Industrial Society and Its Future," by FC. It sounded just like Ted. She shared the text with David, who reluctantly agreed. Here were Ted's ideas and ponderous arguments, largely borrowed from the pop sociologist Jacques Ellul, and Ted's manner of expression—the mathematically precise phrasing and repetitive syntax, the almost schizoid appeal to logic as a justification for avenging personal resentments. The entire overlong treatise was structured like a badly edited academic dissertation—or like one of Ted's angry letters from Montana. For example, from paragraph 18: "cool-headed logicians." How many times had Ted blamed his parents' liberalism, and David's, on a "leftist's feelings of inferiority" while praising himself as a "cool-headed logician"? Ted wrote that paragraph. David did not have to study the whole 35,000-word document from beginning to end. He had heard it all before, and he recognized the voice.

GOOD REASON

> Some of the people around here certainly have their faults, but I'll
> have to give them credit for this: They are perceptive enough to rec-
> ognize my preference for solitude, and considerate enough to respect
> that preference. I've rarely had anyone bother me with a visit unless
> it was for a good reason.
>
> —TED KACZYNSKI, ON HIS CANYON CREEK NEIGHBORS (1984)[4]

On the morning of April 3, 1996, I was still busy explaining why
"W.S." could not be an assortment of alternative W.S.'s. Joe Klein was
still in the midst of his "I am not 'Anonymous' " tour. But Ted Kaczynski was in trouble. A parade of vehicles carrying dozens of federal
agents was silently snaking its way along the unpaved road toward
Stemple Pass in the Montana Rockies. The Kaczynski residence,
H.C.R. 30, was the last cabin on the Humbug Contour, a logging skid
road, a dirt track made muddy with the April thaw. Ted Kaczynski
built the house by himself in 1971—plywood walls, brown-red paint
now long-faded, a tar-paper roof, mossy green. One door, three locks.
Daylight was supplied by two small, square window holes (one north,
one south) high up near the eaves. No one could see in, nor could
Ted see out. The cabin had a small woodstove for heat and cooking,
but no electricity, no phone, no running water. Ted would sometimes
stay inside for weeks without coming out. The house smelled of human waste.

As the first rays of sunlight struck the cabin's front side you could
make out the heaps of trash and scorched food cans. Also, a fifty-
gallon drum, a chopping block, a stone-ringed fireplace. Off to the
left, a small lean-to shelter, designed as a drying shed but serving now
as a garage for Ted's rusty red bicycle, makeshift bike trailer, and
scavenged parts. The hermit's fire pit and the surrounding aspen grove
were littered with the bones of animals, victims of the hunt.

There would be no more hunting for Ted Kaczynski. Agents Max
Noel and Tom McDaniel approached the cabin on foot, accompanied

by Jerry Burns, a ranger with the U.S. Forest Service. With cover provided by a dozen heavily armed agents hiding behind trees, the three men slipped around to the front of Ted's cabin and stood by the door. Burns called out a hearty good morning, identified himself, and announced that two of the mining guys from Phelps Dodge were here with a question about Ted's property line.

Kaczynski slipped the dead bolt, opened the door, and stepped out into the morning light. He sized up his visitors, said "Just a minute," and turned for the door. Quick as a flash, Burns and McDaniel grabbed Kaczynski by the arms as Noel drew down on him with his service revolver. While Burns cuffed the suspect and frisked him for weapons, Noel and McDaniel showed their badges and served him with a warrant: "FBI—Mr. Kaczynski, we have to talk."

The suspect did not look much like a former math professor—or, for that matter, like a present threat to society. His black jeans and black shirt were in tatters, practically falling off. His face and hands were grimy, his complexion chalky pale. He stood before them with a wooden face. For a moment Max Noel stared back, not at the hermit's face but at his bush of wild and dirty, weedwackable hair. Kaczynski's reddish-gray mop was visibly crawling with fleas and head lice.

Wily as a cornered fox, the suspect looked down at his sandaled feet. "May I go back inside for a moment and get better shoes?"

"Sorry."

This was not the way that Ted had imagined it would end.

WARRANTED PURSUIT

> Through a series of false statements, material omissions, and irrelevant information, the Government improperly attempted to suggest that there was evidence that Theodore Kaczynski was the author of the Unabom manuscript.
>
> —KACZYNSKI DEFENSE,
> "MOTION TO SUPPRESS EVIDENCE" (3 MARCH 1997)[5]

The first strategic question raised by Quin Denvir and Judy Clarke, Ted Kaczynski's court-appointed attorneys, concerned the validity of the warrant. Did the comparative text analysis of SSA James Fitzgerald, which cataloged similarities between the defendant's known writings on the one hand, and writings by the Unabom subject on the other, establish probable cause for the search of Kaczynski's Montana residence? Kaczynski's attorneys did not think so—and if Fitzgerald's attributional work was seriously flawed, then the warrant ought never to have been issued. Kaczynski's counsel moved for the court to suppress all inculpatory evidence found inside the cabin, alleging that the April 3 search was illegal, the warrant having been obtained under false pretense.

In November 1996, four months after Joe Klein finally confessed to his authorship of *Primary Colors,* I received a surprise telephone call, an invitation to join the Kaczynski defense team as an expert witness. Known writings by FC and by Kaczynski were composed as much as a quarter-century apart. Why should the court have countenanced chance similarities in phrasing as evidence of common authorship? Theodore Kaczynski had no criminal record. The FBI should not have set foot inside his Montana home without more compelling evidence than the opinion of one or two government agents that Kaczynski wrote the Unabom manifesto. Would I be willing to inspect the analysis of SSA Fitzgerald, to identify methodological errors?

Having never served as an expert witness in a criminal trial, I requested a few days to think over the invitation. In the interim I studied the FBI affidavit, prepared by Assistant Special Agent in Charge Terry Turchie, together with various writings ascribed either to Ted Kaczynski or to the Unabom subject that had been made available on the Internet. The Turchie affidavit, which included much of Fitzgerald's text analysis, had supplied the court with probable cause for issuing the April 3 search warrant.[6] In my inspection of those documents it appeared altogether likely that Kaczynski was indeed the FC who wrote "Industrial Society and Its Future." It appeared also that agents Turchie and Fitzgerald had done a careful job of laying out the evidence. I declined the invitation to assist. The defense team found someone else.

EVALUATION

> The teacher took out a book, leafed through it frantically, and found what he was looking for. . . . "I'm putting next to your name," he continued, opening his booklet, "a very bad grade." Since then, this little error has always pursued me. It has ruined my career.
>
> —"HERCULES" (TED KACZYNSKI), LETTER TO
> PROF. LOUIS DE BRANGES, NOT SENT (1985)[7]

March 1997. A few months after hearing from the Kaczynski defense team I received a second invitation, this one from Stephen Freccero, one of the federal prosecutors. In their motion to suppress evidence, Kaczynski's lawyers had blasted SSA James Fitzgerald's comparative text analysis as a worthless, even fraudulent, report. Freccero asked if I would be willing to respond for the prosecution side. Having never seen an expert witness declaration, having no clue how to write one, what to include or what to leave out, I had some doubts about whether I was the best person for the job. Mr. Freccero said he could advise me on the formal conventions and legal language, though not, of course, on substantive matters. Not wishing to see thoughtful attributional work discredited, I agreed to see what I could do.

There were reams of documents to examine: the defense motion, with attached declarations by expert witnesses (nearly 300 pages), the Turchie affidavit (106 pages, partly redacted), and the Fitzgerald analysis (53 pages). Fitzgerald's work was based in turn on the 14 "U-docs" (known writings by the Unabom subject), including FC's "Industrial Society"; 178 "T-docs" (known writings by Ted Kaczynski); a text archive that included Ted's 1966 doctoral thesis and professional publications; teaching notes from a 1968 math class at UC Berkeley; Ted's unpublished sociological and anthropological essays; family correspondence, 1966–1994; an angry letter to Joe Visocan, a former employer; various letters in Spanish from "Teodoro Kaczynski" to his Mexican *"amigo,"* Juan Sanchez Arreola; plus a cornucopia of bitterly clever short stories, illuminating dream narratives, and two copies of a Swiftian novella called *The Adventures of H. Bascomb Thurgood.*

I did not examine any writings found inside Kaczynski's Montana residence, nor did Stephen Freccero ever mention to me that such documents existed. While preparing my declarations for the prosecution, I knew nothing of Ted Kaczynski's 1979 "Autobiography," nor had I heard of his journals or hit list, nor learned that Unabom-related books were found inside the cabin. It was not my task to determine for prosecutors whether or not Kaczynski ever built or mailed a bomb, nor to comment on his mental health. My commission was limited to just two questions: Was the FBI affidavit reasonable, fair, and accurate in having characterized as "very similar" the writings of Theodore Kaczynski and of the Unabom subject? And were the defense witnesses correct in alleging that the FBI substantially misrepresented the attributional evidence?

Kaczynski's attorneys argued in their motion to suppress that the Unabom correspondence and manifesto might have been written by almost any thoughtful opponent of modern technology. SSA James Fitzgerald had observed, for example, that Kaczynski and FC both cited such texts as *The Ancient Engineers* (1963) by L. Sprague De Camp; *The Technological Society* (1964) by Jacques Ellul; *Violence in America* (1969) by Hugh Graham and Ted Gurr; and multiple issues of *Scientific American* magazine. That the Unabomber and Ted Kaczynski read and cited the same books (including volumes long out of print) was not, in the eyes of the defense, reliable evidence. Various scholars declared for the defense that these texts were known to thousands of readers and that the common citations by Kaczynski and the Unabomber should have been viewed by the court as inconsequential.[8]

Fitzgerald took his hardest hit from Robin Lakoff, a well-known linguist at UC Berkeley retained by the defense. In a ten-page declaration peppered with scholarly jargon, Professor Lakoff dismissed

SSA Fitzgerald's compilation of textual evidence as "untenable and unreliable, at best."[9] She alleged "at least seven" categories of systematic error in Fitzgerald's work and gave examples of each type. Lakoff's first categorical objection was to the FBI's alleged "double use of content-linked lexical choices" as evidence of common authorship. To put that in layman's terms: the Unabom subject and Theodore Kaczynski both discussed a similar topic (electronic technology), but when any two individuals write about electronics (a similarity) they might hit upon the topical word *electrodes* (but that's still only one textual similarity, not two). Ted's mention of *electrodes* is thus a *content-linked* word choice, prompted by the topic—technology— irrespective of authorship.

Lost in the academic mumbo jumbo is the extraordinary fact that Ted Kaczynski and FC both wrote of "electrodes" being "inserted" in the human head as *brain implants,* which is indeed unusual, even in a discussion of technology. Kaczynski in a 1971 essay fretted over the future prospect of "Direct physical *control* of the emotions via *electrodes* and *chemitrodes inserted in the brain*" (my emphasis). The Unabom subject, writing a quarter-century later, opined that it is now possible for "people to be *controlled*" by means of *"electrodes inserted in their heads."* Fitzgerald had simply listed this as "a similarity" between the known writings of Ted Kaczynski and FC. Kaczynski is probably not the only person ever to have considered the vast potential for the improper use of electrodes—Oklahoma City bomber Timothy McVeigh, for one, feared surreptitious implantation of computer chips in his body—but the identified similarities between FC's manifesto and the writings of Ted Kaczynski were not, in my opinion, "absolutely meaningless" as stated by the defense.[10]

Professor Lakoff also pummeled Fitzgerald for having mentioned that Kaczynski and FC both prefer such spellings as "analyse," "skilful," "wilfully," "licence," "instalment" (instead of the more common American spellings, analyze, skillful, willfully, license, installment). Observing in her declaration for the defense that many American dictionaries permit the Kaczynski/Unabom spellings as acceptable variants, Lakoff condemned Fitzgerald's inclusion of such orthographical evidence as another type of "categorical error." The other five types of categorical error were more of the same. Discounting one by one the items of textual and linguistic evidence presented by Fitzgerald, Professor Lakoff denied seeing the forest for the trees, dismissing each identified similarity as slight or circumstantial: Kaczynski and the Unabom subject, she concluded, wrote nothing that was not found in the ordinary language of law-abiding citizens. But Fitzgerald had made no claim for the uniqueness of any particular similarity between the T-docs and the U-docs. It was the sheer magnitude and detail of the similarities between those documents that provided probable cause for a search of Kaczynski's Montana cabin.

Having dismissed Fitzgerald's work as worthless, the defense alleged further that the T-docs and the U-docs exhibited "readily apparent" discrepancies. For example: Kaczynski misspelled *chlorate* ("clorate"), not just once but three times in a single document. In his manifesto, the Unabomber twice spells *chlorate* correctly (FC boasts of using "a *chlorate pipe bomb to blow up* Thomas Mosser" and "a *chlorate explosive . . . to blow up* the genetic engineer Charles Epstein and the computer specialist David Gelernter").[11] The defense complained that this "important distinction" between Ted's language ("clorate") and FC's ("chlorate") passed unnoted by Fitzgerald. But Ted wrote "clorate" in 1970.[12] By 1986, he had learned to spell *chloride* and *chlorine* (in his letters); one may guess that he also learned, by 1995, how to spell *chlorate*. And while Ted may have misspelled *chlorate* in 1970, he already recognized its potential usefulness. Like the Unabomber, Ted Kaczynski had a fantasy of making people "blow up," and with the same material: all three of those 1970 instances of "clorate" appear in an original short story by Ted called "How I Blew Up Harold Snilly," submitted to *Harper's* for publication, and rejected.

As a supplementary assault on the competence and legality of the FBI's case against Kaczynski, the defense submitted a lengthy "Critique of the FBI Analysis of the T-documents and the U-documents."[13] This declaration introduced much new evidence—or seemed to—noting, for example, a fine point of English grammar: Ted Kaczynski frequently splits his infinitives, writing "to all go" and "to voluntarily change" instead of "all to go" and "to change voluntarily." The Unabomber, according to the "Critique," does not. Reporting *twenty* split infinitives in the T-docs versus just one in the U-docs, the defense's "Critique" characterizes that 20–1 discrepancy as an important distinction between Kaczynski's writing and the Unabomber's—a stylistic difference that Fitzgerald ought to have acknowledged, but is alleged to have suppressed.

As it happens, the defense overlooked five of six split infinitives in the U-docs. The defense also neglected to consider sample size: twenty split infinitives in a text sample of roughly 150,000 words (the T-docs' total word count) is not significantly different from six split infinitives in a sample of 43,200 words (the U-docs' total word count). Moreover, the one Unabom instance actually cited by the defense, "to just turn" (FC), finds close analogues in the T-documents: "to just dump," "to just sort of look," "to just shove," "to just go down."[14]

Most "normal" folks—English teachers and editors naturally excepted—do not care much about grammatical conformity. As exhibited in all fourteen U-documents (1978–1995), the Unabomber had a zeal for correct grammar, a passion shared by Ted Kaczynski. In his known writings as far back as 1966, except in his private journals, Ted attempts to catch and correct every vague pronoun reference, every error of subject-verb agreement, every misplaced comma. Sometimes, especially on those occasions when David's letters included something that Ted did not wish to read, he returned the letter like a marked-up classroom assignment, each typographical or grammatical error duly circled. But he missed the split infinitives.

Though prepared to acknowledge any occasional or systematic flaws in the FBI's comparative text analysis, I found that it could be faulted for nothing worse than citation errors—some mistaken document numbers, and a few inadvertent citations to the FBI's own English translation of Ted Kaczynski's original Spanish. Far from stacking the deck, Fitzgerald had cautiously understated the case for common authorship of the U-docs and T-docs. The textual evidence as presented in the Turchie affidavit spoke for itself: there was every likelihood that "Industrial Society and Its Future" was written by

Theodore J. Kaczynski of 30 Humbug Contour, Lincoln, Montana. The defense had no case.

On April 11, 1997, when the "Declaration of Donald W. Foster, Ph.D.," was signed, sealed, and delivered to the federal district attorney to be filed with the court, I returned to Shakespeare, thinking my Unabom assignment at an end. I was mistaken. Kaczynski's attorneys filed a blistering Reply Memorandum, renewing the attack on SSA Fitzgerald's work while adding mine to the dartboard. The Foster declaration did "not address, much less refute, any of [the] errors, flaws, and omissions" identified in the defense motion to suppress and in the declarations by expert witnesses. Foster had merely "opined" that those statements were unreliable. "Incredibly, Professor Foster fails to back up this opinion with even a *single* example of a false or misleading statement or material omission in the defense submission. . . . Foster's failure to do so demonstrates the hollowness of his opinion."[15] The defense even went so far as to question whether my declaration was truly based on "a detailed examination of all the relevant documents."[16]

Attached to this defense riposte was a "Second Declaration" by Robin Lakoff, reasserting "Seven Types of Systematic Error" in SSA Fitzgerald's work. In her second declaration, Professor Lakoff made a surprising admission, freely acknowledging that her original opinion was based on a reading of the Turchie affidavit, one U-doc (the manifesto), one T-doc (the 1971 essay), and commentary prepared by Ted's attorneys. In short, Lakoff had read only two of the two hundred documents on which Fitzgerald's analysis was based. She affirmed it unnecessary to read all of the original documents: "Doing so would in no way have altered my conclusions."[17]

As a novice expert witness, still somewhat naive, still idealistic about the objectivity of expert witness testimony in a criminal trial, I was startled by this development. My first declaration was five pages long without detailed examples because I had been instructed to keep it short, but I had done the necessary homework. The defense's argument seemed audacious (We don't believe that the prosecution witness even *read* these documents—we know *ours* sure didn't!).

I knew that if the case ever came to trial, Professor Lakoff, an accomplished scholar—having published six books in her field—would be a formidable opponent on the witness stand. In preparing a detailed response, I went about my work with the earnestness of a schoolboy hoping to produce an exemplary exhibit for the school science fair, preparing (as I had time, between classes) a second declaration that spelled out the evidence in full, rebutting the defense allegations item by item, with representative illustrations from the original texts. This was my first performance in the high-stakes game of criminal justice, and I did not wish to blow it through careless oversight or a hasty inference.

That second, detailed report, fifty pages, was duly submitted to the U.S. Attorney's Office but not filed with the court, being rendered unnecessary on May 23, 1997, when Judge Garland Burrell denied the defense motion to suppress, citing my first declaration in the judicial opinion. I felt good about that. Even if Theodore Kaczynski never stood trial for killing Hugh Scrutton, Thomas Mosser, and Gilbert Murray, the Unabom case had led to a benchmark decision regarding the legitimacy of attributional evidence in a criminal prosecution. It seemed almost a shame that the second declaration then was not needed, but it was not lost labor, nor uninteresting work. By the time I was done studying thirty years of Theodore Kaczynski's writings, I felt as if I knew him.

SEARCHING FOR FC

> With a briefcase-full or a suitcase-full of explosives we should be able to blow out the walls of substantial buildings. Clearly we are in a position to do a great deal of damage. And it doesn't appear that the FBI is going to catch us any time soon. The FBI is a joke.
>
> —FC TO *NEW YORK TIMES* (20 APRIL 1995,
> ONE DAY AFTER THE OKLAHOMA CITY BOMBING)[18]

The Unabom investigation became a priority for the FBI only after the death of Hugh Scrutton in November 1985, prior to which there were no fatalities from FC's booby-trap devices, no substantial leads, nor any mention in the press of the Bureau's quiet search for a serial bomber. In the seventeen-year period during which the Unabom case remained open, there were 30,000 bombing incidents in the United States with 500 fatalities, not counting the 168 deaths in the Oklahoma City catastrophe. FC was a little fish in a big pond. The "Unabomber" eventually gained notoriety not for his ingenuity or deadly force, but for his extreme weirdness—the story of his life.

It is, however, true that when the FBI began searching in earnest for the Unabom suspect, none of the Bureau's time-tested methods for investigating serial crime was especially helpful. Ted Kaczynski's cleverness in avoiding apprehension, and the FBI's difficulty in catching him, have become part of the Kaczynski legend. By 1995, the search for the Unabomber had become the most expensive manhunt in U.S. history, topping $50 million before there was an arrest. FC launched sixteen "raids" in seventeen years, delivered antipersonnel bombs in seven different states, plus one in the air (an "experiment"), and detonated trial bombs in Montana by the dozen. At the time of the arrest, one completed bomb was already wrapped and ready for a post office drop box, with another under construction. Had his manifesto not been both published and noticed by Linda Patrik and David Kaczynski, the Unabomber might yet have made good on plans to turn his one-member terrorist organization into a bulk mail operation. (His cabin inventory at the time of his arrest included some 40 pipes, 200 feet of copper tubing, 23 identical initiators, and dozens of timing devices and switches.) Contemptuous of the FBI, underestimating the investigative value of his own manifesto, the Unabomber fancied that a coolheaded logician like himself would never be apprehended.

Kaczynski was indeed a thoughtful adversary, withholding the kinds of evidence that the FBI is best equipped to handle—fingerprints, voiceprints, fibers of clothing, eyewitness testimony, and a coherent geographical zone for his field of operation. His bomb components could not be traced, because the devices were largely constructed of scrap material scavenged from junkyards. He sanded the stickers and labels off purchased parts, such as batteries. He wore disguises when purchasing supplies or delivering pipe bombs. From the first Unabom incident in 1978 until the Murray homicide in 1995, the Task Force received no fruitful tips from the public. The bomber was spotted in February 1987, in Salt Lake City, after which he lay low until 1993. Until 1995 he was careful not to lick a stamp or an envelope. (He once pulled a hair from a public rest room and taped it to a Unabom device to throw the FBI off track. The hair was not found, however, and we would not have known about it had Ted not boasted of the stratagem in a journal discovered after the arrest.)

Kaczynski never attacked a personal acquaintance or someone who could identify him. He moved around, planting or mailing his parcels when far from home. His telephone could not be bugged because he did not own one. Nor could anyone squeal on him, because he had no accomplice, no confidant. He did not socialize, had no friends, and regularly deceived his own family concerning his whereabouts. He gave investigators nothing that would turn their attention to the state of Montana. On balance, discounting the evidence of FC's writing, all clues pointed to a craftsman, possibly an airline mechanic, or a university facilities man, but no mathematics scholar. If it were not for his compulsion to write, the Unabomber might still be a free man.

UNIDENTIFIED SUBJECT

> So I thought, "I will kill, but I will make at least some effort to avoid detection, so that I can kill again."
>
> —TED KACZYNSKI, UNDATED MONTANA JOURNAL[19]

On my visit to Quantico, Jim Fitzgerald posed an interesting question: Linda Patrik, then David Kaczynski, then others, came to recognize the words and thoughts of FC as those of Theodore Kaczynski—but what if that hadn't happened? What if David and Linda had dismissed their fears, assured by published profiles that the bomber was not really like Ted? What if the Kaczynskis had been simply too busy to take an interest in a criminal matter out west that seemed to have no bearing on their placid life in Schenectady, New York? Or missed the story altogether while vacationing in France? Could the author of the manifesto have been discovered without the cooperation of the *Washington Post* and the *New York Times* and the invaluable assistance of Ted Kaczynski's own family? Putting our heads together, SSA Fitzgerald and I discussed how the Unabomber might have been apprehended without that crucial break.

Equipped with the advantage of hindsight, and with a full set of Known Documents (KDs) for Kaczynski as well as for the Unabomber, I resumed close study of FC's writing and writing behaviors as time allowed. Beginning with that visit to Quantico, I reviewed the Unabom case history and spoke with agents who had been assigned to the Task Force. Taking advantage of Jim Fitzgerald's expertise and intimate knowledge of the investigation, I came to believe that the authorities might have been led to Ted Kaczynski without fingerprints, without DNA, without eyewitnesses, without the forensic analysis of bomb components—even without known writings by Ted Kaczynski—just by paying extraordinarily close attention to the bomber's own words. With a little persistence, the Unabom case might even have been solved using no other resource than a good academic library.

TYPING BEHAVIORS: CRIMINAL PROFILING AND THE QUESTIONED DOCUMENT

> The Unabomber probably drives an older car but keeps it in good condition. He may have a wife or girlfriend. . . . It's June—maybe he's off from school, he's traveling, he won't be available for the summer. And since he's traveling, maybe flying, he realizes he doesn't

want a hardening of security at the airports. . . . He also would be obsessed with the investigation. While other people would want to talk about the Cubs, he would want to talk about the bombings.

—JOHN DOUGLAS ON FC'S CANCELED THREAT
TO BOMB A COMMERCIAL JET (1995)[20]

Throughout North America, the analysis of criminal behavior, especially of serial offenders, has mushroomed into a cottage industry, driven in part by popular mythology of the "criminal profiler" as represented in box-office hits (*The Silence of the Lambs*), television series (*Profiler*), and memoirs such as John Douglas's *Mindhunter*. Hundreds of self-styled profilers, only a few of whom have successful track records, now advertise their services on the Internet. Police detectives, even those who remain skeptical of the claims made by these independent agencies, are often forced to take advantage of the service, if only to demonstrate to an impatient public that every avenue is being explored.

Certain sorts of crime—including arson, child molestation, rape, serial murder, and terrorist attacks—are most often committed by persons sharing particular socioeconomic or psychological traits. With a personal crime, including most rapes and homicides, one must begin from the crime scene and work outward, through the victim's circle of acquaintance. With a stranger crime, one must begin with a profile that may include a million possible suspects and narrow the field as new information becomes available. A majority of bomb builders in this country are white, medium-framed, lower-middle-class males, high school graduates, often with military training. Bombers tend to be neat in their dress and hygiene, and are generally nonconfrontational, even cowardly, but also deeply resentful, being motivated by low self-esteem or by a sense of injured narcissism. A serial bomber is likely to be a loner, unathletic, unsuccessful with women, and to live alone or with a female relative.

Criminal profiling as practiced by the FBI is based not on the profiler's wizardlike intuition (as glamorously represented by Hollywood) but on a statistical model, augmented by practical experience.

No bomber fits the archetype in every particular. Without specific information about the offender, profiling can be unproductive or even misleading. In my opinion, the best way to gather knowledge of the perpetrator's age, movements, educational background, work record, and circle of acquaintance is to engage the offender in communication, from which a particularized linguistic and textual profile may be constructed. At the investigative level, a single piece of anonymous writing from a violent criminal can be as useful as fingerprints, and far more reliable than a profile based on similar crimes by other offenders. That's because a language and text profile depends on patterns of evidence generated by the offender's own brain.

Every investigative strategy has its limits. When Richard Jewell discovered a nail-wrapped pipe bomb in Atlanta's Centennial Park on July 27, 1996, he was celebrated as a hero—briefly. He was the first person to find the device. He also fit the profile of an attention-seeking bomb builder.[21] The authorities quickly focused their attention on Jewell as the likely perpetrator, someone out to make himself into a hero by "finding" a bomb of his own construction. But he was innocent. The Centennial Park device was followed by the bombing of abortion clinics in Atlanta and Birmingham, and of a lesbian bar called The Other Side. The FBI Explosives Unit determined that the same individual may have been responsible for all four attacks. Letters followed, signed "A.O.G." and "Army of God." Having learned from the Unabom case that an offender can be identified by his words as well as by handwriting or fingerprints or DNA, the Southeast Bomb Task Force located other suspects besides Jewell, gathered writing samples, and asked me if I could help identify an author for those "Army of God" letters. I could, and did.

Though sometimes described in the press as a "handwriting expert," I rarely concern myself with writing pressure, or slant, or pen strokes. I concentrate on the text itself (irrespective of whether it was recorded by a pen, typewriter, or computer), and with the behaviors that produced the text. It is not just the mechanics of writing or the words chosen, but any distinctive writing behavior

New York newspapers—and could not get an audience. On Christmas Eve 1956, the same day on which the *New York Times* published the Brussel profile, another FP bomb was discovered (number 32, found in the New York Public Library) and safely disarmed. The NYPD detectives were exasperated, their efforts being complicated by hundreds of bomb hoaxes. Editors of the *New York Journal American* tried another tack. Without the angst suffered forty years later by editors of the *New York Times* and the *Washington Post,* editors of the *Journal American* offered the Mad Bomber column space in which to air his grievances. FP took them up on that offer.

In his first letter, written on cheap paper bearing the figure of a snowman, the Mad Bomber volunteered a Yuletide truce, thanking the editors for their concern. At the close, he asked not to be called "the Mad Bomber": "CALLING ME NAMES—IS JUST FRUSTRATED STUPIDITY IN ACTION—FP."[26] The bomber sent two more letters to the *Journal American,* one on January 15, 1957, the other on January 19. Acting on clues culled from FP's first two letters, a Con Ed clerk named Alice Kelly searched old personnel records for employees with health complaints. On January 18 she found the file of George Metesky, who claimed to have been injured at work on September 5, 1931, by an updraft of hot gases. Taking sick pay for months at 80 percent pay, he was finally dismissed. He then filed a disability claim that was disallowed because the statute of limitations for filing had expired. Kelly spotted none of the Mad Bomber's most colorful vocabulary ("dastardly acts," "slimy creatures," "ghoulish deeds"). What caught her eye in the Metesky file was the plural word "injustices," followed by a threat "to take justice in my own hands," fairly ordinary language that appeared in the Mad Bomber's prose a quarter-century later.

Members of the NYPD Bomb Investigation Unit at the time were still looking for the Mad Bomber in White Plains, poring over local records, or in Albany, investigating license and car registrations for White Plains residents. Three days after being informed of Alice Kelly's find, NYPD detectives dropped by Con Ed to pick up the Metesky file. On that same day, the *Journal American* received another letter from FP, in which he poked fun at the Brussel profile ("The nearest to my being 'Teutonic,' " wrote FP truthfully, "is that my father boarded a liner in Hamburg for passage to this country— about 65 years ago"). FP in this letter gave the exact date of his Con Ed injury: "September 5, 1931." NYPD detectives checked the George Metesky record for the date of *his* Con Ed injury: "September 5, 1931." That was pretty good evidence. Pulling up stakes in White Plains, the Bomb Investigation Unit dispatched detectives to Waterbury, Connecticut. Alice Kelly modestly renounced the $26,000 reward: "I was just doing my job," she said.

SPOTTED EVIDENCE: EYEWITNESS ACCOUNT VERSUS QUESTIONED DOCUMENTS

> You see what happened to the engineer. What a misfortune, Patron!
> . . . He came down turning over and over in the air like a shot bird.
> —JUAN CARLOS DAVALOS (TED KACZYNSKI, TRANS.),
> "THE FORT OF TACUIL"
> (TO DAVID, "FOR CHRISTMAS," 1985)[27]

From a legal point of view, eyewitness testimony is privileged information. When someone speaks to police detectives in an interview or takes the stand at trial and vows to speak the truth, the whole truth, and nothing but the truth, at least you know for sure who's speaking, which is not always true with a Questioned Document (QD). Following a homicide or a bombing, when police or the media receive an anonymous communication (a confession, explanation of motive, ransom note, or instructions of any sort), whether from the actual offender, or an impostor, or an unidentified informant, the first questions to be asked of the QD include "Is this information accurate?" and "Who wrote it?" Often, the answer to the one may depend on the answer to the other. Many such documents are hoaxes. Examples in the Unabom case include two handwritten love letters from "Ted Kaczynski" to "Tess," documents ignored by Jim Fitzgerald but used by John Douglas to predict Kaczynski's behavior while in prison.[28] As it happens, the "Tess" letters, obtained by a newspaper shortly after Ted's April 1996 arrest and duly forwarded to the FBI, were forgeries.

If traditional means for answering "Who wrote it?"—fingerprints, typeface, handwriting—cannot establish authorship, the QD is typically set aside, considered no further for investigative purposes, and omitted from consideration by the courts. But when gathered and systematically studied, the documents supplied by a serial offender, even when brief or deceitful, may lead investigators to discover the offender's age, gender, native region, socioeconomic background, educational level, and other critical information, while at the same time providing a check to mistaken profiles or inaccurate eyewitness accounts.

The evidence to be gleaned from an offender's writing, whether signed or anonymous, is often more dependable, always less changeable, than the testimony of an eyewitness. Two different guns or faces or hats may look alike, causing a witness to misreport what he or she has observed. A second witness may forget or misremember much of what transpired, or tell first one story then another. He might come to the stand looking strong and then falter under cross-examination. A third witness may lie outright, or equivocate. A fourth may drop dead or flee the country. Linguistic and textual evidence is not subject to such vagaries. As long as the written document is properly preserved, the information that it contains will remain as stable as fingerprints.

Eyewitnesses in the Unabom case entailed a run of bad luck. The first, Professor Don Saari of Northwestern University, did not recognize the significance of those 1978 visits from a Morton Grove, Illinois, mystery man until 1994–1995, when it was too late for his tip to be fruitful. On February 20, 1987, FC was spotted again, in Salt Lake City, outside the CAAMS computer store where Gary Wright was injured by a Unabom device. Members of the Task Force were jubilant—at last, a welcome break in the investigation! This second eyewitness (the first to be identified and questioned) helped to construct the composite sketch of a slender fellow, twenty-five to thirty years old, about six feet tall, with white hands, a reddish complexion, and fuzzy, strawberry-blond hair; wearing "teardrop-shaped" sunglasses, jeans, and a hooded sweatshirt.[29] But the bomber's unwashed face was partly concealed by the hood and dark glasses; the fuzzy blond hair was probably part of a disguise (one of the wigs mentioned by Kaczynski in his Montana journals); and though the man had a youthful, wiry frame, he was under five-ten and almost forty-five years old when spotted in Salt Lake City.

The CAAMS incident, no lucky break after all, introduced an unidentified problem for the ongoing work of the Unabom Task Force, a mistaken description of the offender. Thereafter, every net thrown by the FBI into its pool of suspects was directed toward the wrong school of fish, with Kaczynski's age group being excluded altogether. For example:

- When the Unabomber's writings and choice of targets indicated likely ties to the University of Michigan and UC Berkeley, employee and student directories were cross-checked, but only as far back as the mid-1970s. Ted Kaczynski, who ended his Ann Arbor teaching fellowship in June 1967 and his teaching post at Berkeley in June 1969, escaped inclusion by virtue of his age.
- A videotape of the crime scene following the 1995 blast that killed Gilbert Murray showed a figure in dark glasses who resembled the FBI's composite sketch. On the instant that the man spotted the camera, he bolted, obviously unhappy at having been filmed. Because the man thus captured on film was too old for the Unabom profile by as much as fifteen years, the lead was never pursued.
- In 1995, Professor Don Saari, a Northwestern University mathematician, persuasively reported a 1978 encounter with the suspected Unabomber. Task Force agents duly gathered yearbooks from northwest suburban high schools. None of the faces seemed quite right, and no wonder. Saari was looking for FC in Morton Grove area yearbooks from the early 1970s. The Unabomber graduated from Evergreen Park High School in 1958.

I do not think it fair to call these missed opportunities "investigative oversights." Working from a well-intentioned though incorrect report that the Unabom subject was a young man in his twenties, Task Force agents covered all bases. FC's communications and choice of victims and identifiable reading pointed to an offender much older than the eyewitness account and working profile, but no one at the time pointed that out.

The first useful clue concerning the Unabomber's intellectual history was supplied by Special Agent James C. "Chris" Ronay, the FBI explosives expert who recognized in 1980 that the "Junkyard Bomber" (as the Unabomber was then called) was imitating, or at least influenced by, New York's Mad Bomber of the 1950s. "FP" pipe bombs, armed with such quirky detonators as a dampened throat lozenge, came concealed or suspended in men's woolen socks. The first "FC" pipe bombs, armed with quirky dowel-and-rubber band detonators, and many later ones, came concealed in wooden boxes. On occasion, FC, like FP, enclosed whimsical messages on notepaper that would perish only if the device performed as designed (e.g., "Con Edison crooks, this is for you---FP" [Mad Bomber]; "Wu---It works! I told you it would--R.V."[Unabomber]). And the bombers' respective signatories, FP and FC, seemed related.

For the work that I do, the apparent indebtedness of FC in the '90s to FP in the '50s raises a question: Where and when would a serial bomber born as recently as 1962 be reading of George Metesky? Possibly in James Brussel's 1968 *Casebook*. I also found a few mentions of Metesky in news stories and magazine articles in the '70s and '80s, most of them written by journalists born in the '30s and '40s. But beginning from a statistical model, the safest initial inference was that the Unabomber *remembered* the Metesky case. (Ted Kaczynski, born in 1942, knew of the Mad Bomber from coverage in the *Chicago Sun-Times*. In fact, it was partly the attention garnered by New York's Mad Bomber in 1951–1957 that inspired Teddy Kaczynski to make explosives his boyhood hobby while other Lombard, Illinois, boys played baseball.)

Each new message, each designated FC target, from 1978 to 1995 supplied imperfectly concealed information about the Unabomber's intellectual abilities and educational history, including his ties to Ann Arbor and Berkeley, and even hints concerning his field of scholarly expertise. Setting aside the "Autobiography," the Montana journals, and the writings supplied by David Kaczynski, taking only those few and infrequent communications from FC known to the FBI as the U-docs, it is nevertheless possible to demonstrate that the Unabomber was neither a mechanic nor a sociologist but an alienated scientist or mathematician, probably someone with a Ph.D. The Unabomber may have taken a sociology course or two as a college student in the late '50s and early '60s (FC in the manifesto misapplies Dennis Wrong's 1961 concept of "oversocialization"), but his knowledge of the social sciences indicates the expertise of an undergraduate exposed to popular texts by Eric Hoffer, William H. Whyte, Aldous Huxley, and Jacques Ellul. FC was trained in the hard sciences, probably mathematics, having an advanced and current interest in topology—as indicated, for example, by FC's unidentified but exhibited familiarity with the catastrophe theory of the topologist Christopher Zeeman. Topology and set theory were Ted Kaczynski's specialty.

PLAY ON WOODS

> I have chosen you as my victim . . . when the first piece is played upside down and backwards, it spells out the letters of my name, over and over, in varying permutations taken from the alternating group on 18 letters. . . . I have almost finished two more marches and am working on a waltz, but I won't be able to quite complete these until I have resolved Fermat's Conjecture.
>
> —THEODORE KACZYNSKI TO A LOMBARD NEIGHBOR,
> IN A COMICAL 1966 LETTER FROM ANN ARBOR,
> SIGNED "H. BASCOMB THURGOOD"[30]

For the first fifteen years of the Unabom investigation, agents had little text to chew on. None of FC's communications seemed truthful, dependable, or even fully intelligible. Until more substantive writing became available, FC's few writing samples invited not mere skepticism or disinterest but a measure of speculative overreading. Unexplained initials, multiple pseudonyms, and cryptic messages may have resisted coherent interpretation, but there was at least one point on which the textual and forensic evidence found early convergence: FC had a "thing" about Wood. Most Unabom devices came encased in a wooden box, usually homemade. Wood plugs were often used for initiators, wooden dowels for the pipe, hardwood splinters for shrapnel. To one of his 1979 bombs, FC attached cherry twigs. The bomb that killed Hugh Scrutton in December 1985 and the one that nearly killed Gary Wright fourteen months later were disguised as discarded blocks of two-by-fours. So, too, with FC's written communications. FC in his 1995 letter to the *San Francisco Chronicle* used the return "Fredrick Benjamin Isaac Wood" (i.e., *F.B.I. Wood*), residing at "549 Wood Street, Woodlake, California." The bomb that killed the timber lobbyist Gilbert Murray had as its return address "Closet Dimensions, Oakland," a phrase aptly describing Oakland's wood-product storage systems as well as the bomber's own woodland abode. FC's wooden boxes, dangerous if pried into, and wood jokes, too clever to be understood, constituted the Unabomber's forensic autograph, his way of identifying himself as the man of his wood.

The problem with such observations is that they don't usually get one any closer to identifying the offender unless the identical or similar language and writing behaviors are exhibited in the known writings of an identified suspect, or can elicit further writing from the offender. In 1995, when it was announced to the press that the FBI had taken an interest in the Unabomber's wood, and wood-wording, FC was made sufficiently nervous to write a 450-word rebuttal in a letter to the *New York Times,* beginning, "The FBI's theory that we have some kind of a fascination with wood is about as silly as it can get. They apparently based this theory mainly on the fact that we've used a lot of wood in the construction of bomb packages. . . ." As for "the name of some species of tree, or a word such as 'wood,' 'forest,' 'arbor,' 'grove,' " said FC, "the FBI must really be getting desperate if they resort to theories as ridiculous as this one."[31]

The Unabomber's continuing word games could have been puzzled out, I think, or at least used to prevent mistaken inferences. On July 2, 1982, four years after Professor Saari's face-to-face encounter with the "Morton Grove" fellow at Northwestern, a Unabom device exploded in Room 411 of the Cory Hall Computer Science Building at UC Berkeley, severely injuring Professor Diogenes Angelakos. Hidden inside the bomb was FC's most cryptic message, a note just nine words long: "Wu---It works! I told you it would--R.V." Thirteen years later, Professor Don Saari of Northwestern was instructed, as he inspected Morton Grove High School yearbooks, to focus on persons with the initials F.C. or R.V. But the offender's pattern of past writing behavior—his habit of addressing bombs and letters from one scholar (forged) to another (the intended victim), with attendant puns—indicates that "Wu" and "R.V." probably denoted scholars, while Morton Grove was probably just another *wood* joke, not his real address (*Mort*-on Grove, the woods of death).

In 1967–1969, Hung Hsi Wu and Robert Vaught were colleagues of Ted Kaczynski's in Berkeley's Department of Mathematics, just two buildings distant from the site of that 1982 blast in the Department of Computer Science. Assistant Professor Wu surpassed Assistant Professor Ted Kaczynski in his teaching evaluations, his publication record, his academic citizenship—and went on to distinguish himself while Kaczynski dropped out of the profession altogether. Robert Vaught, a colleague senior to Wu and Kaczynski in the same department at the same time, was an expert in the foundations of mathematics. The Department of Mathematics was chaired at that time (1967–1969) by the senior scholar in Ted Kaczynski's own field, Professor John Addison, whose surname was echoed in the FC bomb sent to Percy Addison Wood in 1983. In the spring of 1996, shortly before the April 3 arrest of Ted Kaczynski, the Unabom Task Force put "Wu" and *Wu* together, along with "R.V." and *Vaught*, "Addison" and *Addison*. By that time, these three UC mathematicians could barely remember an assistant professor named Theodore Kaczynski.

But Ted remembered his Berkeley colleagues well enough and "had no respect for any of them," believing them to be serving the advancement of science and technology to the detriment of individual freedom.[32]

The last thing Professor Kaczynski did before leaving Berkeley back in 1969, for a farewell prank, was to send a hostile letter from one math department colleague (whose name he forged) to another. In 1970, when David Kaczynski first heard that story from his brother, Ted, he thought it sounded pretty strange. A quarter-century later, when hearing about the Wu-R.V. note, David thought it sounded pretty familiar.

GETTING IT: VICTIMOLOGY AND THE QUESTIONED DOCUMENT

> I often had fantasies of killing the kind of people whom I hated (e.g. government officials, police, computer scientists, behavioral scientists, the rowdy type of college students who left their piles of beercans in the Arboretum, etc., etc., etc.) . . . Knowing my revengeful fantasies are not being realized, completely spoils them for me.
>
> —TED KACZYNSKI, MONTANA JOURNALS[33]

Victimology is a field of research that covers a wide range of offender-victim relations and attendant issues, such as social attitudes toward victims of rape. In a criminal investigation, the victimologist studies the victim as a means of understanding the offender, drawing on techniques developed by such experts as Brent Turvey and Robert Ressler. By assessing the type of victim that a serial offender prefers, investigators may identify what kind of person stands at risk of being targeted so that the public may be duly warned. Tracing the victims' conference zone (home area, circle of acquaintance), movements, job history, and past conflicts may lead detectives to the offender even when the victim has no names to offer.

The designated recipients of package bombs are usually known to their assailant. That did not appear to be so in the Unabom case. The difficulty of assessing FC's manner of targeting victims is encapsulated even in the name Unabom, a tag originally assigned by the FBI to designate the "*UN*iversity + *A*irlines *BOM*ber." The offender could not easily have known Edward Smith, Buckley Crist, Percy Wood, LeRoy Bearnson, *and* Patrick Fischer—the first five persons named in Unabom communications. The process by which FC selected these and other scholars and businessmen remained an unsolved puzzle.

Close study of a criminal's writing can be as useful to the victimologist as to a behavioral profiler. FC inadvertently disclosed information about his manner of choosing targets. The first Unabom device (May 1978) was addressed to E. J. (Edward John) Smith, RPI (Rensselaer Polytechnic Institute), Troy, New York, ostensibly from Professor Buckley Crist of Northwestern University. In 1980, after the FBI became involved, agents interviewed a reluctant Ed Smith concerning his circle of personal, professional, and classroom acquaintances, seeking to determine why this Rensselaer engineer should have been selected as a target. The Unabomber seemed to have pulled Smith's name out of the air. Long after the arrest was made, an Associated Press story out of Troy (May 12, 1998) reported that an RPI catalog was found in Ted Kaczynski's Montana hideaway, but that story was mistaken (it was a catalog for Carroll College in Montana, and Smith's name was not in it). The FBI never determined how or why Ed Smith came to be chosen as the Unabomber's first target.

When approaching an anonymous document, I usually begin with the assumption that nothing is irrelevant. I am obliged to ask, even of the postage stamps, "What, if any, evidence can be gleaned from these words and phrases?" From 1978 through 1995, FC used a variety of $1 Eugene O'Neill stamps from the "Prominent Americans" series, sometimes long after their initial date of distribution. How do I explain the Unabomber's evident preoccupation with Eugene O'Neill? FC's evident tendency to buy stamps and to keep them for a long time before using them is one behavior to consider. Another is the Unabomber's self-proclaimed anarchism—O'Neill was an outspoken supporter of the anarchist movement of the 1920s and 1930s. But it was not for his anarchism that O'Neill was featured by the U.S. Postal Service, it was for his plays, arguably the most famous of which is a tragedy called *The Iceman Cometh*.

In 1912, it was an unwary Edward John Smith, captain of the *Titanic*, who steered that floating exhibit of modern technology into an iceberg. A half-century later, RPI's Edward John Smith was among the first to develop an orbital guidance system for large spacecraft. Those Eugene O'Neill postage stamps were a typically sinister FC joke, a literary allusion, a warning to all Edward John Smiths: *The Iceman Cometh*—to take you down, to sink your technological society. It would even be interesting to learn, though I'd never have mentioned it in a court document, whether FC's Iceman-*Titanic* theme was cognitively prompted by FC's recollection or review of original news coverage of the Mad Bomber case: as reported in January 1957, George Metesky's three letters to the *Journal American* included paper illustrated with a snowman and a comment about transatlantic passage on a "Teutonic" ocean liner.

The *Titanic* became a central if unacknowledged theme of the Unabom campaign. After his unsuccessful attempt to blow a commercial jet out of the sky (another bomb mailed with "*Iceman*" postage), FC sent a pipe bomb to Percy Addison Wood, president of United Airlines. This fourth Unabom device was concealed in a hollowed-out copy of a book called *Ice Brothers*. All that remained of the book, after being gutted, was the matter appearing on the novel's spine: its title (*Ice Brothers*), author (Sloan Wilson), and publisher (Arbor House). Those clues were followed by others. The June 1985 bomb mailed to Boeing Aircraft was sent from "Wei*burg*" Tool and Supply, a fictitious company. The November 1985 bomb mailed to Professor James V. McConnell at the University of Michigan was sent from "Kloppen*burg*," a fictitious scholar. The bomber's jesting repetition of icebergs and other burgs escaped notice.

A writer of short, unpublished fiction and expository prose for more than thirty years, Ted Kaczynski received enough rejection slips to have wallpapered his entire Montana residence. His first and only success with original fiction came in September 1999, in an alternative press magazine called *Off!* Tim LaPietra, the editor—a twenty-one-year-old SUNY-Binghamton student and self-styled anarchist—admired Ted Kaczynski because "he wasn't just a serial killer, he had something to say."[34] LaPietra wrote to Ted in prison, inviting him to say it all in *Off!* Ted obliged with an original fable called "Ship of Fools"—the story of an ocean liner whose whining passengers fail to notice, while variously demanding fair play for animals, for women, for homosexuals, for racial minorities, that their insane captain is steering them toward an iceberg. "All this is just awful!" cries a leftish college professor, wringing his hands at the crew's indifference. "It's immoral! It's racism, sexism, speciesism, homophobia, and exploitation of the working class! It's discrimination!" But when a cabin boy urges the passengers to revolt, "the professor elevated his nose and said sternly, 'I don't believe in violence. It's immoral.'

"The ship kept sailing north, and after a while it was crushed between two icebergs and everyone drowned. THE END."[35]

The moral of Kaczynski's story is that the captains of our technological society have gone quite mad. The Unabomber was that prescient cabin boy whose attempted mutiny was thwarted by the momentum of modern technology and by the stupidity of liberals.

"Ship of Fools" is not terribly original. Kaczynski stole the plot and most of the details from "El Conductor del Rapido," a parable by his favorite Spanish author, Horacio Quiroga. In November 1994, just before he boarded the bus for California with the bomb that killed Thomas Mosser (another bomb mailed with Eugene O'Neill postage), Ted in a letter to his brother, David, recommended "El Conductor" as "good entertainment . . . though I don't think Quiroga intended for it to be comical."[36] If James Cameron's 1997 film, *Titanic,* ever comes to the ten-by-twelve-foot supermax prison cell that Ted Kaczynski now calls home, you can bet that Ted won't be rooting for Leonardo DiCaprio or Kate Winslet, and he won't be cheering for the boat. He'll be pulling for the iceberg.

DIRECTORY ASSISTANCE: ZEROING IN

> They were greatly exercised about the sound of explosions heard
> when half the ship was underwater already. Was there one? Were
> there two? They seemed to be smelling a rat there! . . . The Titanic,
> if one may believe the last reports, has only scraped against a piece
> of ice which, I suspect, was not an enormously bulky and compar-
> atively easily seen berg . . . a perfect exhibition of the modern blind
> trust in mere material and appliances.
>
> —JOSEPH CONRAD, "SOME REFLECTIONS ON THE
> LOSS OF THE *TITANIC*" (1912)[37]

There are many unexplicated puns in Ted Kaczynski's choice of victims and pseudonyms, but a more critical interpretive challenge is
that of discovering the actual procedure by which FC targeted individuals for death. There were more than two hundred Edward J.
Smiths in this country in 1978. Why choose Edward John Smith of
Troy, New York, as the first victim of intended serial murder? The
answer to that, I think, may be found in virtually any college or
university library. Ted Kaczynski chose his designated victims
(those whose names he actually put on a parcel) by searching for
them in academic reference works. In the case of Edward John
Smith, Kaczynski was looking, I believe, for anyone sharing a name
with the captain of the *Titanic* who also happened to be a scientist
or engineer. He knew where to look, and he did not have to look
very hard. While Professor Smith of RPI was not widely published,
nor well known in his field, nor known personally to Kaczynski,
his name and field of expertise appear in a reference work called
Dissertation Abstracts International (the *DAI*), a useful research tool
containing a trove of information about newcomers to academic dis-
ciplines. The *DAI* identifies "Edward John Smith (1966), RPI" as a
computer and aerospace engineer with a pilot design for "Attitude
Control" intended for guiding the pitch of large orbital spacecraft.[38]
If there's one phrase that Ted Kaczynski had hated since childhood

more than any other (even "technological society"), it was "attitude control." Edward John Smith, the "attitude control" engineer, was a perfect first target for Ted the Iceman, a.k.a. coolheaded logician Kaczynski.

What's important about tracing FC's selection of his first target is not just the information concerning the Iceman-*Titanic* theme, but the acquired knowledge that this offender was someone comfortable with library research and familiar with a reference work ordinarily consulted only by persons with advanced degrees. Whoever FC might turn out to be, he or she was someone turning to academic reference works in order to assault other academics—which I hesitate to call "scholarly" behavior, but it is certainly not behavior that points toward an airline mechanic. (And in fact, Edward J. Smith, RPI, and Theodore J. Kaczynski, UCB, contributed their respective dissertation abstracts to the *DAI* only a year apart, one in 1966, the other in 1967, volumes that are shelved side by side in most university libraries.)

The fourth Unabom device, concealed inside the hollowed-out copy of *Ice Brothers,* was mailed to the home of Percy Wood, president of United Airlines, just in time for his birthday, and heralded by a letter from "Enoch W. Fischer":

> Enoch W. Fischer
> 3414 N. Ravenswood
> Chicago, IL 60657

Mr. Percy Addison Wood
887 Forest Hill
Lake Forest, IL 60045

Dear Mr. Wood:

I am taking the liberty of sending you, under separate cover, a book which I believe to have great social significance. I am sending copies of this book, "Ice Brothers," by Sloan Wilson, to a number of prominent people in the Chicago area because I believe this to be truly a book for our time, a book that should be read by all who make important decisions affecting the public welfare.

I realize that a man in your position does not have time to read every book that is recommended to him, so that I may have wasted time and money in sending you a copy of Mr. Wilson's work. But I feel sure that it will be worth your while to at least glance through the book. Since it is as entertaining as it is significant, perhaps you will then decide to read the entire work.

Sincerely,
Enoch W. Fischer

The sender and address are fictitious. At "3414 N. Ravenswood" agents found only a vacant lot on the North Line tracks, halfway between the Chicago Loop and Northwestern University. The White Pages were searched nationwide for an Enoch Fischer against whom the bomber might hold a grudge, but again the net came up empty. A useless document? Not quite.

First, what kind of radical would mock books of "social significance" by urging community leaders to read a novel of Coast Guard comrades, a story without political import? And how did the bomber seem to know such details as Wood's home address and middle name? When interviewed by the FBI, Percy Wood had no idea why he should have been targeted for assassination.

Looking for an appropriate victim, the Unabomber had once again visited a library, consulting the 1978–1979 edition of *Who's Who in America,* and selected "WOOD, Percy Addison" as the best target for a bomb from among the seventy-five famous Woods listed there. *Who's Who* supplied Wood's middle name, home address, and June 7 birthday; the name of Wood's yacht (the *Knollwood*), his wife's maiden name (Sherwood), and even his mother's maiden name (Baum, German for *tree*). A native Californian, Wood was born and raised in Oakland. In 1968, he was named the Bay Area's "Industry Man of the Year." He now lived on Forest Hill Road in Lake Forest. He ran a commercial airline, and was a member of two clubs plus the Society of Automotive Engineers. Targeting, for Ted Kaczynski, was nothing personal. He disliked everybody. With so many people, so few bombs, and so little time, FC chose victims' names for their symbolic value, their "type." Percy Wood was exactly the kind of industrialized "Wood" that FC hoped to nail.

NEXT

> [I]nside a luxurious ship carrying wealthy passengers, a parrot was looking at a Magician that was entertaining an auditorium full of rich men. First, he made a fish disappear, then a female assistant and, later on, three strong seamen inside a coffin. In that precise moment, a German torpedo hits the ship, and the parrot suddenly finds itself in the middle of the Pacific Ocean, standing on a floating piece of wood. "How wonderful," it said, "And what trick is this Magician going to do now?"
>
> —TED KACZYNSKI, IN A LETTER TO HIS BROTHER, DAVID (1989)[39]

When confronted with a Questioned Document, I've learned to look first for what's unusual about the text or physical document, which in the Enoch W. Fischer letter includes the continued trope on "Wood" and "Ice," and evidence of another library visit by a bomber in search of a victim's name and address. But what of that unexpected use of the victim's middle name: "Percy *Addison* Wood"? No middle name or initial was necessary for correct postal delivery, nor had Wood's middle name appeared in published sources, except in *Who's Who in America*. In 1968, the year of Wood's award for contributing to industrial society and its future, twenty-six-year-old Ted Kaczynski was laboring unhappily in Berkeley's Department of Mathematics under a department chair he resented, Professor John Addison, the department's senior professor in Ted's own field, topology and set theory. It was also in 1968 that Ted's father was hired to manage a foam-cutting plant in Addison, Illinois. A decade later, Ted followed suit, leaving Montana to work as a foam cutter, joining his father and brother at the Addison plant in June 1978.[40] And it was in Addison, two months later, that Ted's heart was broken by Ellen Tarmichael.

By 1979, "Addison" was a name that Ted Kaczynski despised. If noisy commercial jets could trespass the airspace over his Montana wood, then he had every right to blast an Addison Wood. Tit for tat.

After trying to kill Percy Addison Wood with an Arbor House book bomb sent by a Mr. Fischer, FC tried to kill a Patrick Fischer from Ann Arbor with a bomb ostensibly mailed by LeRoy Wood Bearnson. Investigators noted the bomber's incessant wordplay. Finding it undecipherable, they concentrated instead on searching for personal or workplace ties between the Unabom subject and Patrick Fischer, but the point of contact was again in a university library. FC acquired his target's name and address from library research, from *Who's Who in America*, the most recent, 1980–1981, edition. FC chose "FISCHER, Patrick C.," an Ann Arbor native and University of Michigan graduate whose father, Carl Fischer, was an Ann Arbor professor of mathematics—not someone he knew personally, just another name acquired through scholarly research having a symbolic resonance for Theodore Kaczynski.

ISOLATING THE SOURCE: GEOGRAPHIC PROFILING AND THE QUESTIONED DOCUMENT

> The FBI has tried to portray these bombings as the work of an isolated nut. We won't waste our time arguing about whether we are nuts, but we certainly are not isolated.
>
> —FC TO *NEW YORK TIMES* (20 APRIL 1995)[41]

Most violent crimes require an intersection in both time and place between the offender and the victim. The investigation of serial crimes therefore requires a geographic perspective on the offender's spatial behavior. Detective Inspector Kim Rossmo, a twenty-two-year veteran of the Vancouver Police Department, has gained an international reputation for his proven ability to track down serial offenders using a computer-assisted method called Criminal Geographic Targeting. When searching for a predatory criminal, Rossmo watches for a tendency to hunt prey in identifiable areas and considers the geographic relation of the various crime scenes, duly considering the impulse of the offender to disguise his home location. Where such information can be traced, Rossmo records the place of origin and path of distribution for every kind of physical evidence—weapons, bomb components, duct tape, rope, tire tracks, clothing fibers, postage stamps. First developed by Rossmo during his graduate study at Simon Fraser University, this computer-assisted technique has been successfully employed around the world and has become a standard investigative tool used by Canadian provincial police departments, the FBI, and Scotland Yard.

Geographic profiling did not work in the Unabom case. The offender's primary residence (Montana) and place of employment (none) could not have been pinpointed even with the help of Rossmo's highly effective computer software. But the same principles that enable Detective Rossmo to close in on a criminal's home or work site by tracing the physical evidence can be extended to include the venue and manner in which a criminal (in this case, the Unabomber) has obtained his words and ideas, pseudonyms, even his mailing addresses. By locating FC's books and magazines, reference works, and principal intellectual influences, something could have been learned of the Unabomber's physical whereabouts—even the particular buildings in Utah and Northern California where the Unabomber was conducting his primary research, including, in a few instances, the probable date of his most recent visit. It was the manifesto, FC's "Industrial Society and Its Future," completed and mailed in June 1995, that led the Unabom Task Force to Kaczynski's Montana cabin. I believe that the same wonderfully verbose document, partly written in California libraries, could have led agents to Ted Kaczynski even without David Kaczynski's invaluable assistance.

It is, of course, easy for me to say that. Nothing is easier than to kibitz on a case that has already been solved by someone else. Nor can anyone fault the FBI for having failed to employ a methodology not made available to the Bureau's agents until after the 1996 arrest.

(Far from resisting this kind of investigative work, the FBI has added text analysis to its investigative repertoire as an economical, efficient, and dependable shortcut to the apprehension of serial offenders.) My objective in these observations is not to suggest I'd have done better than others in locating the Unabomber, but only to illustrate with the advantage of hindsight how the FBI might have got its man using only the words of FC himself.

On a Saturday morning in December 1994, just before leaving with his wife and kids to buy a Christmas tree, Tom Mosser of North Caldwell, New Jersey, went through the mail that had been gathered for him on a kitchen countertop. There was a parcel from "H. C. Wickel," evidently a professor of economics at San Francisco State University. When Mosser opened it, he never knew what hit him. A pipe bomb blasted gaping holes in his torso, pierced his organs with nails, and nearly severed his head, killing him instantly. His wife and children were in another room.

Mosser was a family man, a good colleague, an advertising executive best known for promoting the Olympics. He seemed an unlikely target for a serial killer. Writing for *Time,* Elizabeth Gleick suggested that FC might have taken his cue from a recent article in the *New York Times* announcing Mosser's promotion at Young & Rubicam.[42] That was not it—the *Times* article ran on December 5, four days after Mosser's promotion, while FC's bomb was mailed from San Francisco on December 2—but Gleick was on the right track by looking for the offender's source of information. I believe that FC was browsing the December 2 *Wall Street Journal*—probably in a library, and surely for some other reason than to check his stock prices—when the article "AIDS-Related Product Enters Mass Media" caught his eye.[43] At the bottom of the article was a note announcing that Thomas J. Mosser of Young & Rubicam had been promoted to become the firm's executive vice president and general manager. Mosser, the article said, had been chief operating officer of Burson-Marsteller until early 1994.

The name rang a bell—not Thomas Mosser, but Burson-Marsteller, a corporation condemned in the *Earth First! Journal* for its abysmal record on environmental issues. That report, seen by Ted Kaczynski, was subsequently alluded to in Unabom correspondence.[44] Just as he'd done when choosing his earlier victims, FC, upon finding a name in the *Wall Street Journal,* visited the reference shelves to look up Thomas Mosser in the 1994 edition of *Who's Who.* The man lived on Aspen Drive in North Caldwell, New Jersey. That same day, FC addressed and sent a package to the home of Tom Mosser. By the time Mosser's promotion at Young & Rubicam was noted in the *New York Times* on December 5, the bomb that would kill him was already in the mail.

FC made it hard for forensic experts and geographic profilers to trace the origin of his physical materials. The "Junkyard Bomber," as he was originally called, was a scavenger. His intellectual and factual sources are more easily identified. In this representative instance, FC on December 2 consulted the *Wall Street Journal* and *Who's Who,* most likely in a Bay Area library (the Mosser bomb was mailed from San Francisco). As for the *Earth First! Journal* (published out of Missoula, Montana), only two libraries in the state of California then carried the magazine—the University Library at UC Davis, which FC had certainly visited on other occasions, and the Bioscience and Natural Resources Library at UC Berkeley.

As FC moved about from Illinois to Utah to California, he borrowed words, ideas, and addresses from particular libraries that he visited along the way. His favorite hangouts included the libraries of UC Berkeley, UC Davis, and Cal State Sacramento, where he browsed academic journals, East Coast newspapers, academic and business directories, and his favorite magazine, *Scientific American.* It was during a visit to the Cal State Sacramento Library, on or about June 16, 1993, that the Unabomber obtained names and addresses for Charles Epstein, a geneticist who advocated the forensic use of DNA, and David Gelernter, developer of the networking software called LINDA. Both scholars were critically injured by Unabom devices a week later. It may have been in the same library that the Unabomber paused to read portions of Gelernter's *Mirror Worlds,* and Epstein's *American Journal of Human Genetics.* Before leaving campus on June 16, the Unabomber vandalized the Science Building and the Pony Express monument with the spray-painted words ANARCHY and FC. Because the Unabomber and FC had not yet made news at this point, the graffiti meant nothing but a cleaning problem to Campus Security at Cal State. Buildings and Grounds dispatched a crew to scrub off the paint. By the time Professors Epstein and Gelernter received their packages, FC was long gone, but he kept coming back.

Members of the Unabom Task Force during this period were dil-igently knocking on the doors of environmental activists and visiting machine shops—including shop facilities at California's university campuses. Tireless in their search for the Unabomber, Task Force agents scoured scrap-metal yards, hotels, and homeless shelters, combing the Sierras and the Bay Area for some trace of FC. Mean-while, the man for whom they were looking relaxed at the library, combing periodicals for new names, new victims.

THE PAPER TRAIL

> Question of too many people. With 3 billion people (or whatever the
> number is) in the world it seems impossible to have a new idea . . .
> —TED KACZYNSKI TO HIS BROTHER, DAVID (JANUARY 1985)[45]

Despite his characterization in the press as a genius, the Unabomber lacked creativity. In his 35,000-word manifesto I cannot find much that's original, or language that cannot be traced. Even the chapter titles are stolen. Chapter 28, for example—"The 'Bad' Parts of Technology Cannot Be Separated from the 'Good' Parts"—recalls a section heading in Jacques Ellul's *The Technological Bluff:* "The Harmful Effects of Technical Process Are Inseparable from Its Beneficial Effects."[46] FC borrows heavily from Aldous Huxley's *Brave New World,* a text that might not be known to FBI agents but that anyone could identify as an FC source with a computer search of a comprehensive literary text archive. FC copies even such minutiae as Huxley's manner of capitalization. Without citing Huxley, FC complains in his manifesto that "the direction of the *development of* any important aspect of *society*" is blocked by "*modern technology,*" "*concentration of political power,*" and the power of "*Big Government to promote the power of Big Business.*"[47] The debt to Huxley, for anyone who reads *Brave New World Revisited,* will be obvious—Kaczynski duplicates Huxley's capitalization along with the phrasing (emphasis added).[48]

All of FC's most unusual diction is borrowed, including such words and phrases as "surrogate activities," "power process," "organization-dependent," "technophile," and "cryptoleftist." The linguistic currency is easily traced with a computer-assisted search of multiple text archives, including electronic libraries of philosophical, literary, social science, and journalistic texts. The phrases "sphere of freedom" and "sphere of human freedom," used repeatedly by FC, appear most often in texts influenced by Kantian and/or libertarian philosophy, including essays by the anarchist Albert Jay Nock—who, like Ted, condemns the illusion that "we may eat our cake and have it" (1935). Living writers who make repeated use of the phrase "sphere of freedom" include the conservative columnists Steve Chapman, Charles Krauthammer, and George F. Will. FC's term "crypto-leftist" has only one recorded precedent appearing in the Lexis-Nexis archive, in George Will's column of August 2, 1992.[49] *Inference:* the Unabomber may not be reading Emmanuel Kant; he may be reading George F. Will—as indeed he was. Will's *Newsweek* colleague Joe Klein opined that Ted Kaczynski's "essential left-wing orientation seems indisputable" (22 April 1996). Klein was mistaken about that, as would become apparent shortly afterward, with receipt of "Industrial Society and Its Future," but the Unabomber's essential disdain for leftism is indisputably apparent even in FC's choice of crypto-conservative vocabulary.

In June 1995, when Special Agent in Charge Jim Freeman received the Unabom manifesto, he recognized the importance of those textual sources to which FC made explicit reference and dispatched a team to gather information about each book and article expressly cited in the manifesto. Agents visited university libraries in Evanston and Chicago, Provo and Salt Lake City, Sacramento, Davis, San Francisco, and Berkeley, making physical examinations of the books and magazines that receive notice in FC's "Industrial Society." Professors in the social sciences were queried concerning which of those referenced texts may have been used in their curriculum, perhaps in a course on the history of science, a field in which FC had professed expertise in his cover letter for a 1985 bomb to an Ann Arbor professor of psychology, and again in the Unabom manifesto. The earnestness with which agents undertook this line of inquiry testifies to the thoroughness of the investigation—no stone was left unturned.

But in their hunt for FC's college reading, agents were thinking as social individuals for whom education is a collective endeavor, a shared classroom pursuit. FC had followed his own school of thought, drawing on his own extracurricular research. The Unabomber's shameless (and, by 1995, quaintly unfashionable) dependence on Jacques Ellul is an intellectual debt possibly acquired on a university campus, though unlikely to have been cultivated in a classroom. No matter what research tool one uses—for example, the *Readers' Guide to Periodical Literature* or the *Book Review Index*—when investigating Ellul's reception in America, one is directed to *Saturday Review,* the magazine to which Ellul owed much of his success in this country. It was in February 1965, in *Saturday Review,* that American readers were first introduced to Ellul's *Technological Society.*[50] *Saturday Review* followed with reviews of Ellul's *Propaganda* (1965), *Political Illusion* (1967), and *To Will and to Do* (1969).

One reader of those extracts and reviews was Ted Kaczynski, a *Saturday Review* subscriber. Years later, Ted wrote his brother, "You'll recall how pleased I was when I encountered Jacques Ellul's book, *The Technological Society,* because his thinking ran so close to my own. I was glad to find the book, but it was another instance of the parallelism of ideas, of the near impossibility of thinking of anything new in such a crowded world."[51] Ted's correspondence was unavailable to investigators in 1995. But when turning to the pages of

Saturday Review for the years in which Ellul was featured, the Task Force would have found the raw materials for FC's "Industrial Society": *Saturday Review* from 1965 to 1971 provides a trove of articles and op-ed pieces on topics addressed in the Unabom manifesto, from harmful technologies, to government and corporate surveillance, to psychological manipulation of children in the public schools, to the impact of scientific research upon American society. The magazine during this critical period also carried reviews of books directly or indirectly referenced by the Unabomber, including Chester Tan's *Chinese Political Thought in the Twentieth Century* (1971), which receives direct mention in the Unabom manifesto twenty-four years later, long after Tan's book had gone out of print.[52]

If the Task Force had been trained to investigate the Unabomber's reading material, agents would have been led inevitably to *Saturday Review* for the years 1965–1971—and, I believe, to a break in the Unabom case. One letter to the editor could hardly have escaped notice. In the issue of February 28, 1970, "Theodore J. Kaczynski," an unhappy resident of "Lombard, Illinois," blasted C. W. Griffin, an "engineer and professional planner," using language that sounds a lot like FC a quarter-century later. The 1970 letter from Theodore J. Kaczynski as published in *Saturday Review* is just 216 words, but it is a compact digest of diction, prose, and ideology repeated in FC's "Industrial Society and Its Future," registering nearly identical thoughts in nearly identical phrasing.[53]

In 1980, after just four Unabom devices, an offender profile based on FC's reading and writing could not have been too specific. The second bomb (planted at Northwestern) provided no textual evidence except the label on a Phillies cigar box; the fourth device (sent by airmail) was destroyed by fire. But FC supplied enough textual and linguistic evidence early on to supply useful leads. Two years after the first Unabom incident, fifteen years before the arrest of Ted Kaczynski, my reading-and-writing profile for the Unabomber would have looked something like this (with mistaken inferences as noted):

Primary conference zone, Chicago area. Familiar with New York's Mad Bomber campaign (1951–1957), and with the Polish-born author Teodor J. K. Korzeniowski, better known to English and American readers as Joseph Conrad (*The Secret Agent,* "An Anarchist," et al.). Offender is a middle-aged male with possible ties, as a student or employee, to the University of Illinois or Northwestern [wrong inference: Ann Arbor and Berkeley]. No coherent political agenda. FC, familiar with the Mad Bomber story, draws inspiration from FP, but with an original twist, identifying himself with wood. Possible anarchist with a literary interest in Eugene O'Neill, *The Iceman Cometh* (1946); possibly familiar with Sloan Wilson, *Ice Brothers* (1979) and the '50s bestseller *The Man in the Gray Flannel Suit* (1955). Resents modern technology and university scholarship but may have past training in both. Offender is highly intelligent and well educated, given to sarcasm and wordplay, possibly a Ph.D. candidate in the hard sciences, someone who failed to secure tenured employment [wrong inference: he quit]. Targets his victims by consulting such library reference works as *Who's Who in America* and *Dissertation Abstracts International.*

Fifteen years later, a linguistic and text profile could have been precise indeed, including FC's probable date of birth (before 1950), educational level (Ph.D., 1960s), dates and places of employment (Ann Arbor, 1962–1967; Berkeley, 1967–1969), the magazines he read, the books he owned, the particular libraries he visited in Northern California, and when. The same kinds of library research that could have yielded a name could have documented the Unabomber's favorite haunts—fewer than half a dozen research libraries in Northern California—and particular books he had handled on particular days at particular libraries. From the moment he began writing, Ted Kaczynski flirted with being caught. With that 35,000-word manifesto he invited arrest. The dilemma of most anonymous writers is that they crave attention without being identified, but "recognition" is a word that cuts both ways.

Speaking from prison about his promised but still unpublished book, *Truth versus Lies,* the Unabomber condemned his brother, David, as a turncoat. "I trust my readers will realize," said Ted to the *New York Times,* "that in comparing my brother to Judas Iscariot, I do not intend any comparison of myself with Jesus Christ."[54] David Kaczynski's reputation as a man of conscience and integrity seems secure, nor will many readers think that the Unabomber sounds like Jesus Christ. But Ted is vain to suppose that by David's silence he could have escaped his cross. As the Unabom campaign entered its eighteenth year, the FBI had analyzed every scrap of forensic evidence, pursued every lead, interviewed every plausible suspect. The leads that remained, and that invited closer scrutiny, were those supplied by FC himself, in thirteen letters and a 35,000-word manifesto that were covered from top to bottom with the stylistic fingerprints and intellectual debts of Theodore John Kaczynski. It was only a matter of time and close reading before agents stood face-to-face with the Unabomber—whether in Montana or in the reading room of a university library—and said, "Professor Kaczynski, we have to talk."

CHAPTER FOUR

Starr-Crossed Lovers

BELOW THE BELTWAY

> Call up the right master Constable! We have here recovered the most dangerous piece of lechery that ever was known in the commonwealth!
>
> —WATCHMAN IN SHAKESPEARE'S *MUCH ADO ABOUT NOTHING*[1]

On a hot day in July 1998, a week or two before Monica Lewinsky signed her immunity agreement with Kenneth Starr and four months before she signed a book contract with St. Martin's Press for *Monica's Story*, there came an unexpected knock on my office door. During the summer months hardly anyone visits my campus office. Expecting it to be a colleague or custodian, I yelled for whoever it was to come in.

The door swung open, and in came no one I recognized—a skinny cowboy-type, dripping from the heat, with a pointy gray beard and grizzled hair down to his shoulders. Sooty black jeans, black shoes. By way of contrast, a white shirt and a wool knit tie. Very animated.

"Professor Foster?"

I nodded.

points to make in affidavit

Your first few paragraphs should be about yourself —
what you do now, what you did at the White House and
for how many years you were there as a career person
and as a political appointee.

You and Kathleen were friends. *At around the time
of her husband's death* (the President has claimed
it was after her husband died. Do you really want
to contradict him?), she came to you after she
allegedly came out of the oval and looked (however
she looked), you don't recall her exact words, but
she claimed at the time (whatever she claimed) and
was very happy.

You did not see her go in or see her come out.

Talk about when you became out of touch with her and
maybe why.

The next you heard of her was when a Newsweek
reporter (I wouldn't name him specifically) showed
up in your office saying she was naming you as a
someone who would corroborate that she was
sexually harassed. You spoke with her that
evening, etc. and she relayed to you a sequence
of events that was very dissimilar from what
you remembered happening. As a result of your
conversation with her and subsequent reports that
showed she had tried to enlist the help of someone
else in her lie that the President sexually
harassed her, you now do not believe that what she
claimed happened really happened. You now find it
completely plausible that she herself smeared her
lipstick, untucked her blouse, etc.

You never saw her go into the oval office, or come
out of the oval office.

You have never observed the President behaving
inappropriately with anybody.

The first few paragraphs should be about me— what I do now, what I did at the White House and for how many years I was there as a career person and as a political appointee.

Kathleen and I were friends. At around the time of her husband's death, she came to me after she allegedly came out of the oval and looked_____, I don't recall her exact words, but she claimed at the time_____and was very happy.

I did not see her go in or see her come out.

Talk about when I became out of touch with her and maybe why.

The next time I heard of her was when a Newsweek reporter showed up in my office saying she was naming me as a someone who would corroborate that she was sexually harassed by the President. I spoke with her that evening, etc. and she relayed to me a sequence of events that was very dissimilar from what I remembered happening. As a result of my conversation with her and subsequent reports that showed she had tried to enlist the help of someone else in her lie that the President sexually harassed her, I now do not believe that what she claimed happened really happened. I now find it completely plausible that she herself smeared her lipstick, untucked her blouse, etc.

I never saw her go into the oval office, or come out of the oval office.

I have never observed the President behave inappropriately with anybody.

You are not sure you've been clear about whose side you're on. (Kirby has been saying you should look neutral; better for credibility but you aren't neutral. Neutral makes you look like you're on the other team since you are a political appointee)

It's important to you that they think you're a team player, after all, you are a political appointee. You believe that they think you're on the other side because you wouldn't meet with them.

You want to meet with Bennett. You are upset about the comment he made, but you'll take the high road and do what's in your best interest.

December 18th, you were in a better position to attend an all day or half-day deposition, but now you are into JCOC mode. Your livelihood is dependent on the success of this program. Therefore, you want to provide an affidavit laying out all of the facts in lieu of a deposition.

You want Bennett's people to see your affidavit before it's signed.

Your deposition should include enough information to satisfy their questioning.

By the way, remember how I said there was someone else that I knew about. Well, she turned out to be this huge liar. I found out she left the WH because she was stalking the P or something like that. Well, at least that gets me out of another scandal I know about.

"I know your work!" he said with a grin. "Shakespeare and the sonnet? Joe Klein and *Primary Colors*? Ted Kaczynski and the Unabom manifesto? Thrilled to meet ya—I'm Jack Gillis!"

Gillis put down his briefcase, leaned forward, grabbed my hand and gave it a vigorous shake.

I carefully closed an open FBI binder on my desk that contained writing samples for the Atlanta-Birmingham bomb investigation. "What can I do for you, Jack?"

"I was just drivin' by on m'way home from Massachusetts, and I thought to myself, I want to meet Professor Foster, so I drove by here just on the chance I might catch you in, and I guess I was lucky 'cause here ya are." Gillis noticed I was in shorts, T-shirt, running shoes. "Stopped off at a gas station to change into a shirt 'n' tie. Guess I didn't have to do that, huh?"

I smiled. "Not at all."

My visitor sat down in a chair beside my desk, popped open his briefcase, and pulled out a maroon folder. I was a little distracted by his feet, a white sweat sock on the left, a bright mustard-yellow sock on the right, under black Levi's. It was the brightest yellow stocking I'd seen on a male leg since Malvolio in Shakespeare's *Twelfth Night*.

"Professor Skip Fox and I have analyzed the Tripp-Lewinsky Talking Points and made the most amazing discovery—"

"Are you from Louisiana?"

"Whoa!" he said, with an appreciative grin. "How'd you figure *that*?"

"I think I may have seen your analysis, a few months ago. Someone faxed me a copy."

Gillis leaned forward in his chair and whispered, "May I ask who?"

"Well, actually, it was a lawyer."

Gillis grinned. "Monica Lewinsky's lawyer? Nathaniel Speights?"

I nodded. Gillis clapped his hands in triumph and fell back in the chair.

"*Yes!* We sent him a copy of our stuff. Kenneth Starr, too. We've got copies floating all over the Beltway, and it's getting noticed. We've had calls from reporters, TV people, you name it. There's a rumor we could get subpoenaed!"

Having since published their material on-line, Fox and Gillis had met with stinging reviews but no systematic rebuttal. "You get one little thing wrong," Gillis sighed, "and they crucify you. Doesn't matter how much you get right." I understood his frustration, and his courage. It's risky in our profession to go out on a limb. I wished him well and promised to read his analysis. I thanked him for sharing it and for stopping by.

"That version you saw?" Gillis said, without getting up. "That was an early draft. Me and Skip have made lots of revisions. Incorporated new information. And came to the same conclusion: Monica Lewinsky and the president's men had nothing to do with the Talking Points. No *way*. It wouldn't even make any *sense*." Leaving the maroon folder on my desk, my unexpected visitor departed for Louisiana as suddenly as he had arrived.

According to John F. X. "Jack" Gillis and Willard "Skip" Fox, Kenneth Starr had made a serious mistake, receiving and introducing a fraudulent document—the Talking Points—to justify his expanded jurisdiction in the Lewinsky matter. The Gillis-Fox argument, twenty-some pages, ended with two probing questions: "Is Starr currently distancing himself from the document? If it is fraudulent, will Starr investigate and prosecute with the same singleness of purpose he has investigated the President?" Those were not bad questions to have asked. Why, after a firestorm of controversy lasting for several months, did the Starr Report sweep the Talking Points under the rug as an insolvable puzzle?

THE MOST INCREDIBLE STATE

The White House This is where I used to work.
This is *My College*, its located in the most incredible state in the world. . . .

Let me know what you think about my page! Send mail by clicking *here.*
— "MONICA'S PLACE," FORGED MONICA LEWINSKY
AOL HOMEPAGE (22 JANUARY 1989)

The name Monica Lewinsky hit the Internet on January 19, 1998, in the *Drudge Report,* an on-line gossip 'zine read by hundreds of Washington officials. Two days later the Internet gossip was translated into world news as Monica Lewinsky made her debut appearance in the *Washington Post.* Within twenty-four hours, Monica was the only news in town, being featured in eleven articles in Thursday's *Post* alone. Arriving at my office the morning of January 22, I found the World Wide Web buzzing with reports of Monica Lewinsky and her friend Linda Tripp. The president and his close friend Vernon Jordan were under investigation for alleged "suborning of perjury or obstruction of justice by encouraging Lewinsky to lie to [Paula] Jones's attorneys." It was said that Tripp may have been told to lie as well. Someone "even provided Ms. Tripp with a set of written 'talking points' to guide her testimony. . . ."[2]

When Monica Lewinsky handed Linda Tripp the Talking Points document on January 13, 1998, in a Pentagon parking lot, Tripp scanned the suggested language, and said it was "brilliant, brilliant." But instead of following those brilliant instructions about what to say in her affidavit, Tripp gave the three-page document to Kenneth Starr, who was now serving as archivist to Tripp's collection of secret audiocassettes. Things seemed to be snapping into place very nicely for Mr. Starr; and, though he did not know it yet, less well for Mr. Clinton.

A reporter let me know that those Talking Points were the talk of Washington. The Clinton-Lewinsky story was raising eyebrows, a tempest, and two questions: "Did the president of the United States have sexual relations with a barely legal White House intern?" and, second, "Who wrote the Talking Points?" If the Office of Independent Counsel (OIC) could prove that someone had instructed witnesses to commit perjury in the sexual harassment lawsuit brought against Mr. Clinton by Paula Jones, then it would be game, set, match, for Kenneth Starr, impeachment and conviction for the president.

ANON., "POINTS TO MAKE IN AFFIDAVIT"
(13 JANUARY 1998)

> HANDSOME:
> "Wild nights! Wild nights! / Were I with thee,
> Wild nights should be / Our luxury!"—M
>> —MONICA'S FEBRUARY 1998 VALENTINE'S DAY AD, NEVER PLACED

Almost everyone to the right of center said it, and even some on the left: the Talking Points, if connected with the White House, could take President Clinton down. Here was documentary evidence of witness tampering, a felony, provided that when the smoke cleared the OIC could figure out who had pulled the trigger. Monica Lewinsky evidently was the culprit who hit the "Print" button on whatever computer had generated the document; but the principal author, OIC agents believed, was someone close to the White House, possibly the president himself. Monica was only a go-between whose task it was to persuade Linda Tripp to rewrite the narrative of what was becoming known as the Kathleen Willey incident, President Clinton's alleged groping of a married woman in the Oval Office, the kind of antics that Kenneth Starr felt obliged to expose.

The Lewinsky-Tripp Talking Points (so dubbed by the *Washington Post*) is a document actually captioned "points to make in affidavit." The document is not really about "talking." It's about *not* talking. Witnesses subpoenaed in a civil suit may file an affidavit stating that they have no information pertinent to the case and request that the subpoena be quashed. The point of the Talking Points was to assist Linda Tripp with an affidavit for the Jones case, a declaration that would discourage the Jones lawyers from deposing Tripp in the Willey matter. Tripp's assignment, in brief, was to state that Kathleen Willey was a liar, the same thing that the president's lawyer, Bob Bennett, essentially had said about Linda Tripp only five months before in the pages of *Newsweek*.

From February through July, when reporters and media organizations called for a comment on the Lewinsky-Tripp Talking Points, I had none to give. Having twice voted for Bill Clinton and considering his private behavior none of my business, having no appetite for a controversy described in the press as one that could topple an elected president, I held the line, declining comment. Later, I had second thoughts and wondered if I should have said something after all, if only because, after all was said and done, Kenneth Starr declined comment as well. In the Starr Report, the Independent Counsel almost forgets to mention the Talking Points, the document that was used to legitimize an OIC probe of the Monica Lewinsky affair.

A CALL FROM JANE DOE

> Who's telling the truth? It is always hard to know in these matters, and painful to find out.
>
> —MICHAEL ISIKOFF, "A TWIST IN JONES V. CLINTON,"
> *NEWSWEEK* (11 AUGUST 1997)

In January 1997, Joseph Cammarata, an attorney for Paula Jones, received what he would later describe to reporters as an anonymous telephone call. The woman on the other end of the line sounded distraught: "What happened to Paula Jones happened to me, too—on November 23, 1993, in a hidden corridor just off the Oval Office." The woman told her story, adding that her husband had committed suicide over financial troubles, a death now cited by right-wingers as one more in "the Clinton body count." She hung up.

Though Cammarata identified his tipster as Kathleen Willey, suspicions would later focus on Linda Tripp (who had feuded with Willey over secretarial subbing at the White House) and on Lucianne Goldberg, Tripp's book agent (a Nixon-era dirty trickster). On Cammarata's tip, Michael Isikoff interviewed Tripp and Goldberg, as well as Kathleen Willey, the alleged victim; Julie Steele, Willey's friend; and Bob Bennett, the president's personal attorney in the Jones suit. Tripp's version was that Willey, after leaving the Oval Office that day, looked "disheveled. Her face was red and her lipstick was off. She was flustered, happy and joyful." Willey said no, the incident was unexpected and upsetting, and her friend Julie Steele could back her up on that. She denied having called the Paula Jones legal team and was "outraged" at having her name dragged into scandal.

Isikoff interviewed Steele in March, again in July. The March version: a distraught Kathleen Willey told Steele of the incident on November 23, the same day it allegedly occurred. The July version: Willey told her to say all of that, but the truth, said Steele now, is that Willey told of the incident weeks after it allegedly occurred, and Willey did not seem too bent out of shape.

Bob Bennett explained to Isikoff that President Clinton may have made a consoling gesture to Kathleen Willey "around the time of her husband's death." It was "preposterous" to suggest that the president made a sexual advance. Bennett remarked that "Linda Tripp is not to be believed," a statement that Tripp neither forgave nor forgot.[3]

Isikoff's "Twist in Jones v. Clinton," when it appeared in *Newsweek* on August 11, 1997, was a humiliation to Kathleen Willey; an embarrassment for Willey's now former friend, Julie Steele; a triumph for Paula Jones and Joseph Cammarata; a hoot for Lucianne Goldberg; and a P.R. disaster for the White House. The president was furious with Tripp. Tripp was furious with the president's lawyer. Monica Lewinsky, a peacemaker, explained to President Clinton that it was all a misunderstanding, that her good friend Linda Tripp was misquoted by *Newsweek*. "Good," said the president, "because it sure seemed like she screwed me. . . ."[4] It sure seemed to Linda Tripp as though she hadn't.

POSSIBLE AUTHOR: LINDA TRIPP

> I can't be involved in this. I can't be a party to all this ugliness that
> will do nothing except destroy people . . .
>
> —LINDA TRIPP TO MONICA LEWINSKY, WHILE TAPING
> THEIR CONVERSATION (22 DECEMBER 1997)

Linda Tripp's idea was to write a tell-all, through-the-peephole pot-boiler called *Behind Closed Doors: Inside the Clinton White House.* The things she knew. The stories she could tell. Transferred to the Pentagon, Tripp was assigned an underground cubicle: "I'm involved in a lot of things," she hinted darkly to her boss when she arrived, "and I know a lot of things and that's why I need privacy."[5] The Department of Defense gave her a private office, as she demanded. The things she knew—alleged sexual encounters behind closed doors—would become Linda's story, ghostwritten, but from Linda's inside information.

Tripp's professional writing—mostly correspondence in her offi-cial role as a "Public Affairs Specialist" for the Pentagon's Joint Ci-vilian Orientation Conference (JCOC)—is businesslike, efficient, and dull, exhibiting few lapses in punctuation, spelling, usage, or gram-mar.[6] When she's "into JCOC mode" (a Talking Points phrase), Ms. Tripp is utterly professional, no-nonsense, even a little dour.

"I look at you as a mom," said Monica to Linda, cheerfully, in one taped message. Linda Tripp's "mom mode" is more personable than the other, as well as patient, helpful, and empathic. Her e-mail to Monica was always well edited, unlike Monica's, and jokey in a mom sort of way, though not what you'd call laugh-out-loud funny ("I am knot ha! particularly into ties").[7] Ms. Tripp was not a laugher; she had seen too much. Washington, for Ms. Tripp, had stopped being funny long before.

Linda Tripp also knew, but others did not, how dangerous it can be to confuse either her JCOC mode, or her mom mode, with her cloak-and-dagger sleuthing mode. Tripp's book for agent Lucianne Goldberg never actually got written, but Tripp gave the Grand Jury an earful of her best cloak-and-dagger material, story after story, for eight days, about what it was like in there, inside the Clinton White House, behind closed doors. In Linda's retelling of Willey's Oval Office experience, it went down like this:

> She said, "Look, I have a problem. Here's what it is. I need help. I need a job." . . . And then just suddenly he got closer and said, . . .

"I've always wanted to do this since I first laid eyes on you." . . . But it was extremely abrupt, it went from Kathleen telling him . . . about the job, to "Whoa, there goes the coffee, what's going to happen with the coffee, and oh, my God!," and Kathleen's tiny and he's huge and she said it was just so *forceful*. . . . "His tongue was down my throat," was the first thing . . . and she kept telling me the powerfulness of it and the forcefulness of it, and she kept saying, "He put my hand on his penis, it was [—]" (deleted by Mr. Starr).

And I said, *"What?"*

And she said, "I am not *kidding*."

And she saw my surprise, and I said, "Are you *serious?*"

"Yes."

[T]he President had his hands . . . all over her backside . . . pulling her tightly, and she kept saying that it was—almost took her breath away, it was so—*forceful*.[8]

HANDSOME AND DELILAH

> *HANDSOME—*
> *With Love's light wings did I o'erperch these walls:*
> *For stony limits cannot hold love out,*
> *And what love can do, that dares love attempt;—*
>   (ROMEO AND JULIET 2:2)
> *Happy Valentine's Day!*   —M

On February 13, 1997, "M" left "Handsome" (a.k.a. "the Creep," "schmucko," or "Mr. P") an anonymous voice-mail message at the White House, directing him to check out the V-Day personals in the *Washington Post*. The paperwork was handled by Monica's senior colleague, Linda Rose Tripp, a.k.a. LRT (as Tripp signed her e-mail), a.k.a. Mary (a code name assigned by Monica), more commonly called Gus (a detested nickname). Tripp paid for the placement of the valentine and saved a hard copy. (M was spending V-Day that year in London.) In her IOU ("Subject: RE: secret message," signed "msl"),

M told LRT that she'd be checking her voice-mail messages, "in the hopes that the Creep will call and say 'Thank you for my love note. I love you. Will you run away with me?' "[9] Exiled to the Pentagon in April 1996 and still lonely, M had no friend at work except LRT; no access to the WH (White House) except through Handsome's personal secretary, Betty Currie (code name: Kay); no known rival in love except Hillary (code name: Babba, after Monica's great-grandmother); and, from April to December 1996, no passionately romantic or Shakespearean moments with Handsome except as facilitated by the telecommunications industry. M at this point had not yet been introduced to Vernon Jordan (code name: Gwen, no relation to my wife of that name), who would later head up Mr. P's endeavor to Find This Girl a Job (Monica hated her job at the Pentagon); nor had Jordan yet introduced M to Frank Carter, the lawyer who would assist with Monica's no-sex-happened affidavit. M liked Mr. P's style, and she liked Gwen's style, but not Frank Carter's style; he dresses, she said to LRT, "like a Radio Shack salesman."

Monica's style is breezy, informal; she writes like she talks. Abbreviations are frequent, exclamation points plentiful, she's been known to comma-splice a sentence now and then, following the example of her favorite poets, Emily Dickinson and Walt Whitman. (In one note to Handsome, M eulogized Whitman as a poet whose words are "so timeless . . . so rich, that one must read him like one tastes a fine wine or good cigar—take it in, roll it in your mouth, and savor it.")[10] But Monica is a writer whose diction relies heavily on the vernacular, as in her e-mail to Linda Tripp, where Monica, voicing frustration with the Creep, repeatedly complains of neglect in the two-word phrase, "FUCK ME!!!!" (A dramatic irony: Linda Tripp, who received these messages, did just that. Mr. P, never.)

On Independence Day 1997, after a fight in the WH between Mr. P and "Kiddo" (Mr. P's affectionate nickname for M) over the job issue, M warned Handsome that her friend at the Pentagon, Linda Tripp, had been getting calls again from a *Newsweek* reporter (code name: Spikey) about the president and a woman named Kathleen Willey. Mr. P knew about that—Willey had informed the WH as well. The Willey situation was being handled by White House Deputy Counsel Bruce Lindsey (White House nickname: the Minesweeper).

A week later, Willey again called Betty Currie: "Michael Isikoff has learned of my call to the White House—how'd he know? Did someone *tell* him?"

Suspicious, Mr. P asked Kiddo if Linda Tripp could be trusted—was she a team player? Kiddo said, "Yes, absolutely." Kiddo wanted to know if Willey could be trusted. Mr. P didn't think so. Kiddo advised Mr. P that his Willey problem might go away if he would just find the woman a job.[11]

ANOTHER JANE DOE

> The dress story? I think I leaked that . . . I had to do something . . .
> I've done it. And I'm not unproud of it.
> —LUCIANNE GOLDBERG, LAUGHING,
> TO THE *NEW YORK DAILY NEWS* (25 JANUARY 1998)[12]

In October 1997, Joseph Cammarata received another anonymous (he says) phone call at Paula Jones Central. Other calls would follow—to the conservative Rutherford Institute, and to various friends and a law partner of Kenneth Starr, but Cammarata heard it first: investigate "a woman named Monica." So Cammarata did that, with help from Michael Isikoff and Lucianne Goldberg.

Lucianne Goldberg's son, Jonah, has said that it was Linda Tripp, not his mom, who made that October phone call, an attribution never confirmed by Cammarata. Either way, Tripp understood what it meant. Now that a new name—Monica—had been put into circulation, she had better buy a Radio Shack tape recorder to protect herself or risk another Team Clinton assault on her character and credibility like that crack Bob Bennett made to *Newsweek*.

"By the way," said Linda Tripp to Monica, on tape, when she received her subpoena to testify in the Jones case concerning what she knew of the Willey incident, "if they ask me about you and the president, I cannot tell a lie." Monica had no clue why anyone in *Jones v. Clinton* should be asking Linda Tripp about anyone but Kathleen Willey. It put the fear of Starr into her heart, together with Psalm 91, a passage that had been recommended to Monica by her spiritual advisor, a Christian Science counselor: "Surely he shall deliver thee from the snare. . . . Because he hath set his love upon me, therefore will I deliver him."[13] On January 16, while detained by agents in Room 1012 of the Pentagon City Ritz-Carlton, it was Psalm 91 in a Gideon Bible that kept Monica from flipping.

BILL CLINTON SPEAKING

> Q. And you're aware that she testified that you took her hand and put it on your penis?
>
> A. I am aware of that. . . .
>
> Q. Do you know why she would tell a story like that if it weren't true?
>
> A. No, Sir, I don't. I don't know. She'd been through a lot, and apparently the financial difficulties were even greater than she thought. . . .
>
> —WILLIAM JEFFERSON CLINTON, DEPOSITION,
> JONES CASE (17 JANUARY 1998)

On January 13, 1998, over lunch, Monica happened to mention to her friend Linda (who happened that day to be wearing a wire) that she had been "taught" how to answer the question "Were you ever alone with the president?" Monica said she was told to say: "Well, *not that I recall, not that I really remember . . .* Um, *it's possible I may have taken a letter on the weekend,* but, you know—I might have, *but I don't really remember.*"[14] (Four days later, in his deposition in the Jones case, President Clinton was asked the identical question: "Mr. President, . . . At any time, were you and Monica Lewinsky together alone in the Oval Office?"—to which he replied, *"I don't recall,* but as I said, . . . She, it seems to me, *she brought things to me once or twice on the weekends... I just, I don't remember... That's possible"* (emphasis added).[15] It's often said that the man and the woman in a good marriage end up sounding a lot alike. After just two years, that was true also of Bill and Monica. Could there have been a conspiracy to lie? And if so, who was putting words in whose mouth?

To impeach the president of the United States, the Office of Independent Counsel required evidence of "high crimes and misdemeanors." By Wednesday, January 14, 1998, four long years after getting started and two busy days after receiving the Tripp-Lewinsky tapes, Kenneth Starr had what was needed—evidence of a crime: a three-page document that (in the OIC's view) instructed Linda Tripp to lie in *Jones v. Clinton,* first about Kathleen Willey, then about Monica Lewinsky. On Saturday, a second offense occurred as the president testified in the Jones lawsuit, first about Mrs. Willey, then about Ms. Lewinsky. The president performed well, though unvirtuously, on the witness stand. (As Nebraska senator Bob Kerry once said, "Clinton is an unusually good liar—*unusually* good.")[16] In the Talking Points, Linda Tripp is instructed to say of Kathleen Willey's story: *"You now do not believe that what she claimed happened really happened."* On the witness stand, President Clinton said of Willey's story, *"I have no idea why she said what she did, or whether she now believes that actually happened"* (emphasis added). That's one of several points at which the president on January 17 sounded not only like Monica Lewinsky but rather like the author of the Talking Points.

President Clinton made those dubious statements on January 17 without knowing that Kenneth Starr had been given the Talking Points document; without knowing that Starr's team also possessed a detailed, taped narrative of the president's affair with Monica Lewinsky. He did not know that Ms. Lewinsky herself had spent much of the previous twenty-four hours in Room 1012 of the Ritz-Carlton with OIC deputies and armed guards who threatened her with twenty-seven years in prison for the crime of filing a false affidavit.[17]

Kenneth Starr had played his cards well: the president lied under oath. Starting on Monday, the Office of Independent Counsel began passing out subpoenas like candy. With the president's deposition in one hand and a grant of expanded jurisdiction to investigate the Lewinsky matter in the other, plus a smoking gun—the Talking Points—in his pocket, Kenneth Starr had every tool necessary to send the nation lurching toward a presidential impeachment.

MONICA CALLING

> From: Lewinsky, Monica
> To: Tripp, Linda
> Subject: RE: secret message
> Date: Thursday, February 13, 1997 11:05AM
> Priority: High
> IF ONLY I COULD PURSUADE [*sic*] THE CREEP AS EASILY!!!!!!

Any attorney worth his fee, when preparing for a civil suit or criminal trial, will shop early for expert witnesses. No confidential details are exchanged until there is a signed agreement that the attorney will supply true and accurate information, and that the witness will keep that information confidential. This is as it should be.

In a high-profile case, there is another common strategy for contacting experts, and another motivation. Plan B: You call for free advice and try out a line of argument that you might use in your client's defense. You then say "Thanks" and "Maybe we'll call."

April 6, 1998, Plan B: "Hello, Professor Foster? This is Nathaniel Speights, with Speights and Mitchell in Washington. I represent Monica Lewinsky and I wonder if I might have a few moments of your time?"

The phone call was unexpected. Monica Lewinsky had not been indicted. She did not need an expert witness or text analyst, she needed an immunity agreement. Faced with possible prosecution for witness tampering, attempted perjury, subornation of perjury, withholding of evidence, and conspiracy to obstruct justice, Monica had one way to get off the stove top, and that was to testify against Team Clinton. On February 1, the Lewinsky team had given the OIC a "handwritten proffer," offering confidential information in exchange for limited immunity. Monica in that document freely acknowledged an "intimate and emotional relationship with the President" that "included oral sex but excluded intercourse," alleging also that "the President told Ms. L to deny a relationship if ever asked about it."[18] Mr. Starr, playing hardball, rejected the proffer because Lewinsky said nothing of the Talking Points. Starr demanded to know who wrote it. Monica refused to tell. Negotiations broke down.

I listened attentively as Mr. Speights explained to me his theory of the crime, his scenario of how the Talking Points came to be written. Monica Lewinsky's involvement, he said, was "more ministerial than collaborative." Insofar as Monica participated in the document, she took her ideas not from the president, nor from the president's counsel, nor even from inside her own romantic head, but from Linda Tripp. Monica was just "a conduit for Linda's ideas."

I wasn't sure I had heard correctly. How could this line of argument be employed in Monica's defense, or even ventured in a revised proffer, without inviting catastrophe? If Mr. Speights were bold enough to name Linda Tripp as the originating author of the Talking Points document, then Ms. Tripp, I surmised, would make bold with him and box his ears.

First, why would Monica deliver the document to Tripp at the Pentagon if the two women wrote the text collaboratively? When pressed, Mr. Speights seemed evasive, but the conversation drifted toward hints of entrapment. These may be Monica's words, Speights implied, but Linda Tripp put her up to it, telling her what to say. The bottom line was that Monica had no thought in her head of trying to suborn perjury. She did not suspect that Linda would give the Talking Points to her lawyers, and her lawyers give them to Kenneth Starr quicker than Paula Jones could say Bingo!

By this time, out of curiosity, not for comment, I had examined the NBC transcript of the document against published articles, press statements, original speeches, and formal depositions by a dozen possible authors or collaborators, including President Clinton. I had culled from on-line news sources just about every published remark that Linda Tripp and Monica Lewinsky had made to the press or to each other. So far, I had found nothing in the Talking Points that looked like Linda Tripp, nor much that looked like Monica Lewinsky.

Nathaniel Speights is a good lawyer. I felt more than a little dubious about his version of events, but the call was on his dime, no point in wasting it. I asked him to fax me an authentic and accurate hard copy of the Talking Points, a printout or photo-facsimile with every jot and dot and comma as it appears in the original. None was available: "Only one copy of the Talking Points exists. We do not have access to Tripp's Pentagon computer." Verbatim quote. Also, a non sequitur. The original document was in Starr's possession. Tripp's computer was off-limits. That didn't necessarily mean that Tripp had the original, electronic text on her computer. I had looked closely at those three pages. I had thought that page one was probably passed to Monica on a diskette, and not by Linda Tripp. I could imagine no scenario by which the original master copy of the Talking Points should end up on Linda Tripp's computer. I still can't.

I was about to say, "But wasn't there a diskette . . . ?" when Mr. Speights said he had some documents he wanted me to inspect. Could we talk again on Friday? Couldn't hurt. I said, "Yes, sure, my pleasure."

The texts that Monica's defense team faxed for my freebie analysis were hardly top secret. They included the August 1997 *Newsweek* article about the Kathleen Willey incident; selected news stories about the Talking Points; and a published transcript of the Tripp-Lewinsky tapes. Also faxed was a thick typescript by Louisiana scholars John F. X. Gillis and Willard Fox, whose research indicated that the Talking Points document was a hoax produced by three hands: (1) a lawyer friendly to Ms. Tripp—"possibly Tripp's first attorney, [Kirbe] Behre, or her second, James Moody"; (2) a Tripp confidante, probably Lucianne Goldberg; and (3) the typist, main author, and editor, Ms. Tripp herself.

Mr. Speights called my office and left a message that reminded me of a tape delivery from *Mission: Impossible:* "Let me explain what I need from you," he said. "I know *exactly* how the Talking Points came into being. I know that *you* do not. I know that you're relying on press reports. It's better for you to continue to rely on them—on the press reports—so as not to taint your evaluation. But what I'm looking for is an opportunity to determine where some of these ideas came from. . . ." My assignment, evidently, was to study a reported (unauthenticated) text of the Questioned Document; to rely on the media concerning its possible authorship and transmission; to study a conspiracy theory; to search the QD for Linda Tripp's "ideas" (not her words, her *ideas*); and then to deliver an opinion that would help to rescue Ms. Lewinsky from the clutches of Mr. Starr.

Calling again four days later, on Friday, Mr. Speights clarified—or at least repeated—the defense position while the central figure in his cause célèbre, Ms. Lewinsky herself, sat at his side and kibitzed. With the fate of an elected president possibly hanging in the balance, I thought it best to be straightforward: "I do not believe that the Talking Points can be ascribed to Linda Tripp."

"The *ideas*," cautioned Mr. Speights.

Monica chimed in: "Well, there's that 'huge liar' thing," she said. " '*Huge*' is like one of [Linda's] favorite words. She was always saying, *huge* this, *huge* that."

The paragraph to which Ms. Lewinsky referred appears at the tail end of the three-page document:

> By the way, remember how I said there was someone else that I knew about. Well, she turned out to be this huge liar. I found out she left the WH because she was stalking the P or something like that. Well, at least that gets me out of another scandal I know about.

But the "huge liar" paragraph, which Ms. Lewinsky was inviting me to study as an example of Linda Tripp's influence on the Talking Points, looked and sounded to me like something Lewinsky wrote while trying to sound like Linda Tripp. Here were Monica's very abbreviations (WH, P). Monica's informal Beverly Hills High diction (e.g., "or something like that"). Monica's syntax, her tendency to begin sentences adverbially ("By the way, . . ." "Well, . . ." "Well, . . ."). Here also is Monica's tendency to omit relative *that* ("I found out [that] she left . . ." "Another scandal [that] I know about . . ."). Above all, here was Monica's point of view, a panicky desire for Linda Tripp to write a false affidavit that would actually rescue Monica, not Linda, from embroilment in a Clinton sex scandal. Those final four sentences, beginning with the phrase "By the way," illustrate so perfectly the prose style of Monica Lewinsky and express so unmistakably her own idea (*Linda, ya' gotta save me!*) that I could not credit Monica's remark that this was quintessential Tripp. When I shared with Mr. Speights my conviction that the "huge liar" paragraph was Monica's, he did not contradict me.

Linda Tripp does often say the word "huge," as in transcripts of the Tripp-Lewinsky tapes that had already appeared in *Newsweek* (TRIPP: "This is so amazingly *huge* to me . . . I know it's *huge* to you . . ."). That's where the Gillis-Fox analysis came in: "*It is hard to believe,*" wrote Gillis and Fox, "*that the last sentence of this paragraph, 'Well, at least that gets me out of another scandal I know about,' was written by anyone other than Tripp herself.*" The Lewinsky defense team evidently wanted me to say that Linda Tripp did indeed contribute to the document, if only by means of a Svengali-like influence over Monica's use of the word "huge."

The phone discussion seemed unproductive and without direction. I cut to the chase: "Okay, Mr. Speights. Let's separate the question of authorship from the question of document production. You believe that the 'ideas' here are Tripp's"?

"That is what we are trying to *determine.*"

"I can believe Monica *typed* much of this document, but—"

"Yes," said Mr. Speights, "but not on her computer, as you may have read in the press."

I sprang the question: "Are you telling me that Monica and Linda sat down and hammered this thing out together on *Linda's* computer?"[19]

This time, Mr. Speights put his hand over the telephone. He

returned a moment later with the answer: "Monica says it wasn't exactly like that. There was a diskette."

Only a minute after we hung up, the phone rang. I thought it might be Speights calling back with an afterthought, but it was MSNBC: "Can you tell us anything yet about the Talking Points?"

"Sorry, no clue."

STARR REPORT IDENTIFIES AUTHOR OF "TALKING POINTS": MONICA LEWINSKY

> It's called "Points to Make in Affidavit." Prosecutors say it might as well be called "How to Commit Perjury in the Paula Jones Case."
> —*NBC NEWS AT SUNRISE* (22 JANUARY 1998)

At 2:00 P.M. on September 11, 1998, the U.S. Congress published, on the World Wide Web, a full-text version of the Starr Report. Thousands of readers, myself among them, tuned in. It was one of the great *ooh-la-la!* moments in the history of American government. Who would have predicted that Ken Starr, a former Bible salesman and born-again Southern Baptist, would have saturated his 450-page statement with so many salacious details, turning "jurisprudence" into a one-word oxymoron? But Starr by this time had exhausted voters' interest in the Whitewater land deal, the Webb Hubbell billing scandal, the Travel Office firings, the Vince Foster suicide. The Starr Report focused instead on sex acts in the White House, its pages splashed with more than eighty instances of "oral sex" and a whole paragraph on the inappropriate use of a presidential cigar. The object, of course, was to demonstrate to the American people that Mr. Clinton was a philandering liar and should be impeached.

Readers seemed to miss Mr. Starr's point. In a matter of minutes, the Associated Press Web site surged to twenty times its normal load as readers zeroed in on the section of the Starr Report captioned "I.C. Sexual Contacts." At CNN's interactive site, the number of hits peaked at 340,000 per minute, a new record. By dinnertime, Americans age twelve and up were sharing tips about which parts you should read first. Meanwhile, I searched the 91,000-word report for the Independent Counsel's answer to a question that had puzzled the nation and the Washington press corps for nearly eight months—"Who wrote the Talking Points?" As recently as July, Starr's team had floated hints that the document portended impeachment. Interested now to learn what Starr had discovered since the story first broke, I was disappointed. The controversial document was buried with a single sentence: "Ms. Lewinsky testified that she wrote the document herself, although some of the ideas may have been inspired by conversations with Ms. Tripp"—a close paraphrase of what Nathaniel Speights told me in April, four months before Monica was granted immunity.[20] Unable to puzzle out the problem of the Talking Points, Mr. Starr had put his eye to the Oval Office keyhole and reported on that.

Not everyone was willing to settle for Mr. Starr's tidy, twenty-three-word dismissal of a document that had prompted one of the OIC's most vigorous and far-reaching investigations. "The notion that Monica wrote those [Talking Points] on her own," sniffed Tripp, "is about as likely as her co-authoring the Gettysburg Address with Lincoln"[21]—a polite way of saying that Kenneth Starr was either incredibly gullible, having swallowed an obvious lie, or a hypocrite, having abetted perjury after he got what he wanted from Monica Lewinsky.

But Monica's definition of "authorship" is like Bill's definition of "sex": a solo performance doesn't mean that no one else was involved. Now that the scandal is history, I think it appropriate for the rest of us to ask certain questions of the Talking Points, and even to ask if the OIC might have gotten to the bottom of this mystery, had Mr. Starr not been so distracted by the bottoms of President Clinton and Monica Lewinsky.[22]

SMOKING GUN

> Like the purloined letter in Edgar Allan Poe's story, the smoking gun
> in the most recent Clinton scandal is in plain sight. The evidence that
> strikes dread in the White House is a three-page document called
> "the talking points."
>
> —WILLIAM SAFIRE, *NEW YORK TIMES* (12 FEBRUARY 1988)[23]

Deep Throat's advice was to "Follow the money." My advice would
have been: "Follow the words." There are three pages in the Talking
Points document. Page one, captioned "points to make in affidavit,"
was written by a lawyer or by someone with advanced legal training,
probably by a defense attorney. Its purpose is to ensure that Linda
Tripp, though subpoenaed, will not be called to testify in *Jones v.
Clinton* concerning the Kathleen Willey incident.

By January 1998, with the alleged groping of Kathleen Willey
having become grist for the Jones lawsuit, it could no longer be
maintained that the president consoled her with a harmless hug
following her husband's death; and now that Willey was herself involved, Linda Tripp could not be blown off as someone who "is
not to be believed." The situation had become explosive. Clinton
would doubtless survive the Jones lawsuit, but if the American public
should be persuaded that he actually grabbed and groped a woman in
the Oval Office while serving as the president of the United States,
he was done for.

Page two is a cut-and-paste duplicate of page one, with only superficial changes.

Page three is a mishmash of ideas, paragraphs one through six ad-
vising Tripp to remember that she owes her employment to Team
Clinton, and reminding her to run her affidavit past Bob Bennett before submitting it to the Arkansas court. A final paragraph on page
three urges Tripp to deny any knowledge of the Clinton-Lewinsky
affair.

Instead of insisting, from February through July, that Lewinsky answer the question "Who wrote the Talking Points document?" (as if one author sat down and knocked out three pages at a single sitting), Starr and his deputies may have done better to take it page by page, or even point by point. So, let's do that.

PAGE ONE

[L]eafing through her school and college essays, which display lucid lines of thought and argument, it takes little imagination to realize that she was the author of the famous "Talking Points," . . .

—ANDREW MORTON, FOREWORD TO *MONICA'S STORY*[24]

It does not take a Shakespeare scholar, or a computer, or a $40 million federal investigation, to see that "points to make in affidavit" (page one) was written by somebody with legal training. The diction and phraseology of the "points" ("as a someone who would corroborate," "a sequence of events that was very dissimilar from what you remembered happening," etc.) is no more similar to the prose manner of Monica Lewinsky than a motion in limine is to a limerick. From the get-go, everyone who perused those page one "points" (including OIC lawyers, the press, and pundits) recognized the language, thought, and expertise of an attorney—most probably, an attorney representing the president, or even the president himself (who also has a law degree, and who actually *taught* law, at the University of Arkansas, in the 1970s).

Writing to Linda Tripp in the imperative mode, the "points" author offers Tripp competent lawyerly advice on how to defuse a delicate situation while remaining on the windy side of a perjury rap. Tripp is advised to stay on the same page with the White House; to accommodate herself to Bob Bennett's version of events as first told to *Newsweek;* to be fuzzy on details; and to deny having any knowledge or observations that would support Kathleen Willey's story. To maintain an air of objectivity, she must not call the president by name; and she should call Willey "Kathleen," claiming to be "friends" who simply "became out of touch," not feuding rivals. That will make the knife slide in more easily when Tripp goes on to say that her friend Kathleen, who lies, and who even tries to get her friends to lie, may have untucked her own blouse and smeared her own lipstick, making up what never really happened. If Tripp's affidavit adopts the recommended equivocal language ("[I] now do not believe" and "[I] now find it completely plausible"), she can avoid demonstrable perjury.

Slipped into paragraph two is what looks like a subtle threat: Bob Bennett, speaking for the president, has said that Mr. Clinton, *"around the time of her husband's death,"* may have consoled Mrs. Willey. In parentheses, a phrase to be deleted from Tripp's actual affidavit, the author of "points" asks, ominously: "Do you really want to contradict him?"

Apart from the question of ethics, those page one "points" are a brilliant piece of legal work, steering clear of outright subornation of perjury. The goal, obviously, is not to make anyone in an Arkansas courtroom fall for a rhetorical ploy, but to let Team Jones know that Tripp, if subpoenaed to testify, will not corroborate the "pattern" of sexually predatory behavior alleged by the plaintiff. If Tripp follows the prescribed text, Team Clinton will be in good shape. But the someone who wrote the "points" didn't really know Linda Tripp.

PAGE TWO

The second page of the Talking Points appears to be a cut-and-paste duplicate of the page one "points to make in affidavit." Having now two electronic copies in the same computer file, someone made superficial changes in the duplicate that would become page two. Based on the internal evidence and her own sworn testimony, I believe that the "someone" can only have been Monica Lewinsky.

In that slightly revised duplicate copy (to become page two), the page one heading ("points to make in affidavit") has been deleted. Punctuation and spelling have been retained. Removing the page one parenthetical phrases—"(however she looked)" and "(whatever she claimed)"—Lewinsky has inserted blank lines instead. She also did a search-and-replace substitution, altering the second person (you) to the first person (I), but in so doing introduced confusion in paragraph four. Time required for the revised (page two) copy: five minutes, tops.

This manner of "editing" is exhibited in other known writings by Monica Lewinsky. The recasting of a document from "you" to "I," or from "I" to "she" (with attendant confusion), is exhibited, for example, in the handwritten proffer, where Monica speaks of herself, inconsistently, in the third person as "Ms. Lewinsky," and "Ms. L." (with an occasional "I" or "me" thrown in). Or take those fill-in-the-blank lines: turning to Tripp for help with her writing, as during her autumn 1997 job search, Lewinsky's way was to insert blank lines where substantive assistance was required. (One such Lewinsky document in Starr's possession, to be completed by Tripp, contained nine instances of fill-in-the-blank underlining on a single page.)[25]

The page two cut-and-paste text should have signaled to Kenneth Starr that the re-editing job was Monica's and the original "points" text probably by someone else. A good place to begin: not *"Who wrote the Talking Points?"* but *"Who wrote those page one 'points to make in affidavit'?"*

The answer to the second question, "How did the original author expect the 'points' to be delivered to Linda Tripp?" seems obvious: Monica Lewinsky.

The third question, then, should have been "How was the original document delivered to Lewinsky (by express mail? e-mail? hand-delivered hard copy or diskette?), and by whom?"

No matter how, I think the author cannot have been someone who knew what Monica Lewinsky would do to his fine-tuned piece of legal work. Monica had a point of her own to make in Linda Tripp's affidavit, one that had nothing to do with Kathleen Willey, or with events in the Oval Office on November 23, 1993. It had to do with Monica Lewinsky.

PAGE THREE

> From: Lewinsky, Monica
> To: Tripp, Linda
> Subject: bye
> Date: Wednesday, December 24, 1997 1:38PM
> LRT—I will miss working with you tremendously! Who will edit my
> letters? Who will tell me my grammar stinks??? . . . You go girl!!!
> All my love, MSL
>> —MONICA'S LAST E-MAIL MESSAGE WHEN QUITTING THE
>> PENTAGON JOB[26]

Page three is confusing, quite apart from its careless regard for standard punctuation and syntax. The text itself shifts back and forth between a seeming report of what Linda Tripp has been *thinking* and advice about what she should *do*. The main points (paragraphs 1–6):

- *Tripp thinks she should look neutral.*
- *She's not "neutral." She's a political appointee, and she wants to remember that. It's important for Tripp to be a team player.*
- *But she believes Bennett already thinks she's on the other side (because she wouldn't meet with him last summer after the* News-week *article).*
- *She should meet with Bennett now.*
- *But she's still upset about that* Newsweek *remark.*
- *She should do now what's in her own best interest: plead that her JCOC job depends on her not taking time off for a deposition; file an affidavit instead, supplying just enough information to satisfy the questions; and submit her affidavit for approval by Bennett's people before she signs.*

My study of Monica's writings and her own sworn testimony confirm that it was she who cobbled together the disjointed text of page three, but the Ping-Pong frame of reference underlying those six paragraphs looks to me like Monica's notes from a conversation with someone representing the president, someone who hoped to neutralize Linda Tripp's testimony in the Jones lawsuit.

There is a notable mistake in paragraph 6. Linda Tripp is advised to "provide an affidavit . . . in lieu of a deposition" (paragraph 4); and her "deposition [*sic;* a mistake for *affidavit*] should include enough information to satisfy their questioning" (paragraph 4). Not many people on the street know that you can sign an affidavit "in lieu of a deposition" and seek thereby to quash a subpoena to testify. The president's attorneys knew it. President Clinton knew it. By January 6, Monica knew it. But what practicing attorney would have made the mistaken substitution, in paragraph 6, of "deposition" for "affidavit"? Not, surely, the canny lawyer who was responsible for those slickly professional page one "points." It's possible Monica would make such a mistake. But President Clinton actually *did* make this error. In his Grand Jury deposition, the president testified: "I didn't know that Ms. Lewinsky's deposition [*affidavit*] wasn't going to be sufficient for her to avoid testifying."[27]

President Clinton's slip of the tongue, the same mistake made in the Talking Points, page three, paragraphs 4–6, piques my curiosity and raises new questions: Did the president and Monica Lewinsky discuss the Tripp subpoena? And if so, did the president advise Monica to massage Tripp's anticipated testimony?

LAST, BUT NOT LEAST . . .

> Well, at least that gets me out of another scandal I know about.
> —ANON., TALKING POINTS, P. 3, PAR. 7
> (ASCRIBED BY MONICA LEWINSKY TO LINDA TRIPP)

By January 14, 1998, "Bennett's people" had supplied all the assistance that Monica Lewinsky would ever get with her own affidavit for *Jones v. Clinton.* Now it was Linda Tripp's turn to write one, as per these easy-to-follow instructions, with just one small addition at the very end, a favor requested by Monica herself, having nothing to do with Kathleen Willey: Tripp must not supply the plaintiffs with information about "someone else." A scandal was brewing. Someone had mentioned Monica's name to Team Jones as a possible Clinton woman. Monica would be denying sexual involvement in her signed and soon-to-be-filed affidavit. President Clinton, too, would deny, deny, deny. Linda must stay on key. She could do that by dismissing Monica (not naming names) as a "huge liar" who told a few harmless fibs out of school, and who then told the truth under oath. Nothing really happened.

The "huge liar" paragraph must have seemed, to Monica Lewinsky, like the single most important statement she would ever write. The whole *point* of the Talking Points, from Monica's point of view, was that final, added paragraph, and she put some evident thought into it. She supplies Tripp with an excuse for the rumors of untoward behavior between President Clinton and "someone else": "I found out," Tripp must say, that Monica "left the WH because she was stalking the P or something like that. . . ."

To compose that sentence, and to ask Linda Tripp to include it in her affidavit, required of Monica some loyalty and swallowed pride. During the winter and spring of 1995–1996, the "Meanies"—Evelyn Lieberman and other heartless White House staffers—took to calling Monica hurtful names like "the Stalker" and "Clutch." Monica hated that. When the Lewinsky rumor was picked up by Team Jones, Monica was told to "Deny, deny, deny," to exonerate the president. She was a "stalker," not a lover.[28] Nothing really happened.

There is a good reason why this quirky postscript was tacked to the end of a document otherwise concerned with damage control in the matter of the Kathleen Willey incident; and there is a good reason why the original author of the "points" did not mention it himself. Monica at this time had a terrible secret. Neither the president nor any of his people knew that Monica had blurted to Tripp the details of her relationship with Clinton. (Monica to Linda, in the secret recordings: "Look, maybe we should just tell the Creep [but] I can't. If I do that, I'm just going to fucking kill myself.")[29] But if Linda could keep it a secret, and lie a little in her affidavit, no one would ever know.

WHO WROTE "POINTS TO MAKE IN AFFIDAVIT"?

Suspected Conference Zone: The Clinton White House. I lack authenticated writings by Bruce Lindsey and Robert Bennett, and one must assume that the president's speeches are mostly ghostwritten. But the Talking Points document affords certain opportunities for attributional investigation even without comprehensive text samples, beginning, as usual, with vocabulary. Most of the language in the "points," even the Beltway jargon ("career person," "political appointee"), is fairly ordinary—all but the phrase "allegedly came out of the oval." The more grand-sounding name, Oval Office, was coined by Richard Nixon, to lend mystique to the Imperial Presidency. Prior to that the room was called, simply, the President's Office. When the Clintons moved in, they clipped it to "the Oval," an epithet formerly reserved for London cricket fields or Arkansas racetracks.

"The Oval" was not current argot in Washington before 1992, not even among White House insiders. Checking wire service reports, I identified half a dozen White House and State Department officials who had used "the Oval" in briefings and press gaggles, most frequently Mike McCurry, who used it all the time. A few reporters seemed to have adopted it from McCurry, but only during the Q&A, not in print. Except for the occasional punning headline ("EVIL IN THE OVAL," "RED HEAD IN THE OVAL"), "the Oval" was a pet name used by President Clinton and his staff and associates, by a few professional reporters on the White House beat, and by no one else.

I was not the first reader to notice "the oval." Philip Weiss, writing for the *New York Observer,* noticed it. Howard Kurtz, author of *Spin Cycle,* noticed it. The whole White House press corps may have noticed it. But you can't get too far with the information, since all candidates for authorship of the Talking Points are persons who were, in fact, connected at some point with the Clinton White House. Any of them, including Monica Lewinsky or Linda Tripp, might have used Clinton-speak in a memo not intended for public view.

Even Kenneth Starr may have noticed "the oval." When Bill Clinton was finally deposed before the Grand Jury on August 17, 1998, Mr. Starr and his deputies introduced the Kathleen Willey matter as follows: "Mr. President, let's move ahead to the episode on November 23, 1993, in which Mrs. Willey met you in your office at the Oval . . ."

Curiouser still: nowhere else in Washington does one find the terminology "your office *at* the Oval." The president's "office *at* the Oval" is a Team Starr coinage, minted in 1998. But if Starr's deputies were baiting the president, trying to get him to say "in the Oval" without the "Office," Clinton didn't bite, not the first time. They tried again, asking about the location of his books ("—in your office at the Oval?"). This time, the president came out with it: "They were in the Oval."[30] But that was it. By this time, Ken Starr had decided to write off the Talking Points as a lost cause in order to obtain other details, taking up a line of questioning, moments later in the president's deposition, concerning the use of "a cigar as a sexual aid." In his Grand Jury testimony, lasting several hours, Mr. Clinton was not asked one question about suborning of perjury or the Talking Points. The critical document that Kenneth Starr had once cited as the cornerstone for his case against the Clinton White House had been set aside as an insoluble puzzle.

In requesting expanded jurisdiction to investigate the Lewinsky matter, Kenneth Starr on January 16 cited the Talking Points as his key piece of evidence of White House witness tampering. Lewinsky's Watergate residence was ransacked. All original writing, whether on paper, hard drive, or diskette, was confiscated. Her Pentagon hard drive was taken as well. Tripp voluntarily supplied a few samples of her own original prose. Then Starr got sidetracked. If, after gathering all of those documents, the OIC made no systematic effort to examine the authorship issue, it is because Kenneth Starr had other fish to fry:

after President Clinton on January 17 lied under oath, denying a sexual relationship with Monica Lewinsky, it became less important to the OIC's objectives to establish authorship of the Talking Points than to establish that Mr. Clinton had sex and lied about it.

Identified Reading Material: Michael Isikoff, "A Twist in Jones v. Clinton," *Newsweek* (August 11, 1997). Readers of Isikoff's "Twist" included Clinton, Lindsey, Bennett, Lewinsky, Tripp, and thousands of other American citizens, but the article was directly referenced five months later, paragraph by paragraph, by whoever wrote the "points to make in affidavit." The phrase *"At around the time of her husband's death"* (italicized in the "points," the only stressed phrase), and the attendant thought (that the president could have been guilty of nothing worse that a gesture of consolement), are assigned by Isikoff not to the president, but to Bob Bennett. The added stress, the insistence that Tripp use phrasing that will not contradict Bob Bennett, is an attributional pointer worth investigating.

Suspected Reading Material: Arkansas Law Review. When I first received a purportedly accurate text of the Talking Points in February 1998, long before speaking with Nathaniel Speights, I searched electronically for a document exhibiting diction and phraseology similar to that of the three-page document in my possession. The most unusual phrase, I learned, was that remark "about when *you became out of touch.*" Most Americans will say "get in touch" or "stay in touch" or "we're out of touch" or even "fell out of touch," but "become out" is odd, and "become out of touch," highly unusual. When I first looked for this phrase on the Web, I found more than 30,000 instances of *out of touch,* only 73 of which were linked to the verb *to become,* in any tense, past, present, or future. The most interesting parallel came from a law review article by Steven G. Calabresi: "Presidents may temporarily *become out of touch.*" Punching in combinations of ordinary words and phrases from the page one "points" document, I found that the same essay kept popping up as one having similar diction: Steven G. Calabresi, "Some Normative Arguments for the

Unitary Executive."[31] The multiple hits suggested that the author of
the "points" might be someone who knew Calabresi's "Normative
Arguments."

The *Arkansas Law Review,* in which Calabresi's essay appeared,
was formerly edited by Clinton chum Webb Hubbell, who was then
doing time for wrongdoing uncovered by Kenneth Starr. The name
Steven Calabresi was new to me: Did he have White House connec-
tions?, I wondered.[32] Far from it. Calabresi viewed Bill and Hillary
Clinton as a danger to the commonwealth. During the 1996 campaign, Calabresi prophesied darkly that a second-term Clinton regime would turn America, from the Supreme Court on down,
"*against* traditional social values, *for* the 'rights' of pornographers
and drug dealers, *against* private property, *for* racial quotas and preferences." Thanksgiving and mottoes on currency could be outlawed,
and normal heterosexual marriage be endangered, as Clinton subjected our nation to "a radical secular humanism that hates religion."[33] But Calabresi is no dummy, his fondness for apocalyptic
hyperbole and political cliché notwithstanding. He is a graduate of
Yale, an attorney, a professor of law at Northwestern, a distinguished expert on constitutional theory. He is also a director and
cofounder of the Federalist Society, an organization composed
mostly of conservative attorneys, including Kenneth Starr, Independent Counsel; Jim Moody, pro bono attorney for Linda Tripp from
January 13, 1998; Richard Porter, Starr's Chicago partner and a Lucianne Goldberg contact; and members of the Paula Jones legal team.
So how does one account for the apparent influence of Calabresi's
essay on the Talking Points?

There are three possibilities: (1) Calabresi is the true author of the
Talking Points and a right-wing conspirator, someone at whom the
Louisiana scholars, Fox and Gillis, should be taking a close look; (2)
the verbal parallels are merely coincidental, due to shared subject matter and conventional lawyer-speak prose; or, most likely, (3) whoever
wrote "points to make in affidavit" was a reader of Calabresi's essay.
Calabresi's "Normative Arguments" has been widely cited since its

1995 publication as the single most important argument, by a conservative, against the "Independent Counsel idea." A conservative, but no ally of Kenneth Starr on this one issue, Calabresi expressly warned against giving the new Special Prosecutor the license and a blank check to investigate the White House Travel Office affair, the FBI files found in Hillary's office, the Arkansas State Troopers matter, "and who knows what else."[34]

Monica Lewinsky may be a reader of Shakespeare, Whitman, Eliot, and *Cosmo,* she may even have read the Isikoff article. She is not an *Arkansas Law Review* girl. But I'd be pretty amazed if members of the president's legal team were neglectful of an essay as crucial to them as Steven Calabresi's "Normative Arguments for the Unitary Executive." That the same essay influenced the language of whoever wrote "points to make in affidavit" is not a certainty, but it is surely a hypothesis that might have been used as an investigative strategy had Starr ever gotten serious about tracing the origins of the Talking Points. When questioning suspected contributors to the document (President Clinton, Bruce Lindsey, Vernon Jordan, Robert Bennett, "Bennett's people," Monica Lewinsky), an important question to have asked would have been "Do you support Calabresi's theoretical opposition to the Independent Counsel?" Later on, you also ask about those "points to make in affidavit" without tipping your hand that the one question may be related to the other.

SUSPECT NO. 1: ROBERT BENNETT

As it happens, not even President Clinton was able to keep pitch with his private attorney, Robert Bennett. In his January 17 testimony, the president acknowledged that his meeting with Kathleen Willey occurred before Ed Willey killed himself, before Ed Willey was even known to be missing. Later in the same deposition, when responding to a follow-through question, the president grew fuzzy on the chronology, suggesting (as per Bennett) that Kathleen's "lie" about sexual harassment may indeed have been invented after the suicide. ("Her husband killed himself, she's been through a terrible time," etc.) This again suggests that the "points" was written by someone in Robert Bennett's firm, not by the president himself. Mr. Bennett may not be the original author, but his name does bob to the surface as the most obvious suspect.

The Starr Report and Supplementary Materials indicate that the OIC never inquired which member(s) of Team Clinton might have known the Isikoff article and the Calabresi essay. Bob Bennett certainly knew the one and probably knew the other. On March 3, 1999, more than a year after the Talking Points changed hands, Bennett appeared before the Senate Governmental Affairs Committee in order to read a prepared statement in which he urged the abolition of the Office of Independent Counsel. For a left-leaning lawyer, Bennett's opinions and phrasing and examples are remarkably similar to those of the right-leaning lawyer Steven Calabresi.

Calabresi (1995):

I do not believe we need an independent counsel law in this country to protect against *partisan* interference with *the law enforcement machinery* . . . [or] judicial review of presidential exercises of . . . nearly unilateral *prosecutorial discretion* . . . able to *politicize law enforcement* and prosecution. . . . [A] politically motivated request for *an Independent Counsel investigation* . . . may be *triggered* by just a few members of Congress. . . . [T]here is an *enormous possibility for partisan abuse* of this law because "independent" counsels are no more nonpartisan than independent agencies. . . . [W]ith this *regime* . . . *separation of powers* concerns are *undermined*. . . . [R]equests for independent counsel investigations

Bennett (1999):

The Independent Counsel Act . . . should not be re-enacted. . . . *I believe it should not be re-enacted* in any form. . . . The first flaw is the hair-*trigger* provision for activating an *independent counsel investigation*. . . . Rather than freeing *prosecutorial discretion* from political bias, the Act has become another weapon . . . in the arsenal of *partisan* politics . . . puts the *scandal machinery* in overdrive . . . create[s] opportunities for actual or apparent *partisan influence in law enforcement* . . . [violates] the *rights of the targeted public official* . . . [and puts] *enormous law enforcement power* of the Executive Branch in the hands of a single individual who for both political and practical reasons is un-of particular named executive officials bear a *frightening* resemblance to Bills of Attainder . . . See *Morrison v. Olson*, 487 U.S. 654 (1988) (*Scalia, J. Dissenting*). . . . This is not only *unfair to those who become the targets of such counsels*, it is also a bad thing for the country. It encourages an excessive *distrust of the government and of government officials*, and it prevents government from addressing the real problems of the nation. . . . What we need is less of an *obsession with scandals* and more of a focus on policy problems.

accountable, unchecked, and who cannot meaningfully be challenged. . . . As *Justice Scalia* stated in his now-prescient *dissent* in *Morrison v. Olson*, "*How frightening*. . . . " [A]ny benefits to be derived from *an independent counsel regime* are outweighed by . . . corrosion of public confidence in our justice system; the erosion of the *separation of powers;* and incursions into the rights of individuals in and out of public office. . . . [T]he independent counsel process . . . has not only *undermined respect for the Department of Justice* but has also led to *disrespect for Congress.*

At least with respect to the Independent Counsel issue, Steven Calabresi and Robert Bennett think a lot alike. The obvious similarities between the Calabresi essay (April 1994, pub. 1995), the anonymous "points to make in affidavit" (January 1998), and Bennett's statement to Congress (March 1999) do not prove that one of President Clinton's personal lawyers in the Jones case contributed to the Talking Points— much of the shared diction is content-linked—but it invites the same old questions: Did Bob Bennett know the Isikoff article? Did Bob Bennett know the Calabresi essay? Did Bob Bennett write "points to make in affidavit"? If not, does he know who did? Good questions!

On May 5, 1999, Kathleen Willey testified that Bob Bennett first asked her to sign an affidavit swearing that she was not sexually harassed by the president and that she refused, signing a more general affidavit stating only that she had no information pertinent to the Jones litigation. When Willey was called to give a deposition anyway, Bennett advised her, she said, to plead her Fifth Amendment rights rather than answer questions about what happened: "It was a threat," she said, "coming from the president."[35] (Bennett, not under oath, said that all of that was an "absolutely bald-faced lie.")[36]

Whether Bennett made an effort to influence the testimony or the affidavit of Linda Tripp concerning the Willey matter may never now be known, but the OIC did learn that Bennett's people made a generous effort to assist Frank Carter (the attorney Vernon Jordan retained for Monica Lewinsky, and who was later fired and replaced by William Ginsburg and Nathaniel Speights). One day after Jordan drove Monica to Carter's office, someone in Bob Bennett's firm graciously faxed Carter a copy of Isikoff's "A Twist in the Jones Case" and some "generic" tips on how to prepare an affidavit.[37] In his Grand Jury testimony, Carter could not recall whether or not those faxed materials from Mr. Bennett's office were useful to him in the preparation of the Monica Lewinsky affidavit.[38]

SUSPECT NO. 2: BRUCE LINDSEY
(nickname: the Minesweeper)

> *Prosecutor:* Did you ever sleep with him in New York?
> *Witness:* I refuse to answer that question.
> *Prosecutor:* Did you ever sleep with him in Chicago?
> *Witness:* I refuse to answer that question.
> *Prosecutor:* Did you ever sleep with him in Miami?
> *Witness:* No, sir.
>
> —"JOKE OF THE DAY" WEB PAGE

When reporters asked Linda Tripp whom she thought responsible for the Talking Points, she said she thought some of it sounded a lot like her former boss at the White House, Bruce Lindsey, Bill Clinton's best friend and pit bull for more than thirty years. Called "the Minesweeper" for his skill in handling the crisis of the moment, Lindsey was a one-man shovel brigade, from Gennifer Flowers right through Monica Lewinsky. Following Isikoff's August 1997 *Newsweek* article about Kathleen Willey, it was Lindsey who handled the fallout and who dealt personally with Linda Tripp, and it was to Lindsey that

Vernon Jordan directed Michael Isikoff's troublesome inquiries about Monica Lewinsky just before the Talking Points story broke in the press.

When Bruce Lindsey was asked about the Talking Points in his February deposition before the Grand Jury, the president's Minesweeper ran circles around his interrogators. On the stand for almost six hours, Lindsey declined to answer most questions, on grounds of executive privilege, or attorney-client privilege, or both. Others were answered with a "Yes" or "No," plus further explanation. A few questions—nine, to be exact—generated a snappy, West Point–like "No, sir." All nine of these answers came at prickly moments, five of them uttered in rapid-fire succession to questions about the Talking Points:[39]

> Q. Mr. Lindsey, Did you help in any way, directly or indirectly, in the preparation of these Talking Points?
> A. No, sir.
> Q. Do you know of anyone who did?
> A. No, sir.
> Q. Do you know of anyone in the White House who did?
> A. No, sir.
> Q. /. . . . / And, again, do you have any information at all about who would have either prepared or helped prepare this document?
> A. No, sir. None.
> Q. None? You have no information at all about this?
> A. No, sir.

There is a lot that Lindsey cannot recollect about what went on in the Clinton White House from 1992 to 2000. Dozens of times in his Grand Jury testimony, he was forced to reply "I don't remember" or "I don't recall." The one thing, however, that he really, really remembers is that he has no clue who wrote "these Talking Points."

The Lindsey deposition may illustrate why Starr won a few battles but lost the war. The prosecutors were imprecise in their phrasing.

Even if he had composed the page one "points" and typed the file to disk, how else should Lindsey reply to questions about "*these* Talking Points" and "*this* document"? The prosecutors gave Lindsey an opening to say "No, sir," and he drove through it.

Lindsey may have been careless too, or just truthful. When first shown the three-page version and asked if he'd seen it before, he replied, "I'm more familiar with the *front page* because it's been published more often . . ." (my emphasis).[40]

He was mistaken. The "front page" ("points to make in affidavit") was published first, but not more often, not by a long shot.[41] The next questions that ought to have been asked: "Why are you 'more familiar,' Mr. Lindsey, with that first page? Did you ever receive an electronic or printed copy of 'points to make in affidavit' from a third party? from Robert Bennett? from anyone in Robert Bennett's law firm?"

When Lindsey voluntarily brought up the Isikoff article, OIC prosecutors asked him to compare that *Newsweek* account with his own knowledge of what really happened, and received a telling answer:

> Q. [E]ven under Linda Tripp's story that it wasn't "harassment," it appeared as if there were some kind of improper activity that went on when Mrs. Willey had been in the Oval Office. Is that a fair statement?
>
> A. We can argue about "improper," but *some activity went on,* yes. . . . I think Linda Tripp included those *facts* [my emphasis].

Had the deputy prosecutors been paying close attention, they might have then followed through with another interesting question: "Mr. Lindsey, the president's personal counsel, Robert Bennett, has claimed otherwise. Are you contradicting him?"

Team Clinton is good when it comes to plausible deniability. President Clinton and Bruce Lindsey did not help to write the Talking Points. Vernon Jordan doesn't do affidavits. Bob Bennett doesn't do employment opportunities. None of these men, certainly, was responsible for the threats Kathleen Willey received, or for the "dozens of nails" pounded into her car tires two days before her Grand Jury deposition.[42]

But how does one account for Monica's confession that she alone wrote the Talking Points? Why should she cop to sole authorship if she was not the prime mover and did not actually write those page one "points to make in affidavit"? If she flipped on Mr. P, a.k.a. the Creep, and testified against him in copious detail about sexual matters, why should she take the fall for one of his pals or for his personal lawyer on the Talking Points, a document that was once the only real issue? Whom was she trying to protect? Possibly Vernon Jordan.

SUSPECT NO. 3: VERNON JORDAN
(code name: Gwen)

Q. Did you ever talk with the President about the talking points?
A. No.
Q. Did you ever talk with anyone associated with the White House in any way about the talking points?
A. No. And that would include Mr. Jordan.
—MONICA LEWINSKY, DEPOSITION, GRAND JURY (6 AUGUST 1998)

On January 22, the day the Talking Points story broke in the *Washington Post*, Vernon E. Jordan Jr. called a personal press conference at Washington's Park Hyatt Hotel. When he appeared, cucumber-cool, he read a carefully prepared statement (346 words, with good soundbites), provided copies of his text to the press (nine short paragraphs, laid out rather like a page of talking points), then turned on his heel and was gone. He took no questions concerning the document that Monica Lewinsky was said to have given Linda Tripp on January 14 at the Pentagon, or the fact that his own name was already in circulation as its possible author. He had called this press conference to say that yes, he helped this young person, Ms. Lewinsky, to find a good lawyer (Frank Carter), and to find a job (with Revlon). So what?

The final Lewinsky visit with Vernon Jordan was on January 13, probably sometime before her famous recorded lunch date with Linda Tripp. About nine that morning, Lewinsky phoned Tripp to say that she had received a job offer from Revlon and would now sign the No-Sex-Happened affidavit (though she may have been lying; the Lewinsky affidavit, not filed by Frank Carter until January 16, is dated and notarized January 7, one day before Mr. Jordan arranged Monica's interview with Revlon).

The next morning, perhaps after a little independent editing work on the document captioned "points to make in affidavit," Lewinsky paged Tripp, pulling her from a meeting at work, to say: We must meet again when you get off work. I have some "pointers" for you.[43] That makes me want to ask from whom Lewinsky might have received pointers on January 13, or even the next morning—from Bob Bennett? Frank Carter? or maybe Vernon Jordan? And if none of the above, then who?

Poor Kenneth Starr. In January, as soon as the Lewinsky story broke in the press, he went before Judge Susan Webber Wright, who presided over the Jones lawsuit, and requested that the interrogation of witnesses by Paula Jones's attorneys be halted and the document search halted as well, until the OIC completed its investigation of the Lewinsky matter. Judge Wright obliged him—by promptly excluding all Lewinsky-related matters from the Jones litigation as "not important" to the case, including the Lewinsky affidavit and the Clinton deposition—testimony that might otherwise have given Starr grounds for indictment. When Wright threw out the Lewinsky matter, and the affidavit with it, Starr's leverage on Monica Lewinsky—by which to flip her as a witness for the OIC, against the president—all but evaporated. A cruel irony then arose: Starr needed the Talking Points to be Monica Lewinsky's work, or she wouldn't be likely to testify against the president—but if she changed sides, testifying against the president in exchange for immunity, and claimed sole authorship of the Talking Points, there went the evidence of White House witness tampering. Starr would then be left with nothing but sex and attempted perjury with which to disgust American voters and the House Judiciary Committee, which is more or less how it turned out.

I don't know if Monica received her text of "points," whether by e-mail, diskette, or hand, from Vernon Jordan. I do know that Lewinsky, following her traumatic twelve-hour interrogation in Room 1012 of the Pentagon City Ritz-Carlton, developed an intense loyalty to Mr. Jordan as "the only one who came through" for her.[44] In her Grand Jury testimony and throughout *Monica's Story,* Lewinsky eulogizes and exonerates Jordan while dwelling on her own remorse for having lied to Linda Tripp, on tape, saying that Jordan told her to lie under oath—because that, like, never really happened. But if Monica was protecting someone, first by refusing to name anyone at all as the author of the Talking Points document, then by claiming sole authorship, her heroism may have been misplaced. If a middleman handed her a diskette or a sealed envelope containing those "pointers" for Linda Tripp, and if that person was Vernon Jordan, Monica can relax. Mr. Jordan did not write "points to make in affidavit." As Vernon Jordan reminded the Senate in his deposition of February 2, 1999: "I don't do affidavits." The evidence of his own original writings (of which I have a fair sample), and of the language used in the "points," bears him out on that. I think he's telling the truth. Because I lack authenticated writing samples by Robert Bennett and his staff, I cannot vouch for President Clinton's personal attorney.

STARR RAPPORT

> If people lack "sufficient virtue for self-government," Madison wrote, "nothing less than the chains of despotism can restrain them."
>
> —KENNETH STARR, "CIVIC VIRTUE" (1996)[45]

> "I'll admit," said a lady named Starr, "That a phallus is like a cigar . . ."
>
> —G. LEGMAN, *THE LIMERICK* (1970)[46]

One day after it was all over but the Senate vote, I sat at lunch with Shelley Ross, discussing her book, *Fall from Grace* (1988), which chronicles the rich and varied tradition of American political scandal. Ross's eye-opening narrative begins in 1702 when Lord Cornbury, New York's hard-drinking governor-general, showed up to open the colonial assembly wearing formal hooped skirts and lady's accessories. The book closes with public affairs of 1988, including Gary Hart's much publicized affair with Donna Rice. As a producer for ABC News (then with *20/20,* now with *Good Morning America*), Ross knew the inside story of political scandals that I hadn't even heard about.

Our conversation turned to the Clinton sex scandals. I had seen a quotation ascribed to Kenneth Starr, widely circulated on the Internet and picked up by city newspapers from coast to coast: "Public media should not contain explicit or implied descriptions of sex acts. Our society should be purged of the perverts who provide the media with pornographic material while pretending it has some redeeming social value under the public's 'right to know.' "[47] Starr was said to have made these remarks in a 1987 interview with Diane Sawyer on ABC's *20/20.* The quotation looked to me like a hoax. Ross confirmed it. She had personally checked the ABC archives, and there was no such interview.

In the interview that Starr that *did* give ABC, on November 25, 1998, Diane Sawyer asked: "I think there were sixty-two mentions of the word 'breast,' twenty-three of 'cigar,' nineteen of 'semen.' This has been called demented pornography, pornography for Puritans. Were there mistakes made in including some of this? . . . I still don't understand what a cigar has to do with whether the president should be impeached."

In defense of his lurid exposé, Mr. Starr invoked the example of Atticus Finch, the lawyer-hero of Harper Lee's American classic, *To Kill a Mockingbird:* "I love the model of Atticus Finch," he told Sawyer. "There is Truth, and the Truth demands respect. And maybe in the fullness of time, after the heat of battle has subsided, that will be the abiding lesson of this episode, that the Truth was important—and don't compromise the Truth."[48]

Even before his appearance on *20/20*, Kenneth Starr had taken this same message to the American people with a stump speech, comparing himself favorably with America's most widely admired, if fictional, attorney. In a lecture called "From Atticus Finch to Grisham's Bruiser," Starr positioned himself against Bruiser Stone, a lawyer in John Grisham's *Rainmaker*, a master of sleaze who owns strip clubs and evades the FBI while dispatching rookie lawyers to chase ambulances. The Independent Councel, a defender of Truth, is more like Harper Lee's Atticus Finch, because "Truth is the legal system's abiding value.... There's no room for white lies. There's no room for shading." But those are Kenneth Starr's words, not Harper Lee's. Starr misremembers the story. Atticus Finch's ultimate decision is to acquiesce in a lie in order to protect the mockingbird-like Boo Radley from criminal prosecution. The author of *To Kill a Mockingbird*, and even the honorable Atticus Finch, might well commend to Mr. Starr the wisdom of Calpurnia, Mr. Finch's housekeeper: "First thing you learn when you're from a lawin' family," says Calpurnia, "is that there ain't any definite answers to anything."[49]

CHAPTER FIVE

Wanda, the Fort Bragg Bag Lady

REAL PYNCHON

And although I met Thomas Pynchon one evening in Berkeley in
June of 1967, I cannot say I really know him.

—ANDREW GORDON, "SMOKING DOPE WITH

THOMAS PYNCHON" (1994)[1]

Little, really, is known about the life, looks, or immortal soul of
Thomas Ruggles Pynchon Jr. Born on Long Island in 1937, he
shares a May 8 birthday with such notables as Harry Truman,
president; Sonny Liston, boxer; Ricky Nelson, onetime teen idol;
and Beat poet Gary Snyder. Scion of an old New England family,
the novelist is believed to be a great-great-great-great-great-
grandson of the William Pynchon whose religious tract, *The Mer-
itorious Price of Our Redemption* (1650), was condemned for its
heretical opinions and burned by the Commonwealth of Massachusetts. Literary historians and cult followers say that Thomas
Pynchon attended Cornell, left school to serve in the Navy, returned
to college, changed his major from engineering to English, and completed his degree in 1959. Pynchon has since been credited with the

authorship of, among other works, five mostly great novels—*V* (1963), *The Crying of Lot 49* (1966), *Gravity's Rainbow* (1973), *Vineland* (1990), and *Mason & Dixon* (1997)—an oeuvre that has become grist for a cottage industry in professional literary studies, including a scholarly journal called *Pynchon Notes*. He does not like having his space invaded.

Everyone who has ever made it through *Vineland,* or read *The Crying of Lot 49* for a college English class, knows the Pancho Villa story. The year was 1963. When *Time*'s book editor dispatched a photographer to Mexico City to take Pynchon's picture to accompany the magazine's glowing review of *V,* the novelist fled to the hills, taking refuge behind an enormous mustache that inspired the locals to call their shy Yanqui guest "Pancho Villa." *V*'s author has been missing in action ever since. The last known (or supposed) photograph of Pynchon is from 1955, or rather that *was* the last, until 1995, when editors for *New York* magazine published a reputed shot of Pynchon's backside as the novelist walked down a Manhattan sidewalk with his only begotten son. But the *New York* photograph only added to Pynchon's reputation for ineffable divinity (cf. God to Moses: "After I have passed by . . . I will take away Mine hand and thou shalt see My back parts, but My face shall not be seen"; Exod. 33:22–23).[2] A year later, the London *Sunday Times Magazine* published a full Monty of Pynchon & Son's violated privacy, an Instamatic point-and-shoot, taken by the aspiring paparazzo James Bone.[3] Not everyone believed it was Pynchon. Some Pynchonophiles (as they call themselves) say that Thomas Pynchon is not even real. Some say that his novels were written by J. D. Salinger, or by the Unabomber, or by an extraterrestrial sapience, or by a secret organization. Or that Thomas Pynchon is really Wanda Tinasky. Or vice versa.

PYNCH. ANON.

"Along with some lesser Counts," the Rev[d] is replying, " 'twas one
of the least tolerable of Offenses in that era . . . the Crime they styl'd

'Anonymity.' That is, I left messages posted publicly, but did not
sign them."

—THOMAS PYNCHON, *MASON & DIXON* (1997)[4]

An age is darkened when truth lies not in what is said, but in who
says it.

—WANDA TINASKY, *MENDOCINO COMMENTARY* (28 JULY 1983)

In the 1980s, a seemingly insoluble mystery perplexed the denizens
of Mendocino County in Northern California: Who is Wanda Tinasky, and who in hell does she think she is? Wanda wrote scathingly
funny critiques of local *artistes* and politicians, publishing her observations in the same periodicals in which community activists, left and
right, agitated, and in which local poets contributed their musings on
the eternal verities. Ms. Tinasky described herself as an elderly Jewish
bag lady, a White Russian émigré living outside the Fort Bragg limits,
under a bridge (Fort Bragg is a foggy coastal hamlet inhabited by
bohemians, loggers, fishermen, and hemp farmers, not to be confused
with Fort Bragg, North Carolina, home of the U.S. Army's Airborne
Division and Special Ops). Ms. Tinasky confessed to being "old and
poor and funny-looking" with "gaposis and halitosis and B.O." She
admitted to eating out of garbage cans and to dressing out of the free
box. But after eighty-some years her mental faculties were still sharp.
"It is a *bas canard*," wrote Wanda, "or in the Queen's English, a duck
fart, that I am an alcoholic escapee from a mental institution."[5]

In 1984, soon after getting started in this epistolary vein, Wanda
was booted from the *Mendocino Commentary* for her biting assessment of the local Literature Industry, and for remarking, ungently,
that the *Commentary*'s poetry editor "wouldn't know a poem if it bit
her in the ass in broad daylight."[6] Wanda promised to continue ex-
ercising her critical rod with welt-raising vigilance: " 'Whom the Lord
loveth, He chastiseth.' (The Lord, *c'est moi*)."[7] Banished from the
Commentary, she found a new home in the *Anderson Valley Advertiser*, an upstart leftist weekly published out of Boonville (an actual
town in the Anderson Valley), a paper whose "old-fashioned maso-

chistic horsewhippable editor," Bruce Anderson (no relation to the Valley), promised to print anything, any time, and did.[8] While professing herself devoted as always to *Reader's Digest* and to the mystical writings of Nicholas of Cusa, Wanda penned a testimonial saying that the *AVA* was absolutely the best paper in Northern California. In fact, after her underwear gave out (she said), she sometimes used the *AVA* for that purpose and was quite satisfied.

In dozens of letters published in the *AVA* from 1984 to 1988, Wanda reviewed American television ("TV is no worse than smack and coke, the slobs just don't know how to handle it, that's all"); media stars ("I admire Phil Donahue for calling himself a 'workaholic.' Phil's idea of work is sitting under a hair dryer"); and politicians ("Ronzo [Reagan] claims he doesn't wear makeup on TV—the likeliest story since Linda Lovelace claimed she thought she was getting a tonsillectomy").[9] Most of Wanda's commentary, however, concerned the lamentable state of the arts in Mendocino County. Week after week, Wanda detailed the *vers libre* crimes of such artsy-fartsy coteries as the Ten Mile River Poets, the Albion Ridge Poets, and even Wanda's own secret society of one member, the Pudden Crick Poets. In her original verse for the *AVA*, Wanda roasted the canonical authors along with the local hempen homespuns (on Ezra Pound's *Pisan Cantos:* "He brought out Joyce & Eliot— / There must be something in this s***!" —Wanda Tinasky").[10] Wanda's sharpest barbs were reserved for the doyennes of local culture, such as Beth Bosk, host of *Eve in the Afternoon,* a controversial radio talk show. (Bosk's advice to listeners included such locally famous advice as "When a woman is bleeding, she should go into the garden and squat. It's good for the plants.")[11] Wanda wrote tolerantly to the *AVA* of being "amused or stimulated" by Ms. Bosk's radio show, "never infuriated or bewildered." ("It is true that once, in trying to say 'fecund,' she spoke a word not commonly met in family broadcasting or publications, but I was not outraged by it.")[12] Despite their differences, Wanda hoped Ms. Bosk would continue to think of her as a *comrade,* although not *in arms.*[13]

In September 1988 Wanda's letters abruptly stopped. The *AVA* carried on without her. But in 1990, while reading *Vineland,* Bruce Anderson felt a shock of recognition. Lights went on. Bells rang. "Wanda Tinasky" was Thomas Pynchon! In a 1986 letter, Wanda had professed to be writing a "thinly veiled novel of life in romantic Mendocino County"—and eureka! here it was: *Vineland.*[14] Pynchon, while researching the novel, had resided somewhere in Northern California, no one knew just where, but *Vineland* was populated with aging hippies like those evidently known to Wanda Tinasky from her wanderings in Mendocino County and from her pit stops at Fort Bragg's Tip Top Lounge. On March 21, 1990, after running the Pynchon-Tinasky attribution past the noses of a few Pynchonophiles, Bruce Anderson announced his discovery: "SUSPICIONS CONFIRMED. The justly famous American novelist, Thomas Pynchon, is almost certainly the pseudonymous comic letter writer, Wanda Tinasky. . . ." The announcement was greeted with a flurry of letters, also published in the *AVA,* one signed "T. Pynchon," another, "T. Pinch," still another, "Wanda Tinasky-Pynchon," each one hinting that Bruce Anderson could be right, or he could be wrong.

QUESTIONS

If they can get you asking the wrong questions, they don't have to worry about answers.

—THOMAS PYNCHON, "PROVERBS FOR PARANOIDS" (1973)[15]

Personally, whenever I see one of those bumperstickers that say, "Question Authority," I always write "Why?" on it.

—WANDA TINASKY, LETTER,
MENDOCINO COMMENTARY (28 JULY 1983)

It was in June 1996, a few weeks before Joe Klein fessed up to *Primary Colors* (but half a dozen years after Bruce Anderson first looked into *Vineland* and saw the spittin' image of a Fort Bragg bag lady), that reporters and book editors began calling me about *The Letters of Wanda Tinasky.* Edited by TR Factor, fully annotated in semischolarly fashion, the *Letters* were now on sale and believed by many, including Ms. Factor, especially Ms. Factor, to have been written by Thomas Ruggles Pynchon. Though interested, I had not yet seen the letters and could not comment.

Following Joe Klein's July 17 *Primary Colors* confession, the calls resumed, on the Literary Influence theory that if Joe Klein or his agent lied about Anonymous, then Pynchon and his agent may have lied about Wanda.[16] In October, after a "Who's Wanda?" call from the *Washington Post,* I finally gave in to my curiosity and wrote to Bruce Anderson, editor of the *AVA,* to inquire how I might obtain a copy of the Tinasky *Letters,* if only to speak in a more informed way when reporters or reviewers phoned. A few days later, I received a package mailed from Oregon, the first of several, from a person who introduced herself to me as "TR [no periods] Factor." (I never did learn what the "TR" stands for. "Thomas Ruggles," perhaps.) The goodwill parcels from Ms. Factor included a digital and hard copy of the *Letters,* plus back issues of the *AVA,* plus reams of material about Pynchon, plus contact information for a dozen Pynchon scholars, all free of charge, and with no strings attached except an obligation to demonstrate, the sooner, the better, that Thomas Pynchon really was Wanda Tinasky, the bag lady of Fort Bragg.

Taking me under her wing, TR for the next three years advised me to get off my academic duff and deliver the inevitable verdict. From Ms. Factor's point of view, Pynchon's authorship of the Tinasky letters was transparently obvious. A firm denial by Pynchon's wife and literary agent, Melanie Jackson, had forced upon TR, and upon the whole Pynchon Establishment, a rhetorical posture of agnosticism ("The Literary Mystery of the Decade!" TR called it in her advertising); but TR felt the proofs were as strong as Holy Writ. Stronger, even. The Wanda Tinasky Research Group had discovered beaucoup evidence that Wanda was Tom, and Tom, Wanda. There was the internal evidence: Ms. Tinasky had employed a highly unusual word, a slang term used also by Pynchon: Wanda, like Tom, wrote "86d" to mean *evicted.* Wanda, like Tom, constructed elaborate puns, tossed off obscure literary allusions, and peppered her work with wacky original limericks and song lyrics. Like Tom, Wanda spoke irreverently of literary book awards & exhibited an unkillable fondness for the ampersand. The two writers employed similarly eccentric symbolism. In one of her earliest letters to the *AVA,* Wanda had suggested that Bruce Anderson rename his paper "The Boonville Bugle." In Pynchon's *Crying of Lot 49* a muted bugle is a central if meaningless symbol, the emblem of "Tristero," a secret postal system. *Lot 49*'s protagonist, Oedipa Maas, finds the bugle emblazoned, among other places, on the walls of a women's latrine. Wanda Tinasky professed to have been a former employee of the U.S. Postal Service, during which time, she said, she had entertained herself by "writing on the walls of unobservable places such as the women's can."[17] How much evidence did one *need,* for god's sake?

Then, too, there was a world of biographical and ideological coincidence. Like Wanda, Pynchon had an ancient interest in the Beat poets and in obscure rock and roll (but in the '50s, I reasoned, among aspiring American writers, who didn't?). Both Wanda and Pynchon waxed nostalgic for the counterculture of the '60s; both were skeptical of modern technology. Pynchon was believed to have composed *Vineland* on a manual typewriter, an Underwood—the same make as Wanda's! (But that was bad information: Pynchon's typewriter was an Olivetti.) TR's smoking gun was a 1985 letter in which Wanda mentions having worked for Boeing Aircraft "about thirty-five years ago."[18] Pynchonophiles knew that while writing *V* the novelist was employed by Boeing Aircraft—from February 1960 to September 1962. (Go ahead, do the math!) For TR Factor and fellow members of the Wanda Tinasky Research Group, you didn't have to be a genius: those little Pynchonian clues added up.

BUT . . .

There are some irregularities, Miz Maas.
—THOMAS PYNCHON, *THE CRYING OF LOT 49* (1966)[19]

While reading TR Factor's annotated edition of *The Letters of Wanda Tinasky*, I was slow to perceive the obvious. Wanda was witty, smart, and well read. She may have read Pynchon, but she did not seem (to me) very Pynchonian. I had trouble hearing, in Ms. Tinasky's blatantly satirical prose, the rhythms of *V* or *Vineland* or *Gravity's Rainbow*. For one thing, Wanda was too funny. Pynchon wields his irony like a rapier, deftly. Wanda's punch lines usually left some Mendocino County poet or other bleeding on the floor. I looked at Wanda's language and texts from every angle—Wanda's diction, grammar, syntax, her political and literary sensibilities, topical allusions, reading matter, internal biographical evidence—all of which seemed (to me) a poor match with what I knew of Thomas Pynchon. But then, I did not really know Thomas Pynchon. Other scholars had vouched for the attribution, one of whom was reported by TR to have ventured "a hundred-to-one, a thousand-to-one odds" against Wanda Tinasky's identity matching that of any writer *except* Pynchon. (Okay, that *particular* scholar had changed his mind the next morning, reversing the odds, but TR felt sure there were other Pynchon scholars who had seen the light, and who would endorse the attribution if they were not such bleep-sucking cowards.)

TR arranged for collectors of Pynchoniana to supply me with photostatic copies of rare letters actually typed and signed by the novelist, but these yielded only fresh cause for alarm. Wanda usually put an unnecessary space between a quotation and the quotation marks, front and rear, or between marks of parenthesis and the bracketed phrase, " like so " and (like so). Pynchon did not. Nor did the typeface for Wanda's surviving letters match that of Pynchon's original typescript of *Vineland*, sample pages of which were sent to me by John Kraft, a scholar who was himself skeptical of the Pynchon attribution. Charles

Hollander, however, a Pynchon expert enlisted by the Wanda Tinasky Research Group, affirmed that the handwriting of Wanda Tinasky and of Thomas Pynchon were "nearly identical," especially the lowercase *c, m,* and *t*.[20] Hollander's remark reminded me of Malvolio's mistaken text analysis in Shakespeare's *Twelfth Night* ("These be her very *c*'s, her *u*'s, and her *t*'s and thus makes she her great *P*'s"). To my admittedly fallible eye, in no way did Pynchon's hand have the cut of Wanda Tinasky's.

Wanda and Pynchon appeared to have followed different paths to the Northern California coast. For one, Wanda seemed older. To illustrate her critical observations, she recalled obscure news stories as early as 1938, from the days when Tom Pynchon Jr. was still in diapers. Topical references in the Tinasky letters placed Wanda in Washington State in the 1950s, Northern California throughout the 1960s. Wanda spoke of her past acquaintance with Lance E. Davis and John R. Meyer, distinguished scholars who graduated with B.A.'s in 1950 from the University of Washington, and with various Beat poets, mostly on the West Coast. None of that sounded to my ears like Pynchon's biography.

Then, too, Wanda was just too damned *mean* to be Pynchon. Most of Pynchon's rare public statements consist of generous book-jacket blurbs for other authors. In his known letters, Pynchon similarly praises other writers while deprecating his own work. Pynchon seems disinclined to take out the kneecaps of aspiring writers (except, perhaps, of journalists who invade his privacy). I could not imagine this man, a successful and critically acclaimed novelist, holed up in Mendocino County dashing off letters to the *AVA*, skewering local poets, harpooning fish in a barrel as a morning warm-up exercise while writing *Vineland*. And the hypothesis that Pynchon would call Alice Walker "a purple-assed baboon" (as Wanda had done) was unthinkable. Was *that* Pynchon's style?

PYNCHON AND THE PYNCHONESQUE
IN MENDOLAND

> You may never get to touch the Master, but you can tickle his creatures.
>
> —THOMAS PYNCHON, "PROVERBS FOR PARANOIDS" (1973)[21]

> And here they are, now. Find the remote, get out the Snapple and Chee-tos, and like the *Love Boat* staff always sez, Welcome aboard.
>
> —THOMAS PYNCHON, LINER NOTES FOR LOTION'S ALBUM
> *NOBODY'S COOL* (1995)

Before opening a parcel from "Fred Gardner" of San Francisco—no one I knew—I matched the address with a phone number and dialed up Mr. Gardner to ask what he had sent me. Enclosed in the parcel, explained Gardner, was the nonexplosive product of his own pains-taking literary research, outlining his reasons for believing that a comic West Coast letter writer calling herself Wanda Tinasky was actually Thomas Pynchon; and that a sexually ambiguous West Coast virago calling herself TR (no periods) Factor was a mendacious, usurping, plagiarizing, typescript-stealing, opportunistic, goddamn bleeping bitch. Or words to that effect. Fred had heard from Bruce Anderson that I was interested in the Wanda phenomenon. Fred was interested, too. *The Letters of Wanda Tinasky* was his baby, snatched from his arms, he said, by his late-arriving editorial assistant. Mr. Gardner had sent me a copy of his work, together with a single-spaced, twenty-page report in which he detailed how badly he'd been bleeped over by Miz bleeping TR Factor. He was thinking, now, about suing her pants off, and it would not be pretty.

Fred Gardner was no Boonville yokel but a man of the world, a sixties radical and a onetime boyfriend of Jane Fonda (1969–1970, after Roger Vadim, before Tom Hayden), back when he was organizing GI coffeehouses to radicalize the U.S. Armed Forces (which was another project that never totally worked out). He works today as

Public Information Officer for the San Francisco District Attorney's Office. In 1994, Gardner intended with his friend and fellow journalist Alexander Cockburn to edit an *AVA* sampler that would feature commentary by Bruce Anderson and other Mendocino County wits. Searching back issues for the liveliest material, Gardner hit upon the Wanda Tinasky letters. Learning from Anderson that Wanda may have been Pynchon, Fred realized that Bruce was sitting on a gold mine. Gardner volunteered to gather the necessary evidence for Pynchon's authorship and to edit the Tinasky letters into a book. The Wanda Tinasky Research Group was born, an organization composed of Fred, his son Marc, and another Pynchon enthusiast, Steve Howland. Alexander Cockburn wisely bailed, wishing them all the best of luck.

In his twenty-page single-spaced history of TR Factor's book-editing caper, Fred explained to me that it was he, not Factor, who did the research for the annotated *Tinasky*. It was he who transcribed and edited the letters, solicited scholarly commentary, and personally interviewed every living individual ever mentioned by Wanda, friend or foe, from Boonville to Seattle to Boston to L.A. and back again. Then he hit a snag. In June 1995, as the typescript neared completion, Gardner wrote to Melanie Jackson to let her know what was coming down. Ms. Jackson wrote back to say that a mistake had been made: that Pynchon was not, in fact, Wanda Tinasky, and had never pretended to be. ("I have conferred with the author and his editors and publishers," said Ms. Jackson, "and no one can see any resemblance between his work and any of these letters. . . . Thomas Pynchon's name cannot be associated with your project in any way.")[22]

The course of true literary detection never did run smooth. Mulling over Melanie Jackson's strong denial, wondering if (just possibly) he had been bamboozled, Fred Gardner, on a tip from Beth Bosk, drove to Oregon to interview TR Factor, a former Mendoland resident and contributor to the *AVA* who Bosk believed was the real Wanda Tinasky. TR denied it ("Be still, my beating heart!" she exclaimed to Fred, upon learning of the attribution. "Thomas Pynchon has read my prose!"). TR graciously volunteered to join the WTRG, assisting Fred with the annotations for $10 an hour, with deferred wages until after the book went to press and started making megabucks.

The Gardner-Factor partnership, rocky from the outset, soon turned acrimonious. Fred thought TR's annotations too long-winded. TR thought Fred too bossy, and deficient in his typing skills. Fred advised caution in ascribing the letters to Pynchon. "Wimp!" said TR. The showdown came in the last week of August, in Boonville. Fred and his new assistant got into a huge screaming match that lasted for two days, hour after shrieking hour, barely avoiding (according to one eyewitness) knockdown fisticuffs, a fight that Fred would probably have lost, if it had come to that. One of them had to go, either Fred or TR. Fred walked.

When *The Letters of Wanda Tinasky* was finally published in June 1996, "Edited by TR Factor," the new editor tipped her cap to Fred in the acknowledgments, then shed his blood in a two-page diatribe in the *AVA*. "Nothing Fred had was usable," she explained, "much less professional . . . not an iota, smidgen or mote of scholarship. . . . A high school typing student could have done a better job and without the scores of errors."[23] And then she took it from there. The thought occurred to me that I could be in trouble with this Ms. Factor if I said that the Wanda letters were not really by Thomas Pynchon. She took her Pynchon very, very seriously. Not wishing to have a falling-out with Ms. Factor, I back-burnered the Tinasky letters while looking for an opportunity to slip out the back door unnoticed. If Thomas Pynchon got himself into this mess, he could probably get himself out of it without my help.

In April 1997, while I was still working, by day, on my report for the Unabomb prosecution and wondering, by night, how to break the news to Ms. Factor that I could not give her the endorsement she had hoped for, Ron Rosenbaum, a columnist at the *New York Observer*, saved the day. Ms. Factor and the Tinaskyites had demanded a cogent, reasoned argument that Melanie Jackson was lying about Pynchon's nonauthorship of the Tinasky letters. Rosenbaum delivered the goods. Appearing on the eve of *Mason & Dixon*'s publication, Rosenbaum's April 1997 article on *The Wanda Tinasky Letters* highlighted Pynchonesque features of Wanda's prose that Rosenbaum himself dubbed "The Cap/Cape of Invisibility Riff," "The riff on reverse Schadenfreude," and "the disappearance of Maxwell Perkins–type editors" (lines of attributional argument that I still do not fully understand or appreciate but that made perfect sense to many Pynchonophiles besides Mr. Rosenbaum). There was also Wanda's don't-lose-your-ass riff. Rosenbaum cited an episode in Pynchon's *V* in which a man born with a golden screw in his navel removes it, only to have his ass fall off. "But think about the name *Tinasky*," counseled Rosenbaum. "Break it down to *tin ass key*. A tin key that unlocks the ass, a golden screw that holds the ass on." Could *that* be a coincidence? I thought it probably could. But it made Ron Rosenbaum wonder aloud "why whoever Wanda is hasn't come forward—unless it is the Man himself."[24]

There was more. Rosenbaum had received an advance copy of *Mason & Dixon,* which had not yet hit the bookstands. Taking advantage of this sneak preview, Rosenbaum made the hitherto unreported observation that one of Pynchon's characters in that book signs a letter (like most eighteenth-century epistlers), "Y'r ob'd't s'v't."[25] That also happened to be Wanda Tinasky's trademark sign-off, or pretty close: "Yr. ob'd'nt Servant, &c., Wanda Tinasky." Rosenbaum's announcement sent a shock wave from New York to Boonville and back, registering ten points on the Richter scale at Tinasky Central. A jubilant TR Factor shot me an e-mail from her Oregon hideout concerning the "Y'r ob'd't s'v't" in Pynchon's soon-to-be-published *Mason & Dixon.* "If this is true," said TR, "Pynchon may as well have autographed the Wanda Tinasky books himself!"

Until Rosenbaum hopped onto the Tinasky bandwagon, it might have been enough for me to say: "Get real, folks. Thomas Pynchon is not, was not, and never will be Wanda Tinasky, not in her wildest dreams." But after six years of a slowly growing Wanda cult, and with new converts being won over daily by Mr. Rosenbaum—who professed also to know that it was not really Shakespeare who wrote "A Funeral Elegy"—it seemed to me that Wanda would never rest in peace, nor Thomas Pynchon in Manhattan, until the author of the Tinasky letters was truly identified. That, however, was easier said than done. Wanda could have been almost anyone—anyone except Pynchon—who lived in Northern California between 1978 and 1988. I had no guarantee that Wanda's creator was still living there, or alive at all for that matter. Finding a retired bag lady, a decade after she quit writing, from my own home three thousand miles from Fort Bragg, with no reliable witnesses, no original documents, no tips from the public, and not so much as an authenticated writing sample, seemed a virtual impossibility, like searching for a good three-dollar bill in Fort Knox. One thing for sure: there would be no confession forthcoming. If Wanda Tinasky intended to reveal her identity, she would have done so by now, if only to gloat over having been mistaken for the Great American Novelist Thomas Pynchon. The odds of finding Wanda Tinasky were minuscule.

In August 1998 I decided to give it the old college try. I applied the methodology that might have been employed to help find the Unabomber before the Unabomber was found, and had freakish good luck. It took only a month to track Wanda down.

RECOGNITION

> And the voices before and after the dead man's . . . searching ceaseless among the dial's ten million possibilities for that magical Other who would reveal herself out of the roar of relays, monotone litanies of insult, filth, fantasy, love, whose brute repetition must someday call into being the trigger for the unnamable act, the recognition, the Word.
>
> —THOMAS PYNCHON, *THE CRYING OF LOT 49* (1966)[26]

An only child, Thomas Donald Hawkins was born in Pangurn, Arkansas, on January 11, 1927. He grew up in Port Angeles, Washington, where he received local acclaim for his acting skill in high school theatrical productions. After graduating in 1950 from the University of Washington, where he majored in English, Tom married Kathleen Marie Gallanar, supporting his bride as an employee of Boeing Aircraft. In 1955 the Hawkinses moved to Beaumont, Texas, where Kathy went to work for an ad agency and Tom became a studio director for the city's new television station, KFDM-TV.[27] On April 24, 1955, pictures of Tom Hawkins appeared in Beaumont's *Sunday Enterprise,* one of them on the front page, the other on page C-6 over an article headed "Food Seen on TV Isn't Edible (Shaving Soap Serves as Cream and Coffee Is Plain Dye)."[28]

Quitting KFDM-TV after just two years, Tom worked with Kathy at the Beaumont ad agency, but they returned to the West Coast in 1960. Eager to join the Beat poetry scene, the Hawkinses settled in San Francisco. Tom took a job with the U.S. Postal Service and shocked fellow workers by growing a beard, something that had not been seen on the face of a San Francisco postal clerk since—who knows—the days of the Pony Express. To entertain himself during breaks, Hawkins wrote poetry on the toilet stalls, signing himself "Dr. Mung."

Searching for a wider audience than those who sometimes sat in a San Francisco post office Employees Only men's room, Tom submitted his poems and letters for publication in Lawrence Ferlinghetti's *City Lights Journal* and *Evergreen,* and Paul Krassner's *Realist*—without success. So he started his own house, the Ahab Press, comprised of a mimeograph machine and a post office box. Inspired by Tuli Kupferberg's *YEAH,* Tom's major publication for the next few years was *Freak,* an underground newspaper (a "little magazine," as they were called in those days) featuring the original writings of "Tiger Tim Hawkins"—film reviews, consumer reports, literary criticism, social satire, scatological limericks, crude cartoons, essays on the etymology of sexual slang. Also, jokes about twins separated at birth, a game that Hawkins was still playing as Wanda twenty years later ("Dashielle Hammett and William Faulkner," "Steve Martin and Governor George Deukmejian," "Patty Hearst and Dan Quayle," "Heather Locklear and Barbie").

In the 1980s, writing as Wanda, Hawkins recycled some of his old "Tiger Tim" material almost verbatim. For example:

Tiger Tim Hawkins, *Freak's Clean Poems* (1964):	Wanda Tinasky, "Parodies & Congeries," *Anderson Valley Advertiser* (1987):
In days of old when knights were bold	In days of old when knights were bold
And rubbers were not invented,	& rubbers were not invented,
They trod the ooze in wooden shoes,	They trod the ooze in wooden shoes,
And waded til they were contented.	& shloshed til they were contented.

Tiger Tim's *Freak* sold for two bits at the few Bay Area bookstores and Beatnik pubs whose managers made room for it on consignment. Sales were disappointing.

Thomas Donald "Tiger Tim" Hawkins *did* know good writing when he saw it, even if it wasn't his own. For the Tiger's money, William Gaddis's *The Recognitions* (1955) was the greatest, most brilliantly original novel ever written. No one else seemed to appreciate that fact except "jack green," publisher of an underground Manhattan newspaper called *newspaper* (published 1957–1965). Tom's attributional epiphany came on December 14, 1962. While browsing in Ferlinghetti's City Lights Bookstore, Hawkins discovered a copy of jack green's *newspaper* no. 12, and began reading. Mr. green, like Tom himself, was a huge Gaddis fan—no, wait, there was more to it!—Tom read on. While studying green's spirited reply to William Gaddis's boneheaded reviewers, Hawkins felt a shock of recognition. Lights went off. Bells rang. The *newspaper* publisher, jack green, didn't just *admire* William Gaddis, jack green *was* William Gaddis!

Hawkins walked home, sat down, and typed Mr. green a letter that very afternoon—on the same manual Underwood typewriter that he would use two decades later when writing as Wanda Tinasky. Typing in lowercase ("as a mark of respect"), Hawkins coyly presented himself to green as a "sweet con fan" of *newspaper*. The true and undisclosed object of this letter, however, was to investigate, discreetly, whether jack green also wrote the Great American Novel *The Recognitions* by William Gaddis. Tom slyly inquired of Mr. green whether "anyone in any publication, to your offhand knowledge, [has] taken notice of the velikovskyan catastrophism in *the recognitions*? . . . I presume that you are in contact with william gaddis; have you discussed this element of *the recognitions* with him?"[29]

Following this curious paragraph, green wrote one word in red pencil—"No"—and mailed the letter back to Tiger Tim. But that handwritten "No" from jack green's red pencil in 1962 had no more effect on Mr. Hawkins than a typed "No" from Melanie Jackson would have on TR Factor in 1995. Hawkins was now convinced that green and Gaddis were definitely the same guy. Escalating his commitment to this wrong idea, he set forth his theory in a little book called *Eve, The Common Muse of Henry Miller & Lawrence Durrell*, a self-published paperback in which "Tiger Tim" Hawkins affirmed that "Eve" Durrell and "Eve" Miller were essentially the same Muse; that Eden's "forbidden fruit" was a hallucinogenic drug; and that jack green and William Gaddis were truly the same person. Selling for $1, *Eve* never achieved bestseller status. Two copies have survived, one at Trinity College (Connecticut), the other at Amherst College (Massachusetts).

More than twenty years later, Hawkins was still trying to win converts for his theory that William Gaddis (author of *The Recognitions, JR,* and *Carpenter's Gothic*), was really jack green. In 1963, theorized Hawkins, the prolific Mr. green also began writing under the nom de plume Thomas Pynchon. In a footnote to a 1985 letter to the *AVA*, Wanda wrote, "The novels of William Gaddis and Thomas Pynchon were written by the same person." Wanda did not disclose who. But a year later, writing to Beth (*Eve in the Afternoon*) Bosk, Wanda enclosed a few essays by someone named "jack green," with the explanation that green "did pretty well in the auctorial line with novels published commercially under the names of William Gaddis & Thomas Pynchon."[30] Who would write *that?*, theorized TR Factor, in 1995—who except Thomas Pynchon, trying to fool Beth Bosk into thinking that he was really some guy named jack green?

TAKING OFF

> fabulate (făb-ye-lāt) *verb* 1. To talk or narrate in fables; 2. To invent, concoct, fabricate:
> - *"a land which . . . had given itself up to dreaming, to fabulating, to tale-telling"* (Lawrence Durrell)
> - *"praise and curse, laugh and cry, fabulate and sing and, when called upon, take off and soar"* (Thomas Pynchon)

It was after Tom Hawkins retired from the U.S. Postal Service that he and Kathy moved north to Mendocino County, buying a small house and three sheds on a lot just north of Fort Bragg. Tom and Kathy's Beal Lane neighbors thought they were a real sweet couple. Tom, granted, was a little eccentric. The Hawkinses had no visible means of support, and no automobile. Tom stretched his budget for food and household supplies by writing letters complaining to manufacturers of defective products, demanding and often receiving multiple replacements. To buy groceries, he thumbed a ride into Fort Bragg, or caught a lift with neighbors, often stopping for solitary drinks at the Tip Top Lounge or browsing Fort Bragg's three bookstores to trade or steal used paperbacks. Lest he should be recognized, he changed his manner of dress and appearance every few months, shifting from clean-shaven to unkempt beard to goatee or bushy mustache and back again. When venturing into town, Tom wore disguises, and always a different hat. His hats, more plentiful than Elton John's collection of sunglasses, were displayed on row after row of Styrofoam heads on the west wall of his writing shed.

Tom Hawkins's opium gardens were lush and flamboyantly beautiful—opium poppies of every color, a scene made more exotic by the strutting peacocks that he kept for watchdogs. (The bane of the neighborhood, the peacocks shrieked at night like crying babies. Tom and Kathleen had no children but treated their peacocks like family.) Tom's favorite pastime, when not in the shed knocking out Wanda letters on his manual typewriter, was to rake the eucalyptus droppings from his yard and poppy plots. Until the back pain got too much for him, he was out there almost every day with the rake, year-round, gathering the eucalyptus pods and leaves and fallen bark into piles. During breaks, he skulked about the neighborhood and would sometimes appear suddenly, unexpectedly, at a neighbor's window, peering in. Sometimes he would say hello. Other days he would just turn and walk away, and go back to his rake, or to his Underwood.

Kathleen Hawkins was a tall, sweet-tempered woman with curly blond hair who looked much younger than her fifty-odd years. Late in life, she came into some money, which gave her a measure of freedom she had not known during her first thirty years of married life. She bought a pickup truck for Tom and an old Honda for herself, learned to drive, and took pottery classes at the College of the Redwoods, where she made new friends. Despite crippling arthritis in her hands, which made every artifact a painful labor of love, Kathleen was naturally gifted in molding clay. With encouragement and assistance from other local potters, she built a kiln, setting up shop at her home on Beal Lane. Tom often puttered about the studio, helping out, sometimes making pots or plates of his own, but Kathleen was the artist. Neighbors said she never seemed happier. Pottery gave Kathy a freedom of expression, a source of recognition and praise, a sense of accomplishment. She produced large plates and vases carved with figures of cranes. At the time of her death she was working on a series of elaborate clay masks, inspired by African models, a few of which still turn up from time to time in Northern California galleries. Her works are signed with a line drawing of a peacock.

Despite their odd ways, neighbors told the Fort Bragg police, and journalists for the *Press Democrat,* that Tom and Kathy Hawkins were just a pair of "old lovebirds," and "real nice, real friendly, willing to help you in any way."[31] No one saw any signs of trouble. One neighbor later speculated that Tom may have been unsettled by the change in his wife and nursed a growing resentment until one day he just exploded. Or perhaps it was the painkillers he took for his bad back, or the opium. In September 1988, three weeks after mailing what would be his last Wanda Tinasky letter to the *AVA*, Tom bludgeoned Kathy in his pickup truck, crushing her skull.

Amazed, perhaps, at his own ghastly violence, Tom carried Kathy's body inside, into the living room, where he mourned over the corpse for several days until it became infested. On Friday, September 23, he arose and set the house on fire. As a column of smoke rose to the sky over Beal Lane, Thomas Donald Hawkins drove north on Route 1 in Kathy's orange Honda at top speed, soaring into space over the cliffs at Bell Point, crashing onto the rocks ninety feet below. His decomposed corpse was found in the surf on October 6 near Ten Mile River Bridge, five miles from the Chadburn Gulch, where Kathy's Honda lay smashed and sunk. No one, perhaps not even Kathy, suspected that Tom Hawkins was also Wanda Tinasky, culture critic for the *Anderson Valley Advertiser*.

POETRY

> *. . . Wanda Tinasky amok*
>
> *like the bodies popped off and*
> *burned in the house at the*
> *top of the hill blazing glory . . .*
> —GORDON LEON BLACK, *Mendocino Commentary* (1986)[32]

Gordon Leon Black, high priest of Mendoland culture, disliked Wanda Tinasky. For one thing, Wanda had adopted the unpleasant habit of calling him "Back Page Black," a nickname inspired by the location in which Gordon's original poems could usually be found in the *Mendocino Commentary*. Mr. Black never figured out who Wanda really was, but he didn't mind saying that he didn't like her Philistine attitude. In fact, he said so all the time. Once, Gordon went so far as to liken Wanda to a killer arsonist. In October 1986, three years into Wanda's epistolary crusade for better poetry, two years before the Hawkinses' domestic tragedy, a former Hell's Angel settled down in Fort Bragg for a virtuous retirement from gang life, along with his motorcycle-mama spouse and their two children. The fellow brought with him a suitcase full of Hell's Angels' money (which he had embezzled) and a trove of borrowed bike parts. In October, someone killed the man's wife and children, then him, then burned the place to the ground with the bodies inside, then vanished.

In a poem for the back page of the *Mendocino Commentary*, Gordon Black compared this horrific crime to Wanda Tinasky's unfair literary criticism—"Wanda Tinasky amok." Those four hapless ("popped off") victims were like the Albion Ridge Poets, and Wanda Tinasky (with her "anonymous attacks in the letters column") was like their cold-blooded killer, still unidentified, a nattering nabob of "negative affirmation" whose mockery was not to be endured by those with truly cultural sensibilities.[33]

Writing to the *AVA*, Wanda Tinasky in the next week's issue loudly objected to the imputation:

Dear Mr. Anderson:

Please don't worry if you don't hear from me for an issue or two, as I am a bit distraught about having to move again. This morning a "law man" crawled under the bridge asking for "Wanda Tinasky," & of course I was co-operative, offering to take a message, & from what he said I gather that some Albion Ridge poet known as Back Page Black published a scurrilous "poem" in the *Mendocino Commentary*, implying that I was involved in the multiple murders-cum-arson that put Ft. Bragg on the map for a day or two recently. "Aw," I told him, "Wanda's too puny to do anything but eat nana pudden, & whine to go on the Donahue show," but I don't know that he was totally convinced & think it the better part of valor to haul ass for a while until this thing blows over—maybe I'll have to sue for a million or two, to defend my goddamn honor. Do you know a cheap lawyer, Mr. Anderson? Would you like to run the *Mendocino Commentary* for me? I'll be in touch, when I get relocated.

> Yr. Ob'd'nt Servant, &c. &c.,
> Wanda Tinasky

The appended "P.S." and "P.P.S." were about other matters.

Wanda at this point in her life was innocent of arson and homicide, and Gordon Black was whistling in the dark about her true identity. But Back Page Black was evidently a shrewd judge of character, even eerily prophetic. In drawing his analogy between homicide and Wanda's literary criticism, Black seems to have known Wanda better than Wanda knew herself. Or perhaps the Hawkins murder-suicide two years later was just another instance of someone's life imitating someone else's art. Even in our secular, unartistic, postmodern age, a piece of poetry or a great novel can sometimes make a small difference, register an influence, change the world.

FISHING FOR WANDA

> *You* hide, they seek.
> —THOMAS PYNCHON, "PROVERBS FOR PARANOIDS" (1973)[34]

The linguist's first order of business—when seeking to identify the elegist "W.S.," or the novelist "Anonymous," or the Unabomber "F.C.," or the bag lady "W.T.," or any other anonymous author—is to obtain an accurate text of the Questioned Document(s). The second step is to obtain known writing samples by possible suspects. In August 1998, when I finally took up the Wanda Tinasky question, much of that labor was already done for me. Most of the authentic Wanda letters had been gathered and edited by Fred Gardner, and published by TR Factor in the 1996 *Tinasky* volume. A few may have been overlooked. Others were missing by legal necessity: Beth Bosk withheld permission for a reprint of the Wanda letters that were addressed to her as the host of *Eve in the Afternoon* and as editor of *The New Settler Interview*—withholding them not because she was embarrassed by the satire but to express solidarity with her ripped-off friend Fred Gardner against rival editor TR Factor. For my purposes I didn't need every letter that Wanda Tinasky ever wrote, but I did need to cull those that were not true Wanda. A few of the Wanda letters that Factor had thought to be authentic, and had reprinted from the *AVA*, were transparent forgeries by Wanda wannabes.

From 1983 to 1988, if you were someone who hung out Wednesdays at the Sea Gull Bar, you could tell when a new Wanda letter had appeared in the *AVA*. Some Albion Ridge or Ten Mile River bard would shuffle into the Sea Gull with a rolled-up *AVA* tucked under his arm. With hand in pocket, fingering an imaginary Smith & Wesson, the dejected poet would ask his fellow *artistes* one by one, "Are you Wanda Tinasky?" ("Not I." "Don't look at me!" "Ain't me." "Nope."). The latest victim of Wanda's serial criticism would then take a seat beside his colleagues at the Gull—many of them fellow victims of Wanda Tinasky's ridicule—and drown his sorrow in Boont Amber Ale or Belk's Extra Special Bitter (local brews), or a horn of zeese. (The Anderson Valley, home of the *AVA*, has its own dialect, called "Boontling," with a homegrown loggers' vocabulary that goes back to the days of the vertical redwoods. A "horn of zeese" is a cup of coffee. A few Mendoland bards have written whole poems in the Boontling tongue, with never a word of praise or encouragement from the likes of Wanda Tinasky.)

Wanda was tough on artistic morale in Mendocino County. In "I Remember Wanda," Karin Faulkner recalls her colleagues at the Sea Gull plotting a futile revenge on Wanda Tinasky, and on Bruce Anderson, too, for giving column space to that bilious witch. Some wrote anonymous replies to Wanda, or even forged Wanda letters of their own for publication in the *AVA*, just to get her goat. (Wanda hated that!) Karin never forged one herself, though she knew she "could imitate the style. Any good writer with an imagination could. Letters to the Editor are so short. And print is such an easy place to conceal identity."[35]

I began my belated search for Wanda ten months after receiving that initial summons from TR Factor. Acting on Faulkner's caveat, I weeded out a few letters signed "Wanda Tinasky" though not penned in her characteristic style. Next I did a quick read through known writings by the local candidates, one of whom was Michael Koepf from the coastal village of Elk, a controversial figure variously described in the *AVA* as a "fisherman," a "pot farmer," and a "Scheiss Koepf." Mr. Koepf was also a novelist, not widely read, but twice accused (by authentic Wanda) of having forged Wanda letters to the *AVA*. Koepf's *Icarus,* once owned by the Fort Bragg Public Library (before it burned to the ground in an arson fire), was rarely checked out. Nor did it check out (when I found a copy in Poughkeepsie) as a text attributable to Wanda Tinasky.

Mike Koepf had told Bruce Anderson and Fred Gardner, and now me, that he knew for a fact that Wanda Tinasky was really Don Shanley, one of the Ten Mile River Poets. According to Koepf, no one in Mendocino County had ever read one of his novels *except* Don Shanley and Wanda Tinasky, who made fun. Beth Bosk told me that Shanley was her suspect as well. From *The Western Edge* (Ten Mile River Press) I learned that Don Shanley wrote his first real poem (inspired by Ginsberg's *Howl*) in 1959. From the *AVA* I learned that Shanley was a friend of Bruce Anderson's by shared sympathies and good times, a seed wholesaler by profession, and "Horticultural Expert to the Stars" by tongue-in-cheek self-description. None of which got me very far. But when I discovered that Shanley favored the ampersand, & that he inserted spaces (*thus*) inside his parentheses, I asked him for a copy of his collected poems, which he kindly sent me by FedEx at his own expense. But Mike Koepf was mistaken. Shanley's a bright and witty guy, just possibly California's most literate landscape artist, but his life-defining experience as a poet was a gut-wrenching tour of service in Vietnam. There was too much human feeling in his poetry, too little glibness, for him to be true-blue Wanda Tinasky; and the prose was no match, either.

Scratch Mike Koepf and Don Shanley. Scratch Bruce Anderson, Devereaux Baker, the Berry Lady, the Bicycle Man, Beth Bosk, Bill Bradd, Lawrence Bullock, and every other local candidate from A to Zeese. I tried for an eyewitness. Wanda, in a 1985 letter, recalled being picked up while hitchhiking and having to share a cramped truck bed with the classical musician Marcia Sloane and her large cello. I called Ms. Sloane. She remembered riding in the back of a pickup with a middle-aged hitchhiker in a sweatshirt but did not recognize him. She said she would not have recognized Thomas Pynchon, either.

FREAK ACCIDENCE

> HERE'S WHAT THEY'RE SAYING ABOUT " EVE " :
> " Orotund pshit ! "   —G. Legman
> " Laughed & laughed "   —L. Ferlinghetti
> ". . . intriguing. Do you take
> hallucinogenics? "   —G. Snyder
> —TIGER TIM HAWKINS, *FREAK'S LITERARY TERTIARY* (1964)[36]

> If you're sap enough to buy a book some whore of a paid reviewer recommends, you get what you deserve.
> —WANDA TINASKY, *ANDERSON VALLEY ADVERTISER* (13 MARCH 1985)

September 7, 1998. It had now been more than fifteen years since Wanda's first letters to the *Mendocino Commentary,* a decade since Wanda vanished from the *AVA,* and three weeks since I began looking for her. I seemed to have reached a dead end. The locals had their private theories but no evidence concerning Wanda's identity. I would have to follow some other line of inquiry than eyewitness accounts or "inside" information. I could look for prior publications, but where, and under whose name? Wanda's principal literary sources were the Beats, especially Gary Snyder, Gershon Legman, Kenneth Patchen, and Kenneth Rexroth, all of whom Wanda appeared to have known and admired, and Paul Krassner, whom Wanda remembered with contempt as a pimple-faced armpit-sniffing "hero of the Kiddie-kar revolution." Wanda professed to have been "ghosting for Krassner while he was ghosting for Lennie Bruce." That seemed as good a lead as any, but Lenny Bruce, the envelope-pushing comedian who wrote *How to Talk Dirty and Influence People* (1965), had died of a drug overdose in 1966; and Paul Krassner knew nothing of the Tinasky letters except what he'd been told by Fred Gardner.

While angling for Wanda in 1995, Gardner had interviewed just about every living person named in one of Ms. Tinasky's letters. His net had come up empty. (E.g., Gardner to Krassner: "Did Thomas Pynchon ever write for *The Realist*?" Krassner: "Oh, no. Never did. I've never met him, never had any contact with him. . . . Nobody ever ghosted for me.")[37] Gardner had asked the right people the wrong questions.

Searching on-line databases for books about Paul Krassner earlier than 1980, I found five titles, one of which was called *Paul Krassner, The Realist, & $crap: Plus a P.S. on it,* by "Tim" Hawkins (San Francisco: Ahab Press, 1964). That sounded pretty interesting. In her postscript to a 1986 letter, Wanda Tinasky promised readers of the *AVA:* "P.S. I'm going to improve myself . . . & learn to write good and not use ampersands & put all I want to say in some coherent hole without doing a P.S. on it."[38] This 1964 book by Tim Hawkins—with its ampersand in the title, and a "*P.S. on it,*" and its apparently hostile reference to Paul Krassner's "$crap"—might shed light on Wanda's cryptic remarks twenty years later.

In a comprehensive computer search, I located only one surviving copy of Hawkins's *Krassner,* at Columbia University—and that was in the first edition (1963), which lacked the 1964 "*P.S. on it.*" No matter. Ordering a photocopy from Interlibrary Loan, I learned that Paul Krassner in 1963 had used some of Tim Hawkins's material, not in the *Realist,* for which the submission was intended, but in a porn magazine called *Escapade,* with which Krassner was then associated as an anonymous contributor. Furious at having been thus ghosted, "Tim" Hawkins wrote the "$crap" essay, denouncing Krassner for involvement with Lenny Bruce; for making crass jokes in *The Realist* about Nazism, racial violence, thalidomide babies, abortion, rape, and incest; for contributing to pornographic magazines; and for pleading poverty while making big bucks off the degradation of women. As puffed by Hawkins, *Paul Krassner* &c. came in "three decorators' shades of yellow."

I wrote Paul Krassner in Venice, California, to ask whether he recalled this episode. Mr. Krassner wrote back, "Don, I vaguely remember the tract but have no recollection of Hawkins. Sorry, P.K."

At the time, however, the Hawkins publication must have jiggled Mr. Krassner, if only a little. On December 17, 1963, Lawrence Ferlinghetti dropped Tom Hawkins a note after hearing the editor of *The Realist* flame Hawkins on a Bay Area radio show: "I wonder if you heard Krassner the other night," wrote Ferlinghetti, "when he spent about two hours talking about your book? I think you kind of upset him...."[39] (But at this point in the investigation, I was still looking for a "Tim" Hawkins, and knew nothing of the Ferlinghetti-Hawkins correspondence. That discovery was still a week away.)

FINDING WANDA

> Once I thought that " literature " was mainly a
> means of communication between isolated human be-
> ings in a world of uninhabited bodies. I no longer
> think that.
>
> —TIGER TIM HAWKINS, *FREAK'S LITERARY TERTIARY* (1964)

Searching on-line databases of library holdings across North America, I found additional works by "T." or "Tiger Tim" Hawkins under his own Ahab imprint: *Eve, The Common Muse of Henry Miller & Lawrence Durrell* (1963), *Freak* (1962?–1964), *Freak's Literary Tertiary* (1964), and *On the Fairy-Fag Doublet* (1964). I ordered copies from Vassar's Interlibrary Loan Office and, while waiting, rang up John Robert Meyer, now a distinguished professor of the history of economics at Harvard—but known to Wanda as an undergraduate at the University of Washington in the late '40s. When interviewed by Gardner in '95, Meyer had suggested that Wanda could be a woman named Anne Orem, whom he knew while at Purdue. Orem didn't check out. I now asked Professor Meyer if he remembered anyone named Tim Hawkins. No, but he did know a *Tom* Hawkins, a prankster who grew up in the town of Port Angeles, Washington. The last time Meyer heard from Tom Hawkins he was working for the U.S. Postal Service and hanging out in Beatnik pubs in San Francisco—but that was a long time ago. Meyer hadn't heard from Tom in years.

In a 1987 "Open Letter to Gary Snyder" published in the *AVA*, Wanda professed to have written a poem, some "18 or 19 years ago," commemorating the birth of Gary Snyder's son ("How big is the moon? Big / As a silver dollar . . ."). Snyder at the time was "living in a basement apartment on the south side of Pine street in San Francisco, by the Zen center." Wanda reminisced, as if addressing Snyder: "I disguised myself as a mailperson & took you some miniature pink roses. . . ."

I e-mailed Gary Snyder, now a professor emeritus, Department of English, at UC Davis in Sacramento. Did he remember a fellow named Thomas Hawkins? Yes, he remembered Tom quite well. Did Hawkins send him a poem on the occasion of his son's birth, a poem beginning "How big is the moon?" Yes, yes, that was Tom's work. But Professor Snyder had not heard from Tom Hawkins in years.

Taking my inspiration from milk-carton ads for missing children, I sent flyers to Fort Bragg's Tip Top Lounge, Fort Bragg bookstores, the Fort Bragg Seniors Center—asking in boldface 24-point type: "Do you remember TOM HAWKINS?" Evidently no one did. In the meantime, I located a phone number for a Thomas Hawkins of Fort Bragg and gave him a jingle. When he answered the phone, I did not ask: "Mr. Hawkins, are you Wanda Tinasky?" but rather, "Mr. Hawkins, are you the same Thomas Hawkins who was known to the Beat poets Lawrence Ferlinghetti and Gary Snyder and Kenneth Rexroth?"

This was the wrong Tom Hawkins, but the call was not wasted.

This Mr. Hawkins remembered that there was another, older, Tom Hawkins, also of Fort Bragg, who passed away, oh, maybe ten years back, in '88 or thereabouts. Drove his car into the ocean and drowned.

I called the Mendocino County Coroner's office. Yes, they remembered the case. "Thomas Donald Hawkins. Killed his wife, then himself." (That did not sound to me like anything Wanda Tinasky would have done.) "No kids. Next of kin was an uncle, same name, Thomas Hawkins, of Port Angeles, Washington. . . ." (*Port Angeles!*)

While waiting for a photocopy of the coroner's report, I turned to the Internet, did a reverse-address lookup for Tom Hawkins's Beal Lane address, and called the current residents, a couple named Ed Sander and Tenaya Middleton. Tenaya, who was not a reader of the *Anderson Valley Advertiser,* asked if I was the same guy who had called her fellow cellist Marcia Sloane only a few days earlier to ask if she had ever traveled with her instrument in a pickup truck, along with a hitchhiker who may have been "Wanda Tinasky." I confessed I was. So who was this calling?, Tenaya silently wondered. Some strange fellow from New York with a thing for placing unsolicited telephone calls to Mendocino County cello players? I had not known that Tenaya was a cellist. I explained that I was actually looking for a fellow named Thomas Hawkins.

Tenaya was a big help. On September 23, 1988, she happened to be in the neighborhood visiting a friend and saw the billows of smoke over Beal Lane. It was only by chance, on a tip, that she came to purchase the Hawkins property when it was auctioned off by the executors. Except for the main house, destroyed by fire, the property when purchased by Tenaya was just as Tom and Kathleen Hawkins had left it. In the shed out back where Tom did most his writing was an old Underwood typewriter and reams of correspondence, most of which Tenaya threw away without reading. But while working through the debris—musty books, unpublished typescripts, back issues of the *Anderson Valley Advertiser*—she discovered and saved a bundle of cards and letters addressed to Mr. Hawkins from Gershon Legman, Kenneth and Miriam Patchen, Lawrence Ferlinghetti, and Gary Snyder. Graciously, trustingly, Ed and Tenaya sent me the correspondence, news clippings, and other papers that documented the life of Thomas Donald Hawkins.

On September 12, 1998, ten years after Tom Hawkins killed Kathy, his partner, lover, and Muse, with a blow to the head, and took his lonely flight over the Chadburn Gulch, I faxed a letter to Melanie Jackson with the news. Apart from a few hoax "Wanda" letters, Wanda Tinasky, the bag lady of Fort Bragg, was a fellow named Thomas Donald Hawkins, deceased. A few days later, by U.S. Post, I received a thank-you letter, typed, corrected, and signed by Thomas Pynchon. It was no joke. The author of *V* and *Vineland* and *Mason & Dixon* really does exist, and he writes exactly like Thomas Pynchon.

PYNCHED COJONES

> You cannot imagine, my friend, the satisfaction I feel at heaving chicken livers at Mercedes, the release. There's nothing quite like that oozing bloodred slug trailing its path across the hood of an expensive foreign car . . .
>
> —C.O. JONES, "SELF-EXPRESSION,"
> *THE LETTERS OF WANDA TINASKY* (1996)
>
> Pynchon's meat, to be sure . . .
> —TR FACTOR, "IS THOMAS PYNCHON WANDA TINASKY?" (1997)

How to break the news? After more than a year of receiving TR Factor's heel-nipping correspondence, the woman remained, for me, a shadowy figure. TR had volunteered no information about herself, no credentials, no résumé, no phone number, no return address. Before saying who Wanda really was, I wanted to learn who TR Factor really was. Searching through back issues of the *AVA*, I hunted for stray writings by TR—and became interested in a contributing writer who signed his or her letters "C.O. Jones." C.O. Jones sounded like TR Factor. And in fact, C.O. Jones *was* TR Factor, born and christened Diane Kearney. This fierce Mendocino County polemicist had peppered her political commentary with ad hominem zingers until 1985, when a fellow contributor ridiculed her nom de plume, a pun on *cojones* (Spanish slang for testicles). "If C.O. Jones needs a pair that bad," wrote her *AVA* critic, "she should get her name on the waiting list at Stanford Hospital where they are transplanting baboon balls. Until then, for accuracy in media, she should be called Sans C.O. Jones. [signed] E.N. Tranas / East Palo Alto." Jones shot off a testy reply, observing that Tranas's name and city could be reshuffled anagrammatically to read: "AN APE SATAN / TOTAL LOSER."[40] In making this witty riposte, Ms. Kearney-Jones/Factor evidently overlooked the fact that "E.N. Tranas" was already a pseudonym on the same model as her own "C.O. Jones" (*entranas:* Spanish for bowels).

Feeling underappreciated, Ms. Jones collected her marbles, moved to Oregon, and changed her name legally to TR Factor, where she was found, still sulking, by Fred Gardner in July 1995, and invited by him to participate in the Wanda Tinasky Research Group. A troublesome thought now occurred to me. If I should disappoint TR by saying that the Tinasky letters were *not* by Thomas Pynchon, what vile anagrams might be constructed from "D. W. Foster / Poughkeepsie" in the letters column of the *Anderson Valley Advertiser,* or on the Internet, or in the planned second edition of *The Letters of Wanda Tinasky*?

I bit my tongue and said nothing. Melanie Jackson and Thomas Pynchon now had the scoop on Wanda Tinasky and Tom Hawkins. Let them do with the information as seemed best. I was done with the residents of Mendoland. But they were not yet done with me. In March 1999, Gordon Leon Black—Albion Ridge Poet, author of "Wanda Tinasky amok," host of classical music on KZYX radio, and all-round high priest of Mendoland culture—wrote to the *Anderson Valley Advertiser* with his assessment of "Foster's literary detection," which was not high. Having read "A Funeral Elegy" by W.S., Mr. Black invited Bruce Anderson to print an "ample sample" of the "Shakespeare" elegy and let readers of the *AVA* decide for themselves whether or not Shakespeare actually wrote it.

I took the occasion of Mr. Black's skepticism to contribute my one and only letter to the *Anderson Valley Advertiser* (March 17, 1999), observing without fanfare that the "Wanda Tinasky" of local memory, believed by many to be the novelist Thomas Pynchon, was actually Thomas Donald Hawkins (1927–1988) of Fort Bragg; and that Mr. Hawkins's five-year gig as Wanda Tinasky had inspired a few copycat letters to the *AVA* and *Mendocino Commentary* that were not really his, including one by Gordon Leon Black. Explaining these matters to a local audience that still remembered Wanda more than a decade after her disappearance, I hoped that no one would really notice, or care, that Ms. Tinasky was not Thomas Pynchon. TR Factor noticed. TR Factor cared. TR Factor went ballistic. She wrote a blistering letter to the *Anderson Valley Advertiser,* using such colorful language that Bruce Anderson, whose free speech policy is to print almost all of the letters that come in, would not print it. In her own original Amazon.com book review of *The Letters of Wanda Tinasky* (copies of which may yet be ordered, while supplies last, from Amazon.com), Ms. Factor let me have it with both shovelfuls, spicing her remarks with opprobious comments on "Don Foster" that she'd picked up on the Internet.[41] Sometimes I just don't know when to bite my tongue.

P.S. ON IT

> But why am I boring you like this with ghost stories
> of the dead and so-well-buried Beat Generation of
> literaries? Oh, yes: jack green . . .
> —TIGER TIM HAWKINS, *EVE, THE COMMON MUSE OF HENRY MILLER &
> LAWRENCE DURRELL* (1963)[42]

When he first learned from Fred Gardner (then from TR Factor, then from major news organizations) of *The Letters of Wanda Tinasky,* Thomas Pynchon speculated, not implausibly, that Wanda was really Bruce Anderson and that the Pynchon attribution was a hoax designed to gain attention for the *AVA.* He was mistaken about that. TR Factor and Bruce Anderson believed that Wanda really *was* Pynchon. They, too, were mistaken. Hawkins, who never intended for Wanda to be misidentified, believed that Thomas Pynchon was really William Gaddis, who was really jack green. Hawkins was only two-thirds mistaken. Gaddis is Gaddis, and Pynchon is Pynchon, but jack green was not really jack green. The publisher of *newspaper* was actually John Carlisle, the son of Helen Grace Carlisle, author of *The Merry, Merry Maidens* (1937). Carlisle adopted the "jack green" nom de plume in 1957 after he quit his job as an actuarial clerk for Metropolitan Life Insurance, grew a beard, and founded *newspaper*.

A few years ago, selections from jack green's *newspaper* were republished under the title *Fire the Bastards!* (1992), edited by Steven Moore. This is the same Steven Moore who wrote the definitive *Reader's Guide to William Gaddis's The Recognitions* (1982), and this is the same Steven Moore who (twist upon twist) wrote the foreword to TR Factor's edition of *The Letters of Wanda Tinasky*. When publishing his scholarly work on jack green and William Gaddis, and when contributing to the Tinasky volume, Professor Moore (who really *is* Steven Moore) never knew or suspected that Wanda was a fellow admirer of jack green. For Moore's money, Wanda was Pynchon. ("Well, if it ain't Pynchon," wrote Moore, "it's someone who has him down cold: his inimitable literary style, his deep but lightly worn erudition, his countercultural roots, his leftist/populist politics, his brand of wit and humor, his encyclopedic range of reference, his street smarts and raffish charm, his immersion in pop culture and sports, and his hatred of all agents of repression.")[43] The inimitable Tom Hawkins would doubtless have been pleased with the epitaph. He was not Pynchon and never pretended to be, but the Wanda Tinasky story was his best laugh ever, and as Pynchonesque as any story *not* by Thomas Pynchon will ever get.

CHAPTER SIX

Yes, Virginia, There Was a Santa Claus

NOT SO JOLLYE OLDE SAINTE NICKE

He heard the crunch of sleigh and hoof
Crisply alighting on the roof.
What good to rise and bar the door?
A shower of soot was on the floor.

What was beheld by Jabez Dawes?
The fireplace full of Santa Claus!
  —OGDEN NASH, "THE BOY WHO LAUGHED AT SANTA CLAUS"[1]

"Improper ideas." That's what some New York parents were putting in the heads of their children. In 1813, standing firm against the crimson tide, the bookseller Samuel Wood published an essay by a boy who (like Ogden Nash's Jabez Dawes) would not believe in Saint Nicholas, a.k.a. "Sinterklaas" (Dutch), "Santeclaus" (New Amsterdam), and "Santaclaw" (Manhattan, by way of colonial corruption). Mr. Wood's pious teen, writing anonymously, condemned "Old Santaclaw, of whom, so often, little children hear such foolish stories, and once in the year are encouraged to hang their stockings in the Chimney at night. . . ."[2]

For the Sentinel.

ACCOUNT OF A VISIT FROM ST. NICHOLAS.

'Twas the night before Christmas, when all thro'
      the house,
Not a creature was stirring, not even a mouse;
The stockings were hung by the chimney with
      care,
In hopes that St. Nicholas soon would be there;
The children were nestled all snug in their beds,
While visions of sugar plums danc'd in their
      heads,
And Mama in her 'kerchief, and I in my cap,
Had just settled our brains for a long winter's
      nap—
When out on the lawn there arose such a clatter,
I sprang from the bed to see what was the mat-
      ter.
Away to the window I flew like a flash,
Tore open the shutters, and threw up the sash.
The moon on the breast of the new fallen snow,
Gave the lustre of mid-day to objects below;
When, what to my wondering eyes should
      appear,
But a miniature sleigh, and eight tiny rein-deer,
With a little old driver, so lively and quick,
I knew in a moment it must be St. Nick.
More rapid than eagles his coursers they came,
And he whistled, and shouted, and call'd them
      by name:
"Now! Dasher, now! Dancer, now! Prancer,
      and Vixen,
"On! Comet, on! Cupid, on! Dunder and
      Blixem;
"To the top of the porch! to the top of the wall!
"Now dash away! dash away! dash away all!"
As dry leaves before the wild hurricane fly,
When they meet with an obstacle, mount to the
      sky;
So up to the house-top the coursers they flew,
With the sleigh full of Toys—and St. Nicholas
      too:

And then in a twinkling, I heard on the roof
The prancing and pawing of each little hoof.
As I drew in my head, and was turning around,
Down the chimney St. Nicholas came with a
        bound:
He was dress'd all in fur, from his head to his
        foot,
And his clothes were all tarnish'd with ashes
        and soot;
A bundle of toys was flung on his back,
And he look'd like a peddler just opening his
        pack:
His eyes—how they twinkled! his dimples how
        merry,
His cheeks were like roses, his nose like a
        cherry;
His droll little mouth was drawn up like a bow.
And the beard of his chin was as white as the
        snow;
The stump of a pipe he held tight in his teeth,
And the smoke it encircled his head like a
        wreath.
He had a broad face, and a little round belly
That shook when he laugh'd, like a bowl full of
        jelly:
He was chubby and plump, a right jolly old elf,
And I laugh'd when I saw him in spite of myself;
A wink of his eye and a twist of his head
Soon gave me to know I had nothing to dread.
He spoke not a word, but went straight to his
        work,
And fill'd all the stockings; then turn'd with a
        jerk,
And laying his finger aside of his nose
And giving a nod, up the chimney he rose.
He sprung to his sleigh, to his team gave a
        whistle,
And away they all flew, like the down of a thistle:
But I heard him exclaim, ere he drove out of
        sight—
Happy Christmas to all, and to all a good night.

December 23, 1823

In the olden days, before Santa Claus left Holland for New Amsterdam, Christmas was a simple affair, no shopping, no sack of toys, no reindeer, no snow. Sinterklaas came and went on December 5th (Nicholas Eve), or 24th (Christmas Eve), or 31st (New Year's Eve), depending on local tradition; or else, if your parents were Puritans, he did not come at all. In the morning when the good children awoke, they would be "told Old Santaclaw has come down the Chimney in the night" to fill their stockings (or wooden shoes) with oranges, Dutch crullers, juicy sweetmeats, cookies, and nuts. "Thus the little innocents are imposed on by those who are older than they, and improper ideas take possession. . . ."[3] Bad little boys and girls would find nothing in their stocking but a birchen rod, the emblem of corporal punishment.

According to the legend, Nicholas of Myra was a stern but generous bishop who secretly provided dowries for three poor girls when their desperate father would have sold them into prostitution. English Protestants were skeptical of that old wives' tale. The English version, dating from the sixteenth century, is that Bishop Nicholas, the old lecher, debauched the maids himself and paid for their services. More tolerant Anglicans conceded that Saint Nicholas may have been a good man, and a Christian, but he lived in the fourth century, which made him a Roman Catholic. Besides, the fellow was dead. Leaving cookies and tea on the hearth for a dead Catholic smacked of black magic, necromancy, and saint worship.

English poets did not trust Saint Nicholas. As early as 1570, Barnabe Googe accused "popish" mothers of sending their children hungry to bed on Nicholas Eve so as to sharpen the little ones' appetites and gullibility the next morning:

The mothers all their children on the Eve do cause to fast—
And when they every one at night in senseless sleep are cast,
Both apples, nuts, and pears they bring (and other things beside,
As caps and shoes and petticoats), which secretly they hide—
And, in the morning found, they say that "This, Saint Nicholas brought!"
Thus tender minds to worship saints and wicked things are taught . . .[4]

It was different in America. In New England, to protect children from this pernicious practice, veneration of Saint Nicholas was made a criminal offense. (Christmas cookies in the State of Massachusetts were not decriminalized until 1681.)

By 1800 urban New Yorkers had all but forgotten the state's Dutch past. The children of Manhattan knew nothing of stockings hung by the chimney with care, and nothing (thank God!) of a pipe-smoking saint. There were no nighttime miracles causing cookies and knick-knacks to appear as if out of the blue—except, of course, upriver, in quaint villages like Fishkill, Poughkeepsie, and Sleepy Hollow, where Dutch Americans, though warned from Episcopal and Presbyterian pulpits, would and *did* hang their stockings by the fire, unrepentantly, while the more virtuous New England Puritans, eschewing idle pleasures, hanged witches.

In 1823, the *Troy Sentinel* in upstate New York published a little poem that changed all of that. " 'Twas the Night Before Christmas" introduced readers to a jolly old elf, a benign Saint Nicholas who whipped no one, not even his own recently acquired Lapland reindeer. By dispensing with the birchen rod, and by translating Europe's crotchety old Nicholas into Saint Nick, the merriest saint in Christendom, the author of that little poem caused America finally to open its heart to Old Santaclaw, and in a very big way. Widely reprinted, "The Night Before Christmas" soon became the New World's best-loved, most well-known poem, turning Christmas into a festival of good cheer and gift-giving by transforming Saint Nicholas from a thin, dour European saint into the plump and jolly American superstar we know as Santa Claus.

ACCOUNT OF A VISIT

And he chuckled, and clucked, "What a great Grinchy trick!
With this coat and this hat, I look just like Saint Nick!"
—DR. SEUSS, *HOW THE GRINCH STOLE CHRISTMAS*[5]

Troy, New York, December 23, 1823. When the *Sentinel* ran some jaunty holiday verses captioned "Account of a Visit from St. Nicholas," not even the paper's editor, Orville Holley, knew whom to thank, or guessed that this poem was destined for greatness. Submitted anonymously, it was not by one of Holley's regular contributors. Resisting the oblivion to which most nineteenth-century newspaper verse was quickly consigned, "The Night Before Christmas" (as it came to be called) reappeared in the *New York Spectator* only nine days after its Troy debut, in a text borrowed from the *Sentinel,* then in New Jersey and Pennsylvania almanacs for the 1825 calendar year, next in a literary magazine called *The Casket,* in 1826.[6] A few years later, when the *New York Morning Courier* reprinted it, the now popular ditty of Saint Nicholas was said by some to have been written by Clement Clarke Moore, a Bible professor at New York's General Theological Seminary. That rumor was reinforced fifteen years later with the publication of Moore's *Poems.* By the time he died in 1863, aged eighty-four, Clement Clarke Moore was known from coast to coast as the father of Santa Claus, an accomplishment for which his name has been revered ever since. But there are people in my town of Poughkeepsie, mostly persons of Dutch descent, who are unhappy with Professor Moore for having laid claim to "Account of a Visit from St. Nicholas." In fact, certain local historians feel so strongly about this issue that they would like to see Saint Nicholas in heaven take Clement Clarke Moore onto his own reverend lap, flip him over, and let the man have it on the bottom with "the birchen rod" for which Saint Nicholas was once famous.

Poughkeepsie, New York, August 6, 1999. One hot summer afternoon I received a call from a resident of the Boston area, Mary Van Deusen, who identified herself as the great-great-great-great-great-granddaughter ("five greats") of Major Henry Livingston Jr. Mrs. Van Deusen cheerfully explained that it was her ancestor Major Livingston, and not Clement Clarke Moore, who probably wrote "The

Night Before Christmas." She was calling me, she said, at the suggestion of Professor Ian Lancashire of the University of Toronto. I stayed on the line, but only to learn why Lancashire, a distinguished Canadian scholar I knew, liked, and admired, would have given this woman my name. Ms. Van Deusen explained that she had no axe to grind. She was building a Major Henry Livingston Jr. Web site. If I could show that "The Night Before Christmas" was written by her ancestor, not by Clement Clarke Moore, that would be terrific. And if not, not.

Mrs. Van Deusen chatted gaily on, telling me more about Henry Livingston and Clement Moore than I thought I needed to know. The two men, she said, were opposites. Professor Moore was a grouchy pedant, a student of ancient Hebrew who never had a day of fun in his whole life. In fact, he was against it. Henry, three-quarters Dutch, was immersed in Dutch American traditions. He was an artist, journalist, and poet; a surveyor and cartographer; an archaeologist and anthropologist; a flute player and a fiddler; a free spirit and all-round merry old soul if ever there was one.

Mrs. Van Deusen said that, in her opinion, the Major's poetry resembled "Christmas" better than anything Clement Moore ever wrote. Most of the Major's comical and children's verses were written in anapests, just like " 'Twas the night before Christmas, when all through the house . . ." (*da-da-DUM, da-da-DUM, da-da-DUM, da-da-DUM!*). To demonstrate, she broke into a lilting recitation of some lines from a two-hundred-year-old verse epistle addressed by Major Henry to his younger brother, Beekman. I laughed when I heard it in spite of myself:

> To my dear brother Beekman I sit down to write
> Ten minutes past eight and a very cold night.
> Not far from me sits with a vallancy [i.e., a wig] cap on
> Our very good cousin, Elizabeth Tappen,
> A tighter young seamstress you'd ne'er wish to see
> And she (blessings on her!) is sewing for me.
> New shirts and new cravats this morning cut out

Are tumbled in heaps and lie huddled about.
My wardrobe (a wonder!) will soon be enriched
With ruffles new hemmed, and wristbands new stitched . . . [7]

"That's just a sample."

"I wish you good luck with your research," I said, "but—"

"But listen to this: 'The Night Before Christmas' was first published anonymously in 1823. When it was ascribed to Clement Clarke Moore in December 1836, probably by mistake, he said nothing. 'Christmas' became a huge hit. Moore remained silent—because the poem 'embarrassed' him. 'Christmas' was in print for more than twenty years before Clement Moore took credit. Now, isn't *that* interesting!"

"And did Major Henry take credit?"

"No—but I can explain that. He was dead. Major Henry's children knew that Clement Moore didn't write 'Christmas,' that their father did, but no one would listen."

I listened, but without much enthusiasm. Who but maybe Jabez Dawes would challenge the credibility of Clement Clarke Moore? Moore was a scholar, a Bible professor, unimpeachable, practically a saint himself, known to millions of Americans as the "Poet of Christmas Eve." His name by this time had appeared on millions of copies of "The Night Before Christmas." There was nothing to be gained professionally by becoming embroiled in a dispute over the true begetter of Santa Claus. Within academia, the inevitable response would entail such questions as these: "Who cares?" and "Why waste your time on the origins of an overrated piece of holiday doggerel?" From a professional point of view, this was a lose-lose situation.

Responding not as a scholar but as a fan of Santa Claus from way back, I told Mrs. Van Deusen I'd give it my best shot.

Pleased, she said she would also have to call Steve Thomas, which she had not done yet.

"*Steve Thomas?*"

"Yes. He has most of the original documents."

My Steve Thomas was a detective with the Boulder Police Department. Mary Van Deusen's Steve Thomas was her distant cousin Stephen Livingston Thomas, a grandson of William S. Thomas, M.D., the Livingston heir who devoted more than forty years of his life to trying to prove that the Clement Clarke Moore attribution was a mistake. Dr. Thomas died in 1941 without having budged the attribution an inch; after which the quest was pursued by his son, W. Stephen Thomas, who was now in his nineties and in no shape to continue. Next in line, having no obvious interest in this crusade, was Mary Van Deusen's fourth-cousin-twice-removed, Stephen Livingston Thomas.

When Mary called him only a few days later, introduced herself by telephone, and requested photographic copies of Major Henry's verse and prose, Steve Thomas seemed apprehensive. Thomas felt that the Livingston torch should be carried by a Thomas descendant, not by a Van Deusen. Mary explained that she had enlisted a college professor who was supposed to be able to figure out who wrote what, and she suggested that we could all three bear the torch together. Thomas, still doubtful, said he might be willing to speak with an English professor, but he'd have to think first about that, too. Something about auras.

Giving her cousin time to think, Mary Van Deusen drove from Boston to Poughkeepsie, taking up lodging at the Route 9 Holiday Inn, directly across from what used to be the Livingston estate and a short hike from Major Henry's final resting place in the Poughkeepsie Rural Cemetery. The Major's property, called Locust Grove (named for its trees, not insects), is a state historic site, though not in honor of Henry Livingston Jr. Samuel Finley Breese Morse, husband to one of Livingston's granddaughters, acquired the land some years after the Major's death. Today, local schoolchildren who have no clue what a telegraph is can visit the home of the man who invented it. Situated opposite a bank, a motel, and apartment buildings, the Samuel F. B. Morse estate does not feel like sacred ground. I had lived in Poughkeepsie for fourteen years without ever knowing that Locust Grove once belonged to a Henry Livingston, and I had picnicked there without suspecting that it was viewed by some local experts as the birthplace of Santa Claus. My one poetical experience at Locust Grove was when I took my kids to see an outdoor production of Shakespeare's *Macbeth,* a violent affair in which young actors in army fatigues ran around the yard shooting toy rifles while my own boys sifted through the grass, looking for four-leaf clovers, bored silly. There had been no tingles, no close encounter with flying reindeer at Locust Grove, no intuition that something special once took place on this plot of land.

On the morning after Mary's arrival, I picked her up at the Holiday Inn and we drove to Clinton House, home of the Dutchess County Historical Society. Inside this old stone structure are two conscientious and capable ladies, Mrs. Eileen Hayden and Mrs. Bernice Thomas, experts on local history. The sign on the door may say OPEN, but you must call first for an appointment or you will not be admitted.

Punctual for our 10:00 time slot, Mary and I knocked once, and waited. The ancient colonial door creaked open, and we were greeted by the archivists, who invited us to step inside, state our names and objective and the time of our appointment, and then to sign the guest book with a no. 2 lead pencil. There were no other visitors. Mrs. Hayden, Executive Director, handed me a pair of white cloth gloves and instructed me to put them on, and not to touch any books or documents until I had, and not to take them off until I was ready to leave.

The Clinton House archivists are solemn and businesslike, even a little grumpy, but both ladies are willing to answer questions of a historical nature. I found it truly remarkable how much information was stored inside their heads. In a municipality whose official motto is "Poughkeepsie: 300 Years of People, Pride, and Progress," there is a lot of history to know, and these two women know it like no one else, in minute detail, from the first Dutch settler right on through to the First or even Second World War. But Mary Van Deusen and I were here to ask about "The Night Before Christmas."

Mrs. Hayden and Mrs. Thomas delivered their verdict crisply, with complete authority, and without hesitation: "That poem," they said, "was written by Major Henry Livingston Junior."

Mary, who blithely agreed, introduced herself as a great-granddaughter (five greats, she added) of Major Henry. She said she had come all the way from Boston to investigate and to gather material for her Major Henry Livingston Jr. Web site. The archivists, though generally cooperative with requests to inspect original documents, were pessimistic in their assessment of Mary's enterprise. Several local historians had already written in Major Henry's defense—Benson J. Lossing (1886), Henry Litchfield West (1920), Cornelia G. Goodrich (1921), Helen Wilkinson Reynolds (1942), even Henry Noble MacCracken (1958), a former president of Vassar College—but the world did not listen. The Clement Moore camp simply brushed them off like Dutchess County deer ticks.[8] What difference could be made by one inexplicably cheerful woman from Massachusetts?

Mary, not I, was doing all of the hard work for this investigation, gathering documents, checking facts. Here at Clinton House she would be inspecting old newspapers, Livingston correspondence, estate records, back issues of the *Dutchess County Historical Society Yearbook*. Excusing myself, I removed my white cloth gloves and left her to her research, returning at one that afternoon to pick her up and to take her to Poughkeepsie's Adriance Memorial Library, Department of Special Collections. Then it was on to the Franklin D. Roosevelt Library in Hyde Park. Before leaving town, Mary deposited two neatly organized piles of documents in my Vassar office—writings "certainly" by Henry Livingston and writings "maybe" by Henry Livingston. A third pile, by far the largest, contained writings "about" Henry Livingston—machine photocopies of newspaper and magazine articles discussing the authorship controversy, plus biographical and genealogical notes, correspondence, account books, and other Livingston family papers.

On December 24, 1998, Mary's cousin Steve Thomas had received a sign, an omen possibly sent by the Major himself. The *Boston Globe* had printed "A Visit from St. Nicholas" on its front page, beneath a silhouette of Santa Claus. To the right was the day's top headline: LIVINGSTON EXIT DEEPENS PARTISAN RANCOR. The story had nothing to do with Steve's illustrious ancestor—it was about contention and partisanship in the U.S. House of Representatives—but the juxtaposed poem and headline grabbed his attention. He thought: We must not give up.

A year later, Steve came home from work one afternoon to find that his wife had decorated their home for the holidays. The old cello stood in the corner as usual, resting beneath the immutably benevolent gaze of Major Henry's 24-by-36-inch framed portrait—when what to Steve's wondering eyes should appear but a *Christmas Album* on the music stand in the corner by the cello, the cover of which depicted Santa and his sleigh and reindeer soaring skyward, toward Major Henry, as if striving to be reunited with their maker. That was sign no. 2. Steve took a photograph of it.

Then came the unexpected telephone call, in September 1999, from an unknown distant relative, Mary Van Deusen, a woman asking to see the Livingston documents. Cousin Van Deusen was either sign no. 3, or competition.

A generous man, Steve was willing to assist by lending us the original eighteenth-century manuscripts, but not without first seeking the advice of his spiritual advisor, a psychic, and the blessing of his elderly father, an Alzheimer's patient. The spiritual advisor said, "Go for it." That Mary Van Deusen had been drawn to a text analyst living in Poughkeepsie, Major Henry's hometown, and that I myself had been summoned to this place from afar, and that I was willing to help— these were good signs. But when Steve asked to borrow the manuscripts, his ninety-year-old dad, W. Stephen Thomas, said that he had hid them, and he would not say where. That was not such a good sign. "Knowing my dad," said Steve, "this search could take a while."

THE CHALLENGER: HENRY LIVINGSTON JR. (1748–1828)

But now comes blithe Christmas, while just in his rear
Advances our saint, jolly, laughing New Year . . .

—HENRY LIVINGSTON, "THE NEWS-BOY'S ADDRESS,"
POUGHKEEPSIE POLITICAL BAROMETER (1 JANUARY 1803)

I boned up on Major Livingston's biography. Born in Poughkeepsie on October 13, 1748, Henry was the eldest son of Dr. Henry Gilbert Livingston, a Scotsman, and Sarah Conklin Livingston, a Dutchwoman, or, as we say in Dutchess County, a Dutchess. His paternal grandmother was a Dutchess as well. Everyone on his mother's side was Dutch. But his father's father was a Scot. Henry considered himself a son of Scotland. (Remember that. I'm not slipping in these little facts for nothing.) The first recorded mention of Henry Livingston after his Poughkeepsie christening comes during his early adulthood, when he was a member of and frequent visitor to the Social Club of New York, a place run by God-Save-the-King Tories. When war broke out with the Motherland, Henry and his Yankee Doodle brother were blacklisted from the Social Club. For official business, the eldest son of Henry Gilbert Livingston, Esq., signed himself "Henry Livingston, Jr.," dropping the "Jr." after his father's death in 1799. About town, in recognition of his service in the War of Independence, he was called "Major Henry"; and in his old age, while serving as a softhearted Commissioner of Bankruptcy Court, "Judge Livingston." But to family and friends and neighbors, he was always plain Harry, the jolliest man in Dutchess County.

Henry's first recorded words are "Happy Christmas," in a love letter dated December 30, 1773, addressed to a creature for whom his heart was stirring, twenty-one-year-old Sarah ("Sally") Welles of Stamford, Connecticut:

A happy Christmas to my dear Sally Welles!

Next Tuesday evening I hope to see the Girl for whom alone I would well bear to live. Yes, my dear creature, next Tuesday evening, if my God spares my life, I hope to tell you I am as sincerely your friend, as constantly your admirer, & as religiously your lover, as when I sat by your side & vow'd everlasting affection to you.

I well know you will call this the "lover's cant." Call it so, my love—call it anything—I know & swear its truth, and wrap myself up in my own Integrity. . . .

The letter ends:

Remember me, my dear Love, to my friends and relations at Sta[m]ford; and remember, my Love, that of all your friends, none loves you so sincerely as your

Harry Livingston[9]

Harry and Sally were married in Stamford, Connecticut, by Sally's father, the Rev. Noah Welles, on May 18, 1774. The couple set up housekeeping at Locust Grove, a mile south of the village of Poughkeepsie, in a house built by Henry's Scottish grandfather. A surveyor and mapmaker by training, Henry also cut and sold lumber from a sawmill on his property, farmed his land, and operated a landing for sloops called Harry's Point, down on the river. By avocation a journalist and illustrator, Henry contributed engravings, poems, and prose satires to Poughkeepsie newspapers and New York City magazines, adopting such quirky pseudonyms as "Seignior Whimsicallo Pomposo," "Wizard," "Professor Zeritef Shoralow," "Henry Hotspur," and "Peter Pumpkineater."

When rising tensions with Britain led to war, there was no question concerning enlistment. Henry's father-in-law had been a pulpit-thumping firebrand for independence, and Henry was himself an American patriot, a New York gentleman of Scots and Dutch descent whose loyalties were to the Federation, not to England. One day Henry opened his music book to "God Save the King"—on page

182—dipped his quill, lined out "King," wrote in the word "Congress," and rode into the village to join the American Revolution.

The Livingstons' first child, Catherine, was born on August 18, 1775, on the eve of Major Henry's departure to fight the British. Next morning, Henry wrote to his commander, Colonel Clinton, that he was now ready to march:

> Dr. Sir:
>
> I have the pleasure to inform you that yesterday afternoon my wife was a Joyfull mother of a fine daughter—a circumstance in providence I highly rejoice at. You know the feelings of a father, Sir, on these occasions! However, I expect to be ready almost or quite as soon as the men here, as no man enters with more zeal into the service of his country than myself. . . .[10]

While serving under Colonel Clinton and General Montgomery, Livingston kept a journal, still extant, providing an account of his military tour—the highlight of which, for Henry, was an elegant dinner that he organized at Mr. Killip's Tavern in the village of Lapraire, Quebec, his guests of honor being six chiefs and twenty others of the Caghnawaga nation. Also invited was the village priest, "a fat Jolly thing of a Curate who did all the preaching and praying." Henry played the host and master of ceremonies, his introductory speech being translated by "a one-ey'd Chief who understood English very well—& they answered me with all that deliberation, firmness & seriousness [*sic*] peculiar to the Indians." Henry adds: "I took especial care that each one had a full plate continually—Soup-Beef-Turkey-Beans-Potatoes—no matter how heterogeneous the mixture, it was equal to them, & all went down." The guests became somewhat less firm and deliberate in their speech after eighteen bottles of claret, and a good time was had by all.[11]

The great tragedy of Henry's early adulthood was the death of his wife in 1783. It took a while for the Livingston household, and Henry's verse, to recover the liveliness that was there before Sally's death, but the Major and his children worked at it, observing the celebration of Saint Nicholas Day, Christmas, and New Year's as it had been before. Henry describes the typical Livingston family holiday during these years:

> Such gadding—such ambling—such jaunting about!
> To tea with Miss Nancy—to sweet Willy's rout,
> New parties at coffee—then parties at wine,
> Next day all the world with the Major must dine!
> Then bounce all hands to Fishkill must go in a clutter
> To guzzle bohea, and destroy bread and butter. . . .[12]

Relatives and guests came from far and near to join in the festivities. Henry and the children sang and played their instruments. There were noisy dinners, wild sleigh rides, knockabout games of Hide and Seek and Keys and the Cushion, with music and dancing till midnight.

On September 1, 1793, ten years to the day after Sally's death, Henry Livingston remarried, taking to wife Jane Patterson, by whom he would have eight children. As the kids grew up, they became scattered by marriage and by the opportunity for cheaper land out west, in Ohio, Illinois, and Wisconsin. The Major, who remained in Poughkeepsie, died in his eightieth year, on February 29, 1828, much lamented by family and friends. His surviving sons and daughters never tired of telling stories to their children, and to their children's children, of wonderful Papa Livingston, of his "fine poetical taste," his "great taste for drawing and painting," and his "Night Before Christmas." Perhaps the tales grew some with the retelling and the passing of years.

Writing to a niece in 1879, Henry and Jane's eldest daughter, Eliza, recalled how her father would "entertain us on winter evenings by getting down the paint-box, we seated around the table. First he would portray something very pathetic, which would melt us to tears. The next thing would be so comic that we would be almost wild with laughter. And this dear, good, man was your great-great-grandfather."[13] In one of the Major's extant drawings, a young lady flies in holy dread from a watercolor bugaboo—a monster having the head of a fire-breathing devil, the feet of a rooster, and a torso made of a large poultry thigh.

Much of the Major's poetry was written for children and never gathered or published. One compassionate lyric from the 1780s is addressed "To my niece, Sally Livingston, on the death of a little serenading wren she admired"; another, to a young second cousin, Timmy Dwight, a boy as "Blythe as Oberon the fairy." Henry urges the lad to party hard on his birthday, to fill his "cormorantal belly" with hasty-puddings and "charming jelly." Fun stuff, fun poetry. You can't read Major Henry Livingston Jr. and not love the man from the top of his jolly head to the tips of his Poughkeepsie feet. His correspondence and published poems and articles are usually witty, sometimes hilarious, never sarcastic; full of love for humanity and driven by an irrepressible joie de vivre—or, to say it more properly in Dutch, *levenslust*.

But it's one thing to recognize a jolly good fellow and something else to identify Livingston as the true author of "A Visit from St. Nicholas." I liked the man—who wouldn't?—but I could hardly credit Major Henry with "A Visit from St. Nicholas" on the basis of warm, fuzzy feelings. The external evidence for Henry Livingston's authorship of the poem depended on the recollections and anecdotes of his children and grandchildren, who seem to have settled on Christmas morning 1808, at breakfast, as the occasion on which Major Henry introduced his family to "a right jolly old elf" with "a round little belly, / That shook, when he laughed, like a bowl full of jelly."

It is the Major's daughter-in-law, Elizabeth Brewer, who is credited with having discovered Professor Moore's alleged theft a half-century later. "The Night Before Christmas" appeared in book form in 1848, with drawings by T. C. Boyd, and in *Harper's Weekly* in 1861, illustrated by Thomas Nast. Both editions were holiday bestsellers. When Grandma Elizabeth first saw one or the other—no one is sure now which one—she calmly announced, "Some one has made a mistake!

Clement Moore did not write the 'Night Before Christmas.' Your grandfather, Henry Livingston wrote it."[14] Word of this injustice passed from the Major's children to his grandchildren and great-grandchildren, none of whom, however, was able to prove that the attribution to Moore was indeed erroneous.[15] It was more a matter of faith. Said one granddaughter, "Of course Grandfather wrote 'The Night Before Christmas.' I believe it just as much as I believe Robert Burns wrote 'Tam O'Shanter.' "[16]

Eliza and Charles, the Major's two eldest children by his second wife, Jane, said that their father wrote and recited the poem for Christmas of 1807 or '08, beating the *Troy Sentinel* text by as much as sixteen years. (One grandson reports from his father, Sidney, an even earlier date of 1805.) The most detailed account comes from Mrs. Edward Livingston Montgomery, daughter of the Major's eldest daughter, Catherine Livingston Breese:

> There was a young lady spending the Christmas holidays with the family at Locust Grove. On Christmas morning Mr. Livingston came into the dining room, where the family guests were sitting to breakfast. He held the manuscript in his hand and said that it was a Christmas poem he had written for them. He then sat down at the table and read aloud to them "A Visit." All were delighted and the guest, in part, was so impressed she begged Mr. Livingston to let her have a copy. He consented and made a copy in his own hand. On leaving Locust Grove, the young lady went directly to the home of Clement Clarke Moore, where she filled the position of governess to his children.[17]

Mrs. Montgomery is said to have learned all of this from her mother, Catherine. But when Catherine died in 1808, Clement Moore was still a bachelor. He could not have required a governess earlier than 1815, when his first child was born. The numbers don't compute.

Benson J. Lossing, a Dutchess County historian, was the first scholar of record to examine the Livingston theory. Hoping to make a case for Dutchess County's native son, if a case could be made, Lossing in the 1880s wrote to Major Livingston's children and grandchildren with a request for more information. His investigation produced only more of the same: lots of fun anecdotes, no proof. The Major's heirs could supply no manuscript copy of the poem, no document of any kind associating the name Livingston with "A Visit from St. Nicholas." Major Henry's daughter Eliza and grandson Henry (son of Sidney) said that the family had owned a manuscript collection of the Major's original poetry, an album that included "A Visit from St. Nicholas." The volume passed from Sidney (who died in 1829, a year after his father) to younger brother Edwin, who lived in Delafield, Wisconsin. It has been said that the Major's poetry book was in nearby Waukesha, in the home of Susan Livingston Gurney (Henry's seventh child by Jane Patterson), when all was lost in a tragic house fire. The original holograph copy of "A Visit from St. Nicholas" went up in a wreath of smoke. That, anyhow, was the story.

Lossing's respondents included a great-great-granddaughter, Cornelia Goodrich, who relayed her favorite Henry and Jane stories, including this one: In 1793, ten years after Sally's death, Major Henry married the spunky Miss Jane Patterson of Connecticut, after a long-distance courtship. She was twenty-four. He was forty-five. On the Sunday morning after their wedding, the young bride came sailing down the stairs dressed for church. "Not wanting to be restricted in the matter of dress and pretty things," she was arrayed in a brightly colored dress, a scarlet cape, and white satin hat with plumes. This was in an age, remember, when married women attired themselves modestly and soberly for Sunday worship, in outfits of black or brown or charcoal gray.

The Major said "My dear, isn't your gown rather gay for church"? "Not at all," was her reply. "You always liked my gowns *before* we were married, why not now? I shall wear just what I have on." Whereupon the Major said not a word; but mounting the stairs, donned his military coat with brass buttons, three-cornered hat, and shoes with paste buckles; and without saying aught, gallantly led his bride to the coach; got in beside her, and told old Joe, the colored coachman—who sat grinning at this amusing scene—to drive down the old Post Road to the Dutch Church in Poughkeepsie.[18]

Cornelia Goodrich had other charming anecdotes, all tending to show that her illustrious great-great-grandfather might indeed have been the true author of "The Night Before Christmas."

One of Cornelia's cousins supplied Mr. Lossing with the not-very-useful information that the Livingston home at Locust Grove, like the house in the poem, had hinged shutters, a chimney, a porch, a wall. The Major, like the Christmas poet, called the mother of his children "Mama." Et cetera. But Benson Lossing by this time had lost confidence in the Livingston legend, and had lost patience with what was being submitted to him as evidence. He wrote back to say: "My dear Miss Goodrich: I thank you very much for your extremely interesting letter with its enclosures. The circumstantial evidence that your G. G. Grandfather wrote 'The Visit of St. Nicholas' seems as conclusive as that which has taken innocent men to the gallows. . . ."[19]

One cornerstone of the Major Livingston theory is the children's recollection that "A Visit from St. Nicholas" was printed in a Poughkeepsie newspaper—the *Country Journal,* the *Political Barometer,* the *Guardian,* the *Republican Observer,* or any one of a dozen others—many years prior to its appearance in the *Troy Sentinel.* Taking up the quest after it was abandoned by Benson Lossing, the Livingston heir, William S. Thomas, searched for that original Poughkeepsie text of "A Visit from St. Nicholas," and searched for forty years, followed by his son, W. Stephen Thomas, who had no better success than his father. Archival collections of those old newspapers were maddeningly incomplete, and stray copies of missing issues were scattered and hard to find. The Thomases in the course of their research found a lot of writing by Henry Livingston, but not the object of their quest—an 1808 text of "The Night Before Christmas" published in Major Henry's hometown.

The examination of old newspapers is made easier today by microfilm archives. With just one sitting at a microfilm reader in the

Vassar Library, working through reels of the *Poughkeepsie Journal,*
1786–1828, I found more than I was looking for. In fact, I found the
wrong poem altogether: On January 3, 1821, three years before "A
Visit from St. Nicholas" appeared in the *Troy Sentinel,* the *Poughkeepsie Journal* published "Sante Claus," an early Saint Nicholas poem
not mentioned by either side in the "Night Before Christmas" controversy. The poem was evidently written by a resident of the village
of Hudson, forty miles upriver from Poughkeepsie. Anticipating that
his mostly English American readers may be unfamiliar with Dutch
tradition, the poet begins by asking, in effect, *Is it a bird? Is it a plane?
No, it's—*

> SANTE CLAUS
>
> Whose form is that in uncouth garb
> With burdens on his back, . . .
> Is't Mordecai the Wandering Jew?
> Or that more recent wight,
> By urchins styled the "Bugaboo,"
> That horrifies the night?
> Oh, no, 'tis good St. Nicholas,
> Just come from Amsterdam! . . .
> I've often heard my grandsire say
> (Kind heart, he knew him well),
> That when he lived in Netherlandt
> This saint, by book and spell
> The lashing surges from the dikes
> In guardless midnight hour
> Back to their angry caverns drove
> And quelled the tempest's power . . .

This anonymous "Sante Claus" poem, appearing first in *The
Northern Whig* (Hudson, New York), then in the *Poughkeepsie Jour-
nal,* is interesting for what it reveals of local tradition. In villages from
Sleepy Hollow to Kinderhook, Dutch Americans are said to invoke
Saint Nicholas "to guard their happy homes" and to "multiply in

every way / The sweetnesses of life," with gifts of "nuts and pies and crulls / And whiskey's jovial flow." But in the village of Hudson, founded by English Protestants, Saint Nicholas is not honored—the strict English will follow no saint but John Calvin, the Protestant theologian "Who strips our virtues all away / And wraps us up in sin!" In a postscript, the author of "Sante Claus" glosses a few Dutch terms, mocks his own shortcomings as a poet, and wishes to all readers of the *Poughkeepsie Journal* a "Merry Christmas and Happy New Year."[20]

William S. and W. Stephen Thomas had searched in vain for an early Santa poem by Major Henry Livingston printed in a Poughkeepsie newspaper. Perhaps, with the passing of years, the Livingston family confused Clement Moore's popular verse with an earlier Santa poem they saw in the *Poughkeepsie Journal* in 1821. That seemed to me like a plausible explanation.

Then came another surprise—same newspaper, same microfilm reader. While searching the *Journal* for Major Henry's 1828 obituary, what should I find but "A Visit from St. Nicholas"! On Wednesday, January 16, 1828, just six weeks before Livingston's death, the editor of the *Poughkeepsie Journal* published "The Night Before Christmas" on the front page, under the title "A Visit from St. Nicholas or Santa Claus"—but this was twenty years later than the date reported by Henry's children and grandchildren.

January 16 seems like an odd moment for "The Night Before Christmas" to have appeared on the front page of any newspaper. With Major Henry on his deathbed, failing fast, might that publication in the *Poughkeepsie Journal* be viewed as a last tribute to the native son who wrote it? Absolutely not. The *Journal*'s text, reprinted from the *National Gazette,* appears without attribution. The text is derived from the *Troy Sentinel,* but corrupt, having been passed around from paper to paper for more than four years. In the 1828 *Poughkeepsie Journal* text, the children are "*nested* [not *nestled*] all snug in their beds," and Santa's sleigh is pulled not by reindeer but "*red* deer." There is no indication that the *Journal*'s editor, Paraclete Power, received the poem from the Livingston family, nor any indication that

Mr. Power or anyone else in Poughkeepsie knew the original to have been written by Henry Livingston. I rewound the reel, turned off the light on the microfilm reader, and walked home, sorry that I had wasted so much time on a family legend.

CLEMENT CLARKE MOORE (1779–1863), THE POET OF CHRISTMAS EVE

Well . . . in Who-ville they say
That the Grinch's small heart
Grew three sizes that day!
And the minute his heart didn't feel quite so tight,
He whizzed with his load through the bright morning light.

—DR. SEUSS, *HOW THE GRINCH STOLE CHRISTMAS*

In 1829, six years after "A Visit from St. Nicholas" first appeared in the *Troy Sentinel,* the paper's editor, Orville Holley, printed it again. Having since received a tip concerning the poem's authorship, Holley teased his readers with a few hints, noting that the author of "The Night Before Christmas" belonged "by birth and residence" to the city of New York, being "a gentleman of more merit as a scholar and writer than many of more noisy pretensions."[21] Holley could not have been thinking of Henry Livingston Jr. of Poughkeepsie. Like Major Henry, Clement Clarke Moore was a poet, but Moore was also a citizen of New York, a scholar of very quiet pretensions, and enormously rich.

It's often been said that the English acquired New York for a handshake, a promise, and colored beads. Clement Moore's great-granddaddies were the men with the beads and the promises, along with Peter Minuit, who bought Manhattan for twenty-four dollars. Rev. John Moore (1620–1657), who talked the Mohawks into forfeiting much of Long Island, received as his gratuity 110 prime acres (augmenting the 40 acres he had already purchased out of pocket); Clement Moore, born in 1779—grandson to Reverend John and the only child of Benjamin Moore, Bishop of the Episcopal Church of America—was the ultimate beneficiary of that largess. On his mother's side, Clement did even better: he inherited from his Grandma Clarke a parcel of Manhattan comprising nearly six hundred choice building lots (an estate called Chelsea), plus thousands of acres of undeveloped land in Saratoga County. Having a better head for business than most college professors, Moore translated his inherited real estate into a stupendous fortune, making himself into one of the wealthiest men in America.[22]

Throughout the course of his adult life, Professor Moore kept daily account books, recording for posterity several dozen, perhaps hundreds of, personal bequests—thousands of dollars to church institutions, plus frequent gifts of $1 or more to street beggars. His gifts were often underappreciated. When St. Peter's Church required a new organ, Clement Moore donated $5,000 for the best instrument money could buy—volunteering to serve thereafter as the church organist. Some parishioners, though grateful, thought the honor of playing it should have gone to Edward Hodges, a professional musician. George Strong remarks in his diary that the music thereafter was poor, for though the organ was "a very fine affair," arguably the best in the New World, "much can't be expected from it when operated on by Clement C. Moore . . . a very scientific musician, but he's sadly lacking in the mechanical department."[23] The Professor felt the sting of such criticism. When his niece Sarah, insensitive of his feelings, became engaged to Edward Hodges, Professor Moore instructed her to break it off or he'd leave the country.[24] Sarah married Hodges anyway—and Moore eventually forgave her. He even wrote Mr. Hodges a long poem about the moral responsibilities of a church organist.

The New York philanthropist John Pintard first met Clement Moore in 1821 while working to establish the General Theological Seminary. Moore not only donated the land, he volunteered to serve as one of the school's four faculty members, and Bishop John Henry Hobart duly appointed him to be the Professor of Biblical Learning. John Pintard disapproved of this appointment, remarking in his diary that Clement Moore was fond of speaking "slightly or disrespectfully of what he was totally ignorant. . . . Is he a sample of the professors of the new school? . . . *Eheu!* Professor!"[25] But in the years to come Pintard learned to think of Clement Moore as a friend. Moore took some getting used to, that's all.

In 1836, Washington Irving and Gulian Verplanck formed the Saint Nicholas Society, to make merry at Christmastime with an annual banquet and to collect gifts for the poor. When they invited Professor Moore to join, he declined. From Clement Moore's point of view, Christmas was no time to be jolly, but a season for worship, for repentance from sin.

The Professor's attitude toward the veneration of Catholic saints, including Saint Nicholas, is exemplified in a letter that he wrote to a seminary student, young Joshua Newton Wattson, on Christmas Eve 1844—the very year in which Moore first claimed authorship of "A Visit from St. Nicholas." Ever-vigilant in policing the minds of the young, Professor Moore suspected Josh Wattson of holding certain "Romish" beliefs that were unbecoming in an Episcopal youth. On December 24, the Professor took action, commanding Joshua Wattson to stand trial before the faculty. Wattson's fate is not recorded; he cannot have had a very happy holiday.

In addition to bearing heavy responsibilities as a church organist and Bible scholar and theological inquisitor, Clement Moore was also a serious poet. "It was the opening springtime of the year . . ." So begins "A Trip to Saratoga," the first entry in his 1844 volume of *Poems.* If Moore too soon abandons this cheerful Chaucerian vein, the fault lies with his children, who after just six lines "broke the comfort of his morning meal." Such "Babylonish noise about my ears," sighs the poet in lines 11–12, "Confounds my brain and nearly splits my head." Moore pauses to lecture these lovely but undisciplined juveniles to shut their yaps ("clamorous girls, as many boisterous boys . . . provoke the gentlest mood"). The next sixty-five pages of the volume narrate the poet's noisy trip, sans Tylenol, with six kids, to see Saratoga's hot springs and mineral baths (a natural wonder), and the village of Saratoga itself (a community dedicated to "the horrors of ennui").

But oh, the noise! There was the hissing roar of the steamboat, and a ridiculous woman who tried to exhibit her book learning, and an incompetent mother who could not silence her sobbing baby—"her brat." (The little beast "paid its mother's scolding lullaby / With kicks and jerks and still a louder riot.") The women both going and coming in Saratoga were insufferable, especially the talkative, plump-visag'd wives. The ideal woman, for Moore, is "noiseless." As for the other kind, "Heav'n help the mortal doom'd by cruel fate / To bide the wordy torrent of her tongue!" Throughout the *Poems,* Clement Clarke Moore sounds less like the scholar who invented Santa Claus than like Dr. Seuss's grumpy Grinch: "Oh the noise! Oh the Noise! Noise! Noise! Noise! / That's *one* thing he hated! The NOISE! NOISE! NOISE! NOISE!"

To say that Clement Clarke Moore was a curmudgeon is not to cast aspersions on his descendants. Moore was the first in a line of Clements, each one more jolly, more Father Christmas–like, than his predecessor. But truly, I think they get it from the mother's side. The world, as represented in Professor Moore's *Poems,* is a place inhabited by loud children, frivolous maids, scolding wives, loud children, lazy mechanics, loud children, soft-spoken rogues, rude barflies, lewd coquettes and prostitutes, rich men ill-clad, loud children, dull schoolmen, manly-treading female would-be-scholars, and loud children— all of whom must be scolded: the little ones, with patience, and the adults, who ought to know better, with sneering sarcasm. No person so seemingly virtuous or beautiful but that Professor Scrooge's pen can detect a rottenness at the core: ". . . clust'ring cherries on the tree appear, / At distance seen, all ripe, and plump, and sound; / 'Tis not till gather'd, and examin'd near, / That many a canker'd blemish may be found."[26] Even toddlers can be spiritually rotten, their "infant pleasures" tainted with "many a stain."[27]

But let us cut the man some slack. Moore published his *Poems* in 1844, when he was sixty-five years old. "A Visit from St. Nicholas" was in print by 1823. Forty years in academia can do strange things to a man's character. May not the old sourpuss have been a bon vivant as a youth? Professor Moore himself answers that question: Absolutely not. To demonstrate, he reprints his juvenilia, poems that are as biting, as self-righteous and caustic, as anything he wrote later on. Young Clement Moore speaks often of sin, and he lets you know that he's against it. In one early poem from his bachelor days, Moore condemns the walk, talk, dancing, music, dress, and cosmetics of the girls of Manhattan ("Shame! shame! heart-rending thought! deep-sinking stain! . . . arts first taught by prostitutes of France!").[28] Or take that time, back in 1804, when a young lady invited him to attend a ball. For an r.s.v.p., the indignant twenty-five-year-old bachelor and Bible student composed "An Apology for Not Accepting":

> To me 'tis giv'n your virtue to secure
> From custom's force and pleasure's dangerous lure. . . .
> For if, regardless of my friendly voice,
> In Fashion's gaudy scenes your heart rejoice,
> Dire punishments shall fall upon your head:
> Disgust, and fretfulness, and secret dread.[29]

Clement Moore at age thirty-four reports that his own mother thought of him as a "woman hater," a scholar like "the long-bearded Jew who . . . could love nothing but musty black-letter books."[30]

William Bard, a friend, describes Moore's Muse as "angry," "surly," "uncourtly," and "waspish."[31] Philip Hone, onetime mayor of New York, speaks of the hotheaded Professor's "attic fire"—which was probably a compliment, meaning something like "Athenian intensity," but it's also true that you never knew when the Professor's roof would blow—the least little sin could set him off.[32] Clement Clarke Moore, in the words of George Strong, was a man "instinct with red pepper, to a high degree of excitement."[33]

It would be hard to find two sons of the American Revolution more different from each other than Professor Clement Clarke Moore of Chelsea House, Manhattan, and Major Henry Livingston of Locust Grove, Poughkeepsie. There is no topic about which the two men can be found to agree, from women to music to politics. Moore opposed most democratic reforms, including the movement for free public schools; Livingston argued that children should have equal opportunity, regardless of their gender or complexion or cultural heritage. A foe to women's education, Moore protected his daughters from the harmful effects of book learning, and speaks of learned women with scathing derision; Livingston, while traveling through Canada in 1775, praised the women's zeal for education while criticizing the illiteracy of the Canadian men.[34] Moore expresses disdain for the American "savages" and condemns their mode of communication as innately deceitful; Livingston was a friend of the Indians, writes of the aboriginal peoples with admiration, and praises the seriousness and courtesy of their speech. Moore unrepentantly defends human slavery as an institution ordained by God for the health and prosperity of American society—in fact, he owned slaves himself, as many as were convenient to keep the Moore household running smoothly; Livingston in his published journalism as early as 1788 calls for emancipation, and writes in his private journal that "A land of slaves will ever be a land of Poverty, Ignorance, & Idleness!"[35] The son of a British loyalist during the War for Independence, Moore as an adult denounced Thomas Jefferson as a subverter of public morals and a danger to the Commonwealth; Livingston was a die-hard Whig whose lifelong theme, in verse and prose, is that "Love, and all its delectable concomitants" can thrive only "where equality is found or understood."[36]

The personal dispositions of Livingston and Moore were as different as their systems of belief. Major Henry celebrates theater, music, and dancing, which combine "to drive far off care and annihilate time / And chase sour sadness away."[37] Moore writes that the man who dances is "like a squirrel cag'd, who, though he bound, / And whirl about his wheel, yet ne'er advances." Women dancers are said to resemble female scholars and prostitutes: "No laws they heed but those which rule the dance."[38]

Santa's pipe—removed from the poem by some recent editors under pressure from the anti-tobacco lobby—is unmistakably Dutch: "The stump of a pipe he held tight in his teeth, / And the smoke it encircled his head like a wreath." As early as 1748, Tobias Smollett writes of a Dutch sailor taking "a whiff of tobacco from the stump of a pipe."[39] Henry Livingston's imagination is similarly populated by Dutchmen who "puff away care" with a "pipe of Virginia" while Clement Moore likens the lure of tobacco ("Virginia's weed," he calls it) to "opium's treach'rous aid."[40]

An overindulgent and playful father, Henry Livingston taught his children by example, without paying adequate attention to the Good Book and without corporal punishment. Clement Moore subscribed to the biblical precept "Withhold not correction from the child; for if thou beatest him with the rod, he shall not die: thou shalt beat him with the rod, and shalt deliver his soul from hell."[41] But the Professor discovered to his grief, in his old age, that the birchen rod failed to make a lasting and consistent impression on certain of the subjects to which it was applied. In September 1848, after vacationing for a month with the Moore family in Sharon, Connecticut, George Strong observed that the Professor's grown daughters were still "very nice indeed," but "the sons, a compound of imbecility deep beyond all fathoming, with an appetite for chambermaids beyond all precedent."[42] It is a cruel irony of history that when Clement Clarke Moore finally became famous, it was not for his philanthropy, nor for his organ-playing, nor for his *Compendious Lexicon of the Hebrew Language* (1809); nor for such learned books as the history of *George Castriot, Surnamed Scanderbeg, King of Albania* (1850), nor even for his parenting. It was for what he called "the Christmas piece," a mere trifle.

The generally accepted history of "The Night Before Christmas," pieced together from multiple sources, runs something like this: On December 24, 1822, during his first year as the Professor of Biblical Learning at the General Theological Seminary, Clement Clarke Moore went shopping in Greenwich Village for a Christmas turkey. While riding in a one-horse open sleigh, he composed in his head the fifty-six lines of "A Visit from St. Nicholas." Upon arriving home, he copied the poem to paper. On Christmas Day he read "A Visit" to his family, just before eating the turkey. A visitor to Chelsea House, a relative, copied the verse into her album without Moore's knowledge, from which a copy was made by a visitor from Troy, and delivered thence to the *Sentinel*'s editor, Mr. Orville Holley, who printed it, anonymously—causing the Professor "regret and chagrin, as he did not wish it to be published."[43] William Pelletreau, in his 1886 edition of "A Visit from St. Nicholas," states that the purveyor of the manuscript was young Sarah Harriet Butler, daughter of Rev. David Butler, rector of St. Paul's Church and a man who, like Moore himself, was an important figure in the Episcopal Diocese of New York. It is believed that Miss Butler wished to have the poem for recitation to her Sunday School class, but her father, the Reverend, was so taken with it that he delivered young Harriet's find to Orville Holley, editor of the *Sentinel*.[44] And the rest is history.

Professor Moore's grandson Casimir deR. Moore, writing in 1920, supplies a few additional tidbits, information that he gleaned firsthand from interviews with his father, uncles, and aunts: When "An Account of a Visit from St. Nicholas" was first published in 1823, "There were at once several persons who claimed to be the author; and it was not until urged that my grandfather acknowledged that he was the author." Noting his granddad's formidable reputation, Casimir concludes, not unreasonably, that this man of God "never could have said he was the author unless he was so in fact."[45]

While investigating these matters I came upon another strong argument that Professor Moore would not have lied about "The Night Before Christmas." In February 1833, the Moore family attended the joyful wedding of Laura Jephson and George Elliot Taylor. The groom, a clerk for the Manhattan Bank, was the younger brother of Moore's wife. John Pintard describes him as "a beautiful young man of 22 or 3." Three days later, George Taylor was dead. In trouble over unpaid gambling debts, he had forged a banknote in the name of "Clement C. Moore," his wealthy brother-in-law, hoping for the best. When the fraud was detected, and Professor Moore unforgiving, George Taylor committed suicide by an overdose of laudanum. The Taylors' physician, Dr. Francis, said he had seen many awful events in his time, but never a scene of such utter distress and wretchedness as was presented by George's distraught family and grief-stricken bride.[46]

Having been dragged into a bitter tragedy when his name was used unlawfully by another in 1833, would Professor Moore let an error stand uncorrected in December 1836, when his name was first placed on "A Visit from St. Nicholas"? And if "A Visit" belonged to another man, another poet, would Moore have proceeded seven years after that to publish the poem himself, as his own composition? If it were a lie, and the lie were exposed in the New York press, could Moore have expected a happier outcome than the misery suffered by his hapless brother-in-law, George Taylor?

According to Neil Sonne, librarian of the General Theological Seminary, the strongest evidence that Professor Moore wrote "The Night Before Christmas" may be an elaborate calligraphic, illustrated manuscript of the poem, created in 1855 by the Professor's daughter Mary Moore Ogden. Sonne observes: "The 'Livingston claim' requires that Clement Clarke Moore had misled his child daughter" (in 1822); that he "carried the lie along through thirty-three years of life, and now looked on with a lively consciousness of guilt as his daughter naively produced this lovely testimonial to his supposed literary skill."[47] Sonne's point is worth considering. There can be no doubt that Mary was a believer: it was her own Papa who wrote "The Night Before Christmas." (As for Mary's brothers, they were big boys now and did not greatly care, having moved on to other interests.)

Professor Moore's 1844 *Poems* registered disappointing sales, but "The Night Before Christmas" continued to prosper in other venues. Newspaper, magazine, and children's book editors capitalized on the poem's enormous popularity with one sellout edition after another. In 1862, following the classic *Harper's Weekly* issue illustrated by Thomas Nast, the New-York Historical Society decided to interview the father of Santa Claus: Who was Clement Clarke Moore, the man behind the myth? The interview was not wholly successful. Professor Moore by this time was eighty-three years old, and more crotchety than ever. With effort, the reporter extracted from Moore a copy of the poem in the Professor's own hand, plus the outlines of the Greenwich Village turkey story on which other storytellers would later build.[48]

The date that Moore gave for his epiphany was December 24, 1822, when "a portly, rubicund Dutchman, living in the neighbourhood," suggested to him "the idea of making St. Nicholas the hero of this 'Christmas piece.' " Professor Moore said that he never intended for the piece to make him famous. He was writing as a father—not for publication, but for the entertainment of his "two children."[49]

Professor Moore's story of the portly, rubicund neighbor smells of fish. Saint Nicholas was conventionally depicted as tall, thin, haloed, and severe, grasping a raised whip or birchen rod. Not until *after* "The Night Before Christmas" became a hit did the public come to think of Saint Nicholas as a plump and rosy-cheeked Mynheer Dutchman. Then, too, on that historic Christmas Day when he is said to have introduced his family to Saint Nicholas, Professor Moore actually had six children, not two—Margaret, Charity, Elizabeth, Benjamin, Mary, Clement Jr., and the baby, Emily—all of whom were alive and well, none of whom was later able to recall the events described by their father on that Christmas Day when he introduced them all (or introduced them both) to Santa Claus. I doubted that the Professor was telling the truth—but you can't call a man a liar when he's no longer around to defend himself, not unless you're certain he deserves it. Moore, at least, had tradition on his side. The documentary evidence for a Livingston attribution was at best unreliable, at worst fraudulent; and in the view of many capable scholars laughable. The internal evidence was incomplete. I had not yet seen proof that Major Livingston wrote a single line of poetry later than 1794. The Livingston children were doubtless sincere in their recollections concerning "A Visit," but may they not have been sincerely mistaken?

In Shakespeare's Christmas comedy *Twelfth Night,* the boy Cesario (who's really the girl Viola, who's really a boy actor) is in love with the Duke Orsino, who's in love with Olivia (who's really a boy actor), who's in love with Cesario (who's really the girl Viola), who sighs, "O Time, thou must untangle this, not I, / It is too hard a knot for me t' untie." My feelings precisely. Setting the project aside, I knew what it meant to pull out. If Henry Livingston was truly the author of "A Visit from St. Nicholas" and Professor Moore an impostor, an injustice had been done and the error would prevail. But it

would take more than family tradition, more than a few clever anapests, more even than a ray of light from on high, for Henry Livingston to dislodge Clement Clarke Moore's name from "The Night
Before Christmas." Where was the evidence?

THE EVIDENCE

> What we may call the *internal evidence* of a passage can exhibit itself
> only to a person familiar with the style and idiom of the original;
> before whom, a sense sometimes arises which, although he may not
> be able fully to impart the evidence of it to others, appears to him so
> just and true, that it seems like a ray of light from a brighter region.
> —CLEMENT CLARKE MOORE, *LECTURE* (14 NOVEMBER 1825)[50]

Steve Thomas had to be in Dutchess County anyway, visiting relatives, the following week. When he offered to pay me a visit on Friday,
December 17, and let me see some of the original documents in Major
Henry's own hand, I couldn't say no. A week later, Steve sat in my
Vassar office with his grandfather's research notes on yellowed, crum-
bling paper, reams of it, piled high on his lap. The poetry, essays, and
artwork of Henry Livingston lay spread out across the floor. As I
surveyed this cornucopia, the Major himself looked on from the corner, a benign observer: Steve had removed his great-great-great-great-
grandfather from the Thomas family living room and brought him
along for the ride from Boston so that Henry could be with us. The
portrait sat propped in my La-Z-Boy recliner, with Henry facing west
toward the Hudson, toward the old homestead, and toward his own
physical remains, which lay just three miles away. I found the Major's
countenance a little disappointing: wooden expression, clean-shaven,
George Washington smile, nothing like Santa. I could not imagine the
man in the picture with a belly that shook when he laughed like a
bowl full of jelly.

When it was time to go, Steve retrieved the Major, shook my
hand, and said good-bye. To my surprise, he insisted on leaving the

documents in my custody, including the Major's original artwork and a music book dating from before the Revolutionary War, handed down in his family from generation to generation. Steve didn't know me from Adam, but he knew my aura to be in good alignment with that of Major Henry. Accepting the documents, I thanked Steve sincerely for his trust and said farewell.

If a case could yet be made for Major Henry Livingston's authorship of "The Night Before Christmas," it would have to be made on the internal evidence—and here was a heap of new material. The Thomas collection indicated that Major Livingston's private and published writing was far more extensive than I would have guessed. Livingston wrote and published more or less continuously from the 1770s until only weeks or months before his death in February 1828. Much of his prose and verse was printed in late-eighteenth- and early-nineteenth-century newspapers and magazines, available in the special collections of the Vassar College Library; and most of it was signed, if at all, with the simple and improbable pseudonym "R." That was pretty interesting. I had already transcribed, from microfilm reels of the *Poughkeepsie Journal* and of the *New York* and *Weekly Museum* magazines, more than a dozen anapestic poems to illustrate that someone other than Clement Moore or Henry Livingston might have written "The Night Before Christmas." Most of these were by an author whom I had no hope of ever being able to identify. They were signed "R."

In a criminal investigation, the perpetrator of a crime may be identified by what has been left behind—fingerprints, shoe prints, clothing fibers, strands of hair, dropped eyeglasses. In textual analysis, the author of a Questioned Document may be identified by what's been *taken*—vocabulary, phrasing, and metaphor lifted from other writers. As it happens, Clement Clarke Moore was a learned man but not terribly original. Plunk a finger down almost anywhere in his book of *Poems*. Select a phrase that describes nature—"clouds of darker hue," "diamond raindrops," "summer's balmy breath," "rustling foliage," "verdant islets," "yielding sand." Or take a phrase that describes people—"lightly tripping feet," "bounding feet," "favonian breath," "listless drones," "noisy pack," "direful wrath," whatever. A quick check of a literary text archive shows that the identical phrases appear in Moore's reading.

If imitation is the highest form of praise, then Moore's poetry is full of high praise, for he lifts his descriptive language from other poets. When Moore in the first one hundred lines of the first poem in *Poems* writes of "dear-lov'd daughters," "vernal clouds," and "roseate light," or begins another in "a jocund hymeneal strain," you can tell he's been reading Robert Southey. When Moore complains in one short lyric of the "din of commerce," life's "motley scene," "glorious contests," and "ruthless Time," or begins another with "hail thy natal day," he's been reading the verse of Bernard Barton. When, in the space of a few lines, one finds Moore writing "welcome to your wish'd abode" and "thought of dread futurity," he has been reading Timothy Dwight's *Conquest of Canaan*, which has "guide us to your wish'd abode" and "through dread futurity." The Professor's verse is highly derivative—so much so that his reading can be tracked, and his poems dated, by the dozens of phrases borrowed and recycled by his sticky-fingered Muse.

It would be unfair to call Moore's extensive borrowings plagiarism. Poetry has less to do with original creation than with reassembling familiar language into something new. No one—not Clement Moore, not Henry Livingston, not Shakespeare—is free from formula. In fact, from an investigative point of view, borrowing is good—the more, the better. By tracing the literary debts of the "Christmas" poet, and of Henry Livingston, and of Clement Moore, I hoped to unravel a still-unsolved mystery that had me stumped.

Searching for the poet's literary roots, I was drawn to two of the most popular anapestic works of the eighteenth century, William King's "The Toast: An Heroick Poem" (1747) and Christopher Anstey's *New Bath Guide* (1766), both of which remained popular well into the nineteenth century. In "The Toast," King describes the sun god Apollo, hungover from too much to drink the night before. His horses are ready to fly more rapid than eagles, but red-eyed Apollo is not:

> ... so swift are the coursers, they think it mere play,
> Or a breathing, to measure the globe in a day. . . .
> Made to prance and curvet with so martial a grace,
> Yet [he's] unable to move half an inch from his place

Rising at last, taking the reins, still hungover,

> In his mounting, what grace! in his driving, what skill!
> Nor his horses he spar'd, tho' the way was uphill;
> Never stopping to kiss a young wife, or to drink;
> Never whistling or swearing—because he can't think.
> As he urg'd on his stage, he revolv'd in his mind
> All the toasts of last night, how his own was defin'd . . . [lines 61–82]

Christopher Anstey's *New Bath Guide* is a collection of verse epistles in which a wickedly funny narrator mocks English high society, poking irreverent fun at lifestyles of the rich, famous, and naughty. Unabashedly influenced by William King's "The Toast," Anstey's work was original enough to make it a runaway bestseller in Britain. Here's Epistle 6:

> This morning, dear mother, as soon as 'twas light,
> I was wak'd by a noise that astonish'd me quite,
> For in Tabitha's chamber I heard such a clatter,
> I could not conceive what the deuce was the matter.
> And, would you believe it, I went up and found her
> In a blanket with two lusty fellows around her . . . [lines 1–6]

King's inebriated anapestic lampoons and Anstey's bawdy anapestic epistles were many times reprinted and widely imitated. Directly or indirectly, for better or worse, "The Night Before Christmas" owes some of its bounce to "The Toast" and the *The New Bath Guide:* the author of "A Visit," whoever that may be, is writing in the King-Anstey tradition. Would Professor Moore, a Bible professor, read such stuff? It's not unthinkable. Moore detested profane literature, but he also thought it his bounden duty, as a faculty member of the General Theological Seminary, to keep close watch on the subverters of public morals, such as Thomas Jefferson. The English poets King and Anstey were probably men to be watched, though dead, if only because college students thought that "The Toast" and *The New Bath Guide* were pretty darn funny.

But would Professor Moore then imitate King and Anstey when writing a Christmas poem addressed to his own impressionable children? Probably not, or at least not consciously. In 1806, in his second publication (following that unprovoked first strike on Thomas Jefferson), Moore condemned the "depraved taste in poetry" of those who read anapestic satire, together with every "bawd of licentiousness" who writes it. Moore at age twenty-five fairly wept over "the influence which nonsensical and immodest verses may have upon the community." According to Moore, poetry ought not to be tolerated at all "if it possess no other recommendation than the glow of its expressions and the tinkling of its syllables, or the wanton allurement of the ideas that it conveys."[51]

Major Henry Livingston Jr. was a religious man as well (Dutch Reformed, not Episcopal). He, too, was a devoted and conscientious father. Would *he* read and imitate another poet's profane anapestic epistles? Yes. Every Christmas, and in between. One of his earliest poems, "Mistress Van Kleeck's Tenant's Letter," is an epistle ostensibly addressed to Major Henry's sister Cornelia (1750–1810), wife of Myndert Van Kleeck. In the Major's Christmas poem, the Van Kleecks' tenant farmer begs to be excused for not making his scheduled payment of three Yuletide hogs:

> My very good landlady, Mistress Van Kleeck,
> (For the tears that o'erwhelm me I scarcely can speak!):
> I know that I promis'd you hogs two or three—

But who knows his destiny? Certain not me!
That I promis'd three hogs, I don't mean to deny—
I can prove that I had five or six upon sty!
Three *hogs* did I say? Three *sows,* I say then—
'Pon honour, I ne'er had a *male* upon pen!

Well, Madam, the long and the short of the clatter
(For mumbling and mincing will not better the matter,
And "Murder and truth," my dear Mammy would say,
"By some means or other, forever [see] day";
And Daddy himself, as we chopp'd in the wood,
Would often observe that "Lying's not good—
Tell truth, my sweet fellow, no matter who feels it!
It ne'er can do hurt to the man who reveals it!")

But stop! While my Daddy and Mammy's the subject,
I am running aside the original object—
The sows, my sweet madam, the *sows,* I repeat,
Which you and your household expected to eat,
Instead of attending their corn and their swill,
Gave way to an ugly *he-sow's* wicked will!
When 'twill end, your good ladyship need not be told,
—For Nature is still as she hath been of old,
And when he cries, "Yes!" mortal may not cry "No!"
So Madam, farewell!—with my holiday bow.[52]

Livingston wrote "Mistress Van Kleeck's Tenant's Letter" about December 1787, thirty-six years before "A Visit from St. Nicholas" made its debut in the *Troy Sentinel,* when Clement Moore was still a young boy. In this and similar epistles written over a fifty-year spread, Livingston appears well familiar with the anapestic satires of Anstey and King. So, too, does the author of "The Night Before Christmas." Clement Clarke Moore does not. In fact, Moore's one undisputed anapestic poem—"The Pig and the Rooster"—appears to have been modeled on the anapestic animal fables of Henry Livingston.

Or take the simple word *all*—which can be used either as a pronoun, to mean *every* person or *every* thing ("All of the children were snug") or as an adverb, to mean *totally* ("The child was all snug"). Most writers use *all* as a pronoun more often than as an adverb, but the "Christmas" poet does not. In the poem's first line, it's "all through the house" (not *throughout*). In line 5 he writes, "all snug in their beds" (not *snugly* or *quite snug* or *so snug*). These examples are followed in turn by "dressed all in fur" and "all tarnished." That's a lot of adverbial "all" for one short poem. Against those four adverbs are five pronouns: "dash away *all*," "fill'd *all* the stockings," "*all* flew," "Happy Christmas to *all* and to *all* a good night." Vintage Henry: in Livingston's early verse, and in Livingston's late verse, and in his verse in between, the pronouns and adverbs are about evenly divided. In Moore's poetry, the pronouns outnumber the adverbs 10 to 1 (and in Moore's prose, by more than 100 to 1). Henry writes "all along," "all blithe," "all blue," "all craggy," "all defenseless," "all delightful," "all early," "all flaming," "all forlorn," "all-hid," "all keen," all this or that, all through the alphabet.

It's worth tracing the history of this quaint phrase, "all snug"— which is as common today as "Tuck me in!" but less familiar in the days of Livingston and Moore. By writing "all snug," the author of "The Night Before Christmas" was using an idiom more common in Scotland and Ireland than in England or America. Turning to the *Oxford English Dictionary,* one learns that "all snug" or "right snug" at first meant *all tidy,* the earliest recorded instance of which is in 1725, in Allan Ramsay's *Gentle Shepherd:* "He kames his hair, indeed, and gaes right snug." Great Scot! Allan Ramsay was one of Henry Livingston's favorite poets. The Major even performed Ramsay's poems, set to music, on his flute and violin.[53]

The *Oxford English Dictionary* reports that "snug" later came to mean not only *tidy* (as in Ramsay) but *cozy* or *comfortable*. As the earliest instance of "snug" for *cozy*, the *OED* cites Christopher Anstey, *The New Bath Guide* (1766), a poem already identified as a major influence on both Henry Livingston and on the author of "A Visit from St. Nicholas" (see *OED*, "snug," ad. 1, ad. 2.). For additional examples, I turned to Literature Online—an archive described by the publisher as a "fully searchable library of more than 260,000 works of English and American poetry, drama, and prose"—and found that the second earliest instance of "all snug" appears in John O'Keeffe's libretto *The Highland Reel* (1789). That's of interest as well: the two latest items in Henry Livingston's music book (1776–1784) are from John O'Keeffe ("Amo Amas," and "Can I declare" [1784], p. 52). Henry Livingston and the author of "The Night Before Christmas" display remarkably similar reading habits.

Henry Livingston is not the only poet who might have written "all snug." In 1801, Matthew Lewis published his *Tales of Terror,* a book of scary bedtime stories for children, one of which is called "The Wolf-King; or, Little Red-Riding-Hood," in which a big, bad wolf-king dons Grandma's nightcap and gets "all snug" in her bed while hoping that the plump little gal in the red suit will soon be there.[54] The same early-American dad who wrote "The Night Before Christmas" for his children quite possibly read to them in 1808 from Lewis's *Tales of Terror.* No one poet had a monopoly on such phrases. But Henry Livingston and the "Christmas" poet not only adopted the same words and phrasing; their respective poems were indebted, directly or indirectly, to the identical poets (including, I think, Allan Ramsay, Michael Drayton, Christopher Anstey, William King, John O'Keeffe, and Matthew Lewis, none of them poets who influenced Clement Moore).

Of all the poems and letters and magazine articles that Henry Livingston wrote during his eighty years on the planet, the earliest to survive begins with the greeting "A happy Christmas to my dear Sally

Welles." "A Visit from St. Nicholas" ends with the greeting "Happy Christmas to all." One might guess that a "happy" Christmas, which today sounds quite ordinary, was as commonplace in Livingston's time as a "merry" Christmas, but the guess would be wrong. Literature Online, for example, locates the earliest "Happy Christmas" in 1823 in a little poem beginning " 'Twas the night before Christmas...."[55] A broader survey of English and American literature, from 1390 ("murie Cristes masse") through the Christmas of 1823, shows that "Merry Christmas" was commonplace and "Happy Christmas" rare. Charles Fenno Hoffman, who ascribed the poem to Moore, changed "Christmas" to "New Year" at lines 1 and 56.[56] Other editors changed the last line of "A Visit" to read "Merry Christmas to all...."[57] Many later editors followed suit, as if "Happy Christmas" were a mistake. But a "Happy Christmas!" sounded just fine to Henry Livingston.

Whether Clement Moore preferred a "Merry Christmas" or a "Happy Christmas" cannot be determined. From what I've seen of his extant writing in verse and prose, including personal correspondence, Moore never said "Happy Christmas" (or "Merry Christmas") to anyone.

"The Night Before Christmas" is as different from Moore's other children's verse as Christmas cookies from steamed spinach. The 1844 *Poems* includes three other poems (besides "Christmas") addressed to Moore's children. In one, he urges his little ones to look on his portrait and remember him after he lies mould'ring in the tomb. In the second, he urges the children to look on the freshly fallen snow and remember that they, too, and their transient joys, must perish from the earth. In "The Pig and the Rooster," written about 1833, Moore allegorizes a "conceited young rooster" and a "lazy young pig" (a fashion-monger and a wine-bibbing glutton), and a "counselor owl" (who despises them both).[58] Moore's supporters always point to the form of this anapestic "Pig and Rooster" fable as evidence that the Professor really *was* capable of writing a children's poem like "A Visit from St. Nicholas." Major Livingston's heirs point to the content as evidence that he couldn't have. Major Livingston's heirs are right.

SANTA'S REINDEER

"All I need is a reindeer . . ."
The Grinch looked around.
But, since reindeer are scarce, there was none to be found.
　　　　　　　　—DR. SEUSS, *HOW THE GRINCH STOLE CHRISTMAS*

Clement Clarke Moore reports that "The Night Before Christmas" was written in 1822, and there may yet be nine reasons to believe him, to wit: his mode of entry—coming down through the chimney—and eight reindeer: Dasher, Dancer, Prancer, Vixen, Comet, Cupid, Donder, and Blitzen. At least two of Major Henry's children said that their father wrote "The Night Before Christmas" in 1808, yet it has appeared to past researchers that "A Visit from St. Nicholas" cannot be that early. In 1813, Samuel Wood published *False Stories Corrected,* in which a teenaged polemicist warned New York parents not to share with children the "improper idea" that "Old Santaclaw has come down [the] Chimney in the night" to fill their stockings. That is the first recorded reference to Santa as an elf-sized saint who comes down with a bound through the chimney. And doesn't that prove that *False Stories Corrected* came before "A Visit from St. Nicholas"?

Eight years later, William Gilley, another New York bookseller and a friend of Clement Moore's, published *A New-Year's Present to the Little Ones from Five to Twelve* (third in a series of booklets called *The Children's Friend*). Gilley's 1821 paperback contains just one poem, a didactic parable beginning "Old Santeclaus with much delight / His reindeer drives this frosty night. . . ."[59] The first of eight color engravings is a sketch of old Santeclaus on a city rooftop covered with snow. In the background is a cathedral spire. Santa sits in a sleigh pulled by a leaping reindeer. Everything else in *A New-Year's Present to the Little Ones* can be found in the earlier literature, but the reindeer was new, entirely original, quirky, and quintessentially American, a newly coined myth for a society where ancient national traditions were all jumbled together, as in "A Visit from St. Nicholas" with its mishmash of fairy lore, religious tradition, and Norse mythology.

In academic and journalistic accounts of Santa's reindeer it has been a commonplace to observe that Moore (or whoever) borrowed the reindeer idea from Gilley's 1821 children's book. As Santa's historian, Charles Jones, has said, "Moore knew how to multiply; he was perfectly capable of turning one deer into eight . . ."[60] It's not so easy as that. Moore could multiply one reindeer into eight, but from whom did the dull wit who wrote Gilley's "Old Santeclaus" poem acquire the original reindeer in 1821? Probably from Henry Livingston.

The sky, in Major Henry's imagination, is a busy place. As in "A Visit," where reindeer like dry leaves "mount to the sky," Livingston writes of children and souls and storms and even lambkins who mount "to the sky," or "to the skies," or "to the bright empire of the sky"; of Oberon, King of the Fairies, whose carriage is a nutshell pulled by a team of katydids; of a handsome white-stocking'd colt who "moves as if he danced on air." In Major Henry's verse and prose, whales gambol above the waves, boats fly, angels hover, kittens bound, gnats flit, dancers float. Even his dinosaurs can mount to the sky. When the bones of a "gigantic quadruped" were discovered in Ulster County's Little Britain in 1783, the locals were awestruck by the awesome majesty of God. Henry was struck by the majesty of the dinosaur. In a short story for *New York Magazine* two hundred years before *Jurassic Park,* Livingston imagines one of these ancient monsters hiding out in the American wilderness, devouring men, flattening villages, ascending to the bluest summit, and leaping over the waves of the west at a bound.[61]

Major Henry's interests extended beyond paleontology and aeronautics. As Dutchess County's local expert on the Arctic, Livingston wrote of northern cultures around the world, from Labrador to Norway to Russia to Siberia, borrowing elsewhere from books that provide accounts of Scandinavian elves, of Lapland reindeers, and of the Norse god Thor, whose chariot was said to have been pulled by airborne "He-Goats."[62] By combining the pipe-smoking Dutchmen of the Hudson Valley with the reindeer of Lapland and the flying goats of Norwegian mythology, our Christmas poet created an American original. Santa has traveled by reindeer-drawn sleigh ever since.

But there's another oddity about the reindeer: Whenever a jolly Dutch burgher and his Dutchess were startled or angry or delighted, the oath "Dunder and Blixem!" would escape their lips ("Thunder and lightning!")—not "Donder and Blitzen."[63] Dutch fondness for this ancient oath was proverbial—but in English and American literary texts earlier than 1836, it's always "Blixem" (or "Blixim" or "Blixum"; in modern Dutch, *Bliksem*). The only recorded instance of "Blitzen" earlier than 1836 is in Sir Walter Scott's novel *Guy Mannering,* first published in America in 1815: Sir Walter, who was no Dutchman, has eight instances of the German "Blitzen!"—each mistaken instance being placed in the mouths of dunderheaded Dutchmen. But Henry Livingston, who was three-quarters New York Dutch and a resident of the Hudson Valley, could not have made such a mistake.

I asked Mary Van Deusen, on whose indefatigable research skills I still depended, to find me a photo-facsimile of the 1823 text of "A Visit from St. Nicholas." I had a hunch that the text did not say "Donder and Blitzen." If it did, we had a problem. Mary was able in a few days time to locate a copy of the original *Troy Sentinel* text, which she sent me in facsimile, via the Internet:

> Now! Dasher, now! Dancer, now! Prancer, and Vixen,
> On! Comet, on! Cupid, on! Dunder and Blixem;

Dunder and Blixem! Orville Holley, editor of the *Troy Sentinel,* got it right.

Holley also got something else right that was thought by later editors to be wrong: the 1823 *Sentinel* text has odd, offbeat punctuation of Santa's giddyap to the reindeer: "Now! Dasher, now! Dancer, now! Prancer, and Vixen, / On! Comet, on! Cupid, on!" (etc.). Early editors weren't sure what to do with that. Mr. Holley left it alone.

The next several editors followed Holley's lead, but successors tinkered with the exclamation points, trying to fix the rhythm; and Holley himself, when he reprinted "A Visit" in 1829, emended the original printed text to read, "Now, Dasher! now, Dancer! now, Prancer! now Vixen! / On, Comet! on, Cupid! on," (etc.).[64] When Clement Moore reprinted "A Visit" in his 1844 *Poems,* he used the standardized punctuation. Modern editors have followed suit, blaming the misplaced exclamation points on Miss Harriet Butler, whom legend credits as the source for the 1823 *Sentinel* text.

Interestingly, Henry Livingston had the same odd practice of peppering his verse with offbeat exclamation marks that interrupt the *da-da-DUM* meter: "And happy—thrice happy! Too happy! the swain / Who can replace the pin or bandana again . . ."[65] Even in his prose Henry puts exclamation points where you don't quite expect them. As a young man, he writes of human existence that our "business is Praise! & Love! the unremitting theme" (1784). Forty years later, aged seventy-eight, he still registers that old exuberance: "Dear, Dearest! son! . . ." (1826).[66] Miss Harriet Butler should not be blamed for the punctuation of the original 1823 *Troy Sentinel* text.

Early reprints of "A Visit" follow the *Sentinel*'s text verbatim. The first major interventions were made by Charles Fenno Hoffman, who in 1837 ascribed the poem to Clement Clarke Moore: Hoffman changed "Blixem" to "Blixen," for a perfect rhyme, and "Dunder" to "Donder," and tinkered with the exclamation points.[67] When Hoffman's text was reprinted in *The Rover,* the hapless printer introduced still another little change—"Now, Dasher! now, Dancer! now, Prancer! now, Nixen! . . ."[68] "Nixen" was a printer's error. But the change from "Blixem" to "Blixen" was a deliberate sophistication by which Hoffman fixed an off-rhyme and corrupted the original author's perfectly correct Dutch.

To the eyes of Clement Clarke Moore, who knew German but not Dutch, neither "Blixem" nor "Blixen" looked right. Reprinting "A Visit from St. Nicholas" with his 1844 *Poems,* Moore called the eighth reindeer "Blitzen":

> Now, Dasher! now, Dancer! now, Prancer and Vixen!
> On, Comet! on, Cupid! on, Donder and Blitzen!

In 1856, and again in 1862, Professor Moore copied out the text of "A Visit from St. Nicholas," signed it, and distributed these autographed copies as gifts (one of which recently sold at a Christie's auction for $255,000). One of the Professor's biographers, Samuel Patterson, describes these autographed copies of 1856 and 1862 as "irrefragable proof that Clement Clarke Moore composed the poem,"[69] but in fact these autographed manuscripts indicate that Clement Clarke Moore did not know the original names of his own Dutch reindeer. In the manuscript copies, as in the printed *Poems,* Moore makes the same telltale error, writing "Donder and Blitzen," not suspecting that Saint Nick is a Dutchman who says "Dunder!" and "Blixem!" Moore's corrupt "Blitzen" is one more indication that he stole "Christmas"—Santa Claus, sleigh, reindeer, and all—from a portly rubicund Dutchman named Henry Livingston.

When the evidence is laid out on the table, one cannot help but wonder how "A Visit from St. Nicholas" ever came to be associated with an old curmudgeon like Clement Clarke Moore in the first place. I think I know.

A HOLIDAY TRIFLE

> The plodding after mere words, and the investigation of minute verbal distinctions, must have a tendency to lower the tone of the mind and to cloud the fancy, to draw the thoughts away from what is noble and elevated, and to turn them upon things comparatively low and trifling.
>
> —CLEMENT CLARKE MOORE, "LECTURE" (14 NOVEMBER 1825)[70]

It is everywhere reported that Professor Moore, when writing "The Night Before Christmas," was inspired by "Old Santeclaus," the anonymous poem featured in Gilley's *New-Year's Present to the Little Ones,* the 1821 children's book containing a sketch of Santa in a one-reindeer sleigh. Another possibility, and a better one, is that Mr. Moore *wrote* "Old Santeclaus." In fact, if "Old Santeclaus" was not written by the original Grinch, Professor Clement Clarke Moore himself, then call me "Rudolph" and never let me play in reindeer games.

Old SANTECLAUS with much delight
His reindeer drives this frosty night,
O'er chimney-tops, and tracks of snow,
To bring his yearly gifts to you.

The steady friend of virtuous youth,
The friend of duty, and of truth,
Each Christmas eve he joys to come
Where love and peace have made their home.

Through many houses he has been,
And various beds and stockings seen;
Some, white as snow, and neatly mended,
Others, that seemed for pigs intended.

Where e'er I found good girls or boys,
That hated quarrels, strife and noise,
I left an apple, or a tart,
Or wooden gun, or painted cart.

To some I gave a pretty doll,
To some a peg-top, or a ball;
No crackers, cannons, squibs, or rockets,
To blow their eyes up, or their pockets.

No drums to stun their Mother's ear,
Nor swords to make their sisters fear;

> But pretty books to store their mind
> With knowledge of each various kind.
>
> But where I found the children naughty,
> In manners rude, in temper haughty,
> Thankless to parents, liars, swearers,
> Boxers, or cheats, or base tale-bearers,
>
> I left a long, black, birchen rod,
> Such as the dread command of God
> Directs a Parent's hand to use
> When virtue's path his sons refuse.[71]

The imagination, for Clement Moore, is a place "Where all things strange and monstrous make their home." A good family, for the "Old Santeclaus" poet, is one "Where love and peace have made their home." Like Clement Moore, the "Santeclaus" poet writes "Mother," not "Mama." Moore asks, "Why should not we store our minds . . . ?"; the "Santeclaus" poet writes of "pretty books to store their mind." Both poets agree that books are for boys, not girls. Moore complains obsessively of "bustle, noise, and rout," "playful strife and noise," "the strife, the tumult, and the noise," "bustle, heat, and noise" (etc.); the "Santeclaus" poet writes that "good girls or boys" are those who have "hated quarrels, strife, and noise." Moore's poetry, like "Old Santeclaus," denounces rude boys and pigs.

When not recycling descriptive phrases picked up from his reading, Clement Moore quickly runs out of modifiers and settles for "various," his favorite original adjective. Moore in the *Poems* employs "various" to denote "sounds," "nations," "arts," "gleam," "parts," "notes," "stimulants," "quality of mind." The author of "Santeclaus" writes of "various beds" and "knowledge of each various kind." Moore loves to use the passive form *seen,* especially at the end of a verse line ("Reflected images are seen," "The muses and the loves were seen," "Dissolve away, or just be seen," "And bids retiring worth be seen.") The "Santeclaus" poet has "And various beds and stockings seen."

In Moore's *Poems* one finds "*long,* black boots" and "a *birchen rod,*" and in "Santeclaus," "a *long, black birchen rod.*" Moore writes of "Jove's *dread command,*" while the "Santeclaus" poet writes of "the *dread command* of God." This one word, *dread,* is hardly unique to Clement Moore—it appears also in "The Night Before Christmas" ("I had nothing to dread") and several times in the writings of Henry Livingston—but "dread," in Moore's verse as in "Santeclaus," is spiritually useful. Clement Moore is big on dread, it's his specialty: "holy dread," "secret dread," "need to dread," "dreaded shoal," "dread pestilence," "unwonted dread," "pleasures dread," "dread to look," "dreaded weight," "dreadful thought," "deeper dread," "dreadful harbingers of death," "dread futurity." (The last, "dread futurity," was stolen from Livingston's kinsman Timothy Dwight, and just goes to show Professor Moore never saw a phrase with "dread" in it that he didn't like.) "Dread," for Moore, is the sinner's ticket to salvation, the child's motivation to be good.

That Clement Moore was well familiar with the "Santeclaus" poem in this 1821 *New-Year's Present to the Little Ones,* and with the bookseller William Gilley, is old news.[72] But if Professor Moore was one of Gilley's best customers, he may also have been one of Gilley's authors. That 1821 Santeclaus poem has the Professor's stylistic fingerprints all over it. Giving credit where credit is due, I think Moore may be credited with having written one of America's first Santa Claus poems—not "A Visit from St. Nicholas," but "Old Santeclaus." Somewhere along the line, perhaps as early as 1829, Moore's name became associated with the wrong Santa poem. There are a number of sources from whom Charles Fenno Hoffman might have obtained his bad information, including his uncle Gulian Verplanck, or Moore himself. But by the time anyone thought to ask Hoffman why he thought Clement Moore wrote "The Night Before Christmas," it was too late to get a straight answer. At the height of his career as a distinguished literary critic, Mr. Hoffman suffered a breakdown and spent the last thirty-five years of his life in a mental asylum.

"MY LYRE, A BIRCHEN ROD..."

But, you know, that old Grinch was so smart and so slick
He thought up a lie, and he thought it up quick!

—DR. SEUSS, *HOW THE GRINCH STOLE CHRISTMAS*

Casimir Moore in 1920 argued that if Henry Livingston wrote "The Night Before Christmas," then his grandfather Clement Clarke Moore "lived a lie his entire life"; but Casimir insists that his granddad did not lie and "never was caught in one."[73] If that's correct—if Professor Moore lived for eighty-four years without ever telling even a little white one, then he's unlikely to be caught in a fib more than a century after his death; but it may be worth examining the Professor's record if only to rid ourselves of doubt on that point.

In 1823, when "A Visit" was printed anonymously, Moore felt "regret and chagrin" that his trifle had come to light.[74] In 1836, when Hoffman reprinted the poem with Moore's name on it, the incident must have really popped his cork. But he said nothing. For the next seven years, Moore allowed the attribution to be widely reprinted, even in national magazines, without issuing a correction. In the meantime, the "Christmas piece" made him more famous than anything he had ever done, said, thought, or written, and readers of all ages loved him for it.[75] In the Christmas season of 1843–1844, his own daughters begged him to publish his *Poems* for posterity, especially "The Night Before Christmas." No other claimant had surfaced, or at least none that could be taken seriously.

A document preserved in the New-York Historical Society indicates what happened next. On February 23, 1844, Clement Moore wrote to Norman Tuttle, former owner of the now-defunct *Troy Sentinel,* with a discreet inquiry: could Mr. Tuttle please account for the provenance of "A Visit from St. Nicholas"?—how and from whom did Tuttle obtain his copy text back in 1823? In a prompt reply, dated February 26, Tuttle informed the Professor that Orville Holley received his 1823 text from Mrs. Sackett, wife of Daniel Sackett, a Troy merchant. (So much for Pelletreau's 1886 Harriet Butler story!) Tuttle further assures the Professor that it was not until much later that he and Mr. Holley learned the poem was Moore's.[76]

The coast was clear. Twenty-one years after that first publication of "A Visit," Henry Livingston, Mrs. Sackett, and Moore's own wife were dead. Tuttle believed the hearsay that the poem was written by Professor Moore. Having now no compelling grounds on which to exclude "A Visit from St. Nicholas" from his forthcoming edition of collected *Poems,* and no one who was likely to contradict him, Professor Moore followed the flow:

Dear Children:

In compliance with your wishes, I here present you with a volume of verses, written by me at different periods of my life. . . .

Dedicating his *Poems* to the children, Moore dates his prefatory epistle March 1844, only a few days or weeks after receiving the all clear from Mr. Tuttle. In his dedication Moore apologizes to the children for having included, together with his "severe or sarcastic" verse, a few poor trifles (e.g., "A Visit from St. Nicholas") but "such things have been often found by me," writes Moore, "to afford greater pleasure than what was by myself esteemed of more worth."[77] "Found," indeed!

Moore entitled his volume *Poems.* Of the thirty-seven printed, only thirty-two are actually his (or thirty-three, if you count "Christmas"). The volume contains one poem by Moore's friend William Bard (urging Moore to temper his poetic fury), another by the former New York mayor Philip Hone (a thank-you note, in verse, for a gift of flowers); these are printed as replies to two of Moore's own verses. Also included are two poems by Eliza Moore, the poet's late wife. Moore does not claim to have written these auxiliary items—all four are scrupulously attributed, both in the text itself and in the table of contents. "A Visit from St. Nicholas," the single most famous poem in the collection, appears without fanfare or introductory note on pages 124–128.

In his letter of dedication to the children, Moore remarks that he has presented his poems in a muddle because he cannot remember how or when they came to be written.[78] That may be a little disingenuous. All are easily datable and most were, in fact, already dated, either in manuscript copies in Moore's own hand or in authorized publications since 1804. (Some of those previously published poems had the dates right in the title; Moore changed the titles, deleting the dates.)

One well-kept secret—unknown, evidently, even to the Professor's many biographers—is that Clement Moore as a young bachelor published many of his poems under the pseudonym "L."[79] In 1844, when publishing his collected *Poems* under his own name, not under his youthful pseudonym, the Professor must have been disappointed in the response: reviews of his *Poems* ranged from sarcasm to tepid praise. But one reviewer, writing for *The Churchman,* the magazine of the Protestant Episcopal Church of America, gave Clement Moore's *Poems* a ringing endorsement, a review suitable for framing.[80] I don't know for sure who wrote it, but the author of that flattering *Churchman* blurb signs himself "L." Perhaps the old Professor wasn't humorless after all. Perhaps he even wrote his own book review.

BAAH, HUMBUG

> *Little lamb, who made thee?*
> *Dost thou know who made thee?*
>
> —WILLIAM BLAKE, *SONGS OF INNOCENCE*

As a trustee of the New-York Historical Society Library, Clement Clarke Moore contributed manuscript copies of his verse, and a few books, to the Society's collections, inscribing each with an autograph note to record the gift for posterity. One of these gifts—a book called *A Complete Treatise on Merinos and Other Sheep* (1811)—is more interesting than its title page suggests.

About the turn of the nineteenth century, Major Henry's wealthy cousin Robert L. Livingston imported from Spain a flock of Merino sheep. In 1809 he published a book called *An Essay on Sheep . . . An Account of the Merinos of Spain.*[81] Two years later, New York's Economical Office School published a book with a similar title, *A Complete Treatise on Merinos and Other Sheep.* This was an unabridged English translation of a manual by the French veterinarian Alexandre Henry Tessier—and it was this volume, not Robert Livingston's, that Professor Moore later donated to the New-York Historical Society.[82] *A Complete Treatise* on Merino sheep may seem like an odd volume to be owned by a Manhattan Bible scholar. Moore's biographer Samuel Patterson suggests that the Professor may have raised sheep at Chelsea, his Manhattan estate (it was big enough to do that, and Moore owned human slaves who might well have kept watch over his flocks by night). But the Professor kept remarkably thorough financial records, from which there is no indication that he kept any livestock except for carriage horses. I doubt that Professor Moore ever came closer to a Merino sheep than roast mutton or woolen underwear.

Autographing his gift of the *Complete Treatise,* Moore includes a handwritten note explaining how he happened to possess such a curious volume: he was himself the anonymous translator! The title page announces that the *Complete Treatise* has been "Translated from the French"—to which Moore adds, in his own hand, "by Clement C. Moore." The Professor donated this trifle to the Historical Society Library as a sample of his original work in French–English translation—a text not previously recognized as his own production, but there it was.

Before inscribing the volume, Professor Moore ought to have read the book from cover to cover. At the back of the *Complete Treatise* is an appendix, the last page of which contains a copyright note easily missed, disclosing the inconvenient information that Francis Durand, who applied for copyright on November 30, 1811, is also the book's sole translator. In presenting this charitable donation to the New-York Historical Society Library, Professor Moore does not just recycle a few borrowed phrases, as in his poetry—he lays claim to an entire book that was the work of another man. John Pintard, founder of the New-York Historical Society, said it best: *Eheu!* Professor!

AULD LANG SYNE

Hail home! sacred home! to my soul ever dear;
Abroad may be wonders but rapture is here.
My future ambition will never soar higher
Than the clean-brushèd hearth and convivial fire . . .
On your patience to trespass, no longer I dare
So, bowing, I wish you a Happy New Year

—HENRY LIVINGSTON, *NEW YEAR'S CARRIER'S ADDRESS* (1819)[83]

The last three documents to have survived from Henry Livingston's pen are two poems of farewell and a Christmas letter. In an original lyric to the old Scots tune "Scots Wha Hae Wie Wallace Bled," penned in the autumn of 1827, Livingston speaks of himself as a poet in the tradition of Thompson, Ramsay, and Burns. He closes, "But, useless now my broken shell, / I bid the land of cares farewell, / Oppressèd with the lapse of time, / I faintly dream of Auld Lang Syne."[84] The Major's other farewell poem, addressed to his daughter Jane, is a hymn of joy, each four-line stanza beginning "I love" ("I love on pity's wing to fly / To soothe the deep-expiring sigh"; "I love to view domestic bliss"; "I love the morning's roseate ray, / I bless the glorious march of day"; "I love the night"; "I love to read"; "I love my feeble voice to raise / In humble prayer and ardent praise. . . ." An old man now, knowing that his days are numbered, Major Henry believes that his love for the world will last forever. He imagines himself on his dying day mounting up, up to the sky, "Where reigns the Eternal Source of Love."[85]

Livingston's last farewell is a Christmas letter addressed to "Dear Son Charles! Dear daughter Eliza! our much respected friend, Mrs. Brewer!" Writing now in a shaky hand, having only a few weeks of life left in him, the Major rejoices over the construction of the Ohio Canal and of the Hudson and Delaware Canal, engineering projects that will bring people together. Old Henry reports on the weather (getting milder, not so cold and wet) and mentions his health (it's just "a small cold"). He does not say: "Charles and Eliza, I'm dying. I wish I could see you again." His last words are "put a few sleighs in requisition. . . ." The letter then breaks off, unsigned, being completed by Henry's daughter Susan, who writes of the recent "Thanksgiving" festivities on Saint Nicholas Day, December 6. As usual the Livingston house was filled with guests, a few of whom stayed on—and then it *snowed!* Susan writes, "We have had pretty gay times, I tell you— 4 horse sleigh, and bells to fly!"[86]

On January 16, the *Poughkeepsie Journal* published a corrupt text of "A Visit from St. Nicholas or Santa Claus," ascribed to no one; and on February 29, Henry slipped away. He was buried by the wife and children and friends he loved, beneath a grove of locust trees he loved, beside the river he loved. An obituary in the *Journal*, unsigned, describes him as "a great lover of the fine arts, and particularly fond of poetry and painting. His best qualities, however, shone in the domestic circle, over which his tender feelings, his warm affections, and his sprightly and instructive conversation shed uncommon interest and loveliness."[87] Sixteen years later, a wealthy stranger, a scholar named Clement Clarke Moore, would lay claim to "A Visit from St. Nicholas." No matter. Henry Livingston gave to his children, and neighbors and friends and readers, much that could not be taken away. Compared to such an extraordinary life, "A Visit from St. Nicholas" is indeed a "trifle," just as Dr. Clement Clarke Moore had said it was. Henry Livingston was the spirit of Christmas itself.

Epilogue: After Words

ICING IT

> You cannot eat your cake and have it too.
>
> —JOHN KEATS, "TWO SONNETS ON FAME" (CA. 1800)

> [O]ur civilization is . . . persuading itself that it can find some means which nature will tolerate, whereby *we may eat our cake and have it;* and it strongly resents the stubborn fact that there is no such means.
>
> —ALBERT JAY NOCK, "OUR ENEMY, THE STATE" (1935)

> We will be sacrificing some of the materialistic benefits of technology, but there just isn't any other way. *We can't eat our cake and have it too.*
>
> —THEODORE KACZYNSKI, UNPUBLISHED LETTER TO
> *SATURDAY REVIEW* (1971)

> As for the negative consequences of eliminating industrial society, well, *you can't eat your cake and have it too.* To gain one thing you have to sacrifice another.
>
> —"FC" (TED KACZYNSKI), THE UNABOM MANIFESTO (1995)[1]

June 22, 2000. I write these words on my fiftieth birthday, a hasty epilogue to my *Author Unknown,* written at the last minute before e-mailing the typescript to my editor to be vetted for book production. I am finishing the project on the fly, just the way I've done everything else for the past four years, always in a race against deadlines.

Gwen and the boys have made me a cake, decorated as a book. After dinner they will make me stop working long enough to celebrate, to open presents and their homemade birthday cards, and to blow out the candles. The cake is a sweet present and it reminds me of what I owe them—the time these adventures have taken away from our lives together. My sons, who finished their high school classes only yesterday, want me to go Rollerblading with them on the Vassar College campus. Eric, fourteen, dangles his in-line skates before me, urging me to turn off the computer and join their fun. Blake, seventeen, tries subtler subversions, quoting a little Shakespeare at me: "Dost thou think, because thou art virtuous, there shall be no more cakes and ale?" Later, boys, I'm on the homestretch.

They have accomplished at least part of their mission: I feel terrible about continuing to work. I am reminded of Ted Kaczynski's 1971 condemnation of scholarly research as an enterprise that devours the cake of "privacy and freedom." Ted may have been on to something there. The attributions I have been able to make have helped make cases and convictions, eliminated suspects and exposed frauds; but they have also brought me media exposure, which for a scholar can be wonderful or disruptive, depending. I have grown accustomed to the daily pleas for assistance with questioned documents, the phone calls from reporters looking for a scoop, the constant barrage of e-mail—in one recent year, thirteen thousand messages were addressed to my Vassar account, more than I could read or acknowledge. There have been moments of weariness in which I have allowed the exposure to disrupt not just my work and family life but the caution and objectivity that every true scholar seeks to embody.

I was once anonymous myself, unknown except to my family and friends, students and colleagues (and the occasional demented Shakespeare correspondent), comfortable in a profession where the most excitement was a robust exchange with other scholars in my field who shared my research interests or damned my conclusions. One day I was bicycling to class, and the next analyzing Ted Kaczynski's Luddite manifesto for the United States government and opening my own mail more carefully. I am the furthest professor from Indiana Jones you could find—even at Vassar—yet my time between classes is often spent with the secret writings of killers and scoundrels. I have had a ride—part dream, part nightmare—through worlds Shakespeare wrote about but few of us ever encounter outside the theater. I'm ready now to get off the roller coaster if the machinery would just stop long enough for me to climb out.

AN ODYSSEY

I used to be numbered without fail among the pilgrims attending the annual meeting of the Shakespeare Association of America. When the conference fell on Gwen's April 11 birthday, we made accommodations. The SAA conference was an event I thought I couldn't miss. I missed it in 1997, though I did not miss it very much. One day in March, just before my trip to Boulder for the JonBenét Ramsey case, a month before the SAA meeting in Washington, D.C., a student stopped by my house to talk about his planned trip to Greece. My older son, Blake, then fourteen, overheard us talking. Blake had studied ancient Greece in school that year. When the student left, Blake spoke up and said, "I'd like to go there."

Gwen looked at me and saw a very tired and tense person. She knew I needed a break, that I was running out of steam. She said: "I think that's a great idea." I had already committed myself to participation in an SAA forum on literary attribution, but excused myself. In April, while other Shakespeare scholars met in the capital to discuss "A Funeral Elegy" and attributional theory and methodology, Blake and I toured Greece, hiked Olympus and the cliffs of Meteora, visited the Acropolis, shopped in the agora, and chowed down on souvlaki.

One day, on the island of Aegina, we rented a motorcycle and rode east to admire the temple of Aphaia, then stopped on our return trip to explore the ruins of Paleohora, a town that served as the island's capital until 1826, now desolate but beautiful, set high on a hill. The only buildings still standing are the churches, more than two dozen, in various states of collapse. It felt good to be out in the sunshine, far from discussions of literary attribution, from Boulder, from the Unabomber, from the Internet.

One church along the way was built into the hillside. Blake climbed up the hill and onto the wall while I stood inside the bare ruin, among weeds and stone rubble. He asked me to take his picture as he stood up there, looking down on me through the collapsed roof. As I focused the shot, taking a step backward, the ground suddenly gave way beneath my feet. I fell into a shallow pit, knee-deep. Blake came scrambling down to investigate as I climbed out of the hole and dusted myself off. He poked his head into the pit, and was spooked by what he saw.

"Uh, Dad? There are *bones* down there," he said.

He wasn't kidding. I had fallen through what used to be the floor of the sanctuary and landed at the head of a neatly laid out skeleton, every bone intact, dry as dust. Is there something about me, I wondered, that leads me from literary to literal skullduggery?

We repaired the tomb as well as we could with a slab of rock and some dirt, returned to our rented motorcycle at the bottom of the hill, and pushed on. Blake had a thousand questions about "the dead guy," none of which I was able to answer. I could say only that the bones were probably 150 years old or more and belonged once to a real person, someone whose stories we will never know.

That night, back in Athens, Blake and I climbed Mount Likovitos. Reaching the top, with the city of Athens stretched out below us, the Acropolis illuminated in the distance, we sat for hours under the stars, just chatting, father and son, about everything, about nothing, as the Hale-Bopp comet made its way across the sky, from the west to the northeast. I recalled for Blake a line from Nietzsche: "He who still sees the stars as 'up' does not perceive with the eye of truth."

But it was I who needed to adjust my perspective, not Blake. It is tempting, when caught up in tense dramas on a public stage, to view oneself as central to the action. For the past few years I have been confronted almost daily with appeals from media organizations seeking my help with controversial writings, or from the victims of anonymous libels, threats, or harassment, or from police detectives seeking assistance with Questioned Documents. For a time, I felt as if I had to solve every attributional riddle that came down the pike. Lately I have come to develop a more modest sense of limit. Everyone has an attributional problem of one sort or another. I cannot solve them all. I have played a role in a few dozen criminal investigations and civil suits but can count on one hand the cases in which my identification of an unknown author was the decisive factor in the decision of judge or jury. Successful prosecution is rarely possible on attributional evidence alone: it is one thing to show who wrote a critical document, and another to prove who committed the crime.

Meanwhile, I find that the constant attention, the escalated workload, have made me less attentive to the words of those individuals who most matter to me—my own family, friends, students, and colleagues, and, of course, Shakespeare. I cannot picture myself doing attributional work for the rest of my life, much less studying the language of criminals. There remains the necessary labor of showing others how to do what I do, and I still have a few cases open. After that, I may give literary forensics a rest, at least for a while. The first item on my agenda after finishing *Author Unknown* is to take a trip with my younger son and to give his every word my undivided attention.

EVER AN ANON.

Anon he comes, and throws his mantle by,
And stood stark naked on the brook's green brim . . .
—FROM A POEM DOUBTFULLY ASCRIBED TO SHAKESPEARE IN 1599

Wanda Tinasky believed that "an age is darkened when truth lies not in what is said, but in who says it." The brightest age, from this radically democratic point of view, may be one in which the "Author" and "Editor" (and even the network "Anchor") have lost their authority. If so, then the future of our culture is looking so bright that we may need to wear shades. In our age of electronic communication and no-holds-barred publication on the Internet, it is an easy labor, and one viewed by many as a constitutional right, to say anything about anybody, any time, for any reason, without having to take responsibility for the utterance. On the electronic superhighway, a social experiment in unlimited free speech, there are no cultural referees to label a text as "good" or "bad" writing, no editorial board to distinguish truth from fiction. We seem to be constructing a postmodern culture from which the "major author" has evaporated, leaving only text, and more text, billions of words, millions of authors, no matter who's speaking and almost no way of finding out who is.

In a culture that encourages anonymous communication and the right to speak without responsibility for the content of the utterance, the spoken message and, eventually, language itself are depleted. But the question of "Who said it?" needs to be asked only of a text that has some special value to its readers, or that introduces real or imagined harm. If it's a question of "Who wrote it?" and if enough people care, I sometimes get a phone call. I'm not always able to supply the answer. But there will always be perceptive readers. It was Professor Rick Abrams whose close reading returned me to "A Funeral Elegy" in 1995, persuading me that it was a text that invited a better understanding and open debate. A month after writing my "Primary Culprit," I learned it was George Stephanopoulos, not I, who first thought that *Primary Colors* sounded a lot like Joe Klein. It was Linda Patrik, a philosophy professor, who first recognized the Unabomber's thought and language to be that of her angry brother-in-law, Ted Kaczynski. Henry Livingston's children and descendants, sure that the Moore attribution was a mistake, found a champion in Mary Van Deusen.

It is never my job, not even in literary studies, to assume the responsibility of judge and jury. All evidence, including words, must be tried. There is no magic in my attributional work, no junk science, no computer wizardry. The words on the handwritten or printed page are more indelible than fingerprints, and more dependable, if carefully assessed, than eyewitness testimony. Until writers can find some other medium than their own language in which to cloak their anonymity, there will always be someone to study the anonymous, or misattributed, text and say—"Gotcha!"

PROLOGUE: On the Trail

1. Anonymous, pseud. (Joe Klein), *Primary Colors* (New York: Random House, 1996), 172; A. Nony Mouse, "The Politically Correct 12 Days of Christmas" (17 January 1995), http://www.in-machina.com/reece/humor/12-days-of-xmas.
2. Edwin Yoder, "Absurd Links in Unabomber Case," *San Diego Union-Tribune*, 15 July 1996.

CHAPTER ONE: Looking into Shakespeare

1. Mark Twain, "October 12. The Discovery," *The Tragedy of Pudd'nhead Wilson* (Hartford, Conn.: American Publishing, 1894), Conclusion.
2. George Steevens, "Introduction," *The Plays of William Shakespeare,* ed. George Steevens (London: T. Longman, 1793), 1.7.
3. Hyder E. Rollins, ed., *A New Variorum Edition of Shakespeare: The Sonnets,* vol. 2 (Philadelphia: J. B. Lippincott, 1944), 166.
4. Leslie Hotson, *Master W.H.* (New York: Knopf, 1965), 13, 16, 9.
5. "The Maker's word, one God doth sole extend / Without beginning, and shall see no end. . . . poets are Makers": Thomas Heywood, *Troia Britannica* (London, 1609, reg. 5 December 1608), 1.41–42, 2.59. For other examples, see John Stradling, *Divine Poems* (London, 1625), and

examples from George Puttenham and others in Donald W. Foster, "Mr. W.H., R.I.P.," *PMLA* (January 1987): 47.

6. F. O. Matthiessen, *American Renaissance: Art and Expression in the Age of Emerson and Whitman* (London: Oxford University Press, 1941), 392.

7. William Martyn, "Deposicons and examynacons of Wittnesses," book 60B, letter 145, Exeter City Archives, Devon Record Office, folios 110–20.

8. Martyn, folio 118.

9. Henry Burton, "Elegie. A Pilgrims Sad Observation," in Joshua Sylvester, *Lachrymae Lachrymarum,* 3d ed. (London, 1613), ed. D. Foster; William Shakespeare, *A Midsummer Night's Dream* 5.1.278–80.

10. W[illiam] S[hakespeare], *A Funeral Elegy* (London, 1612), ed. D. Foster (1989, 1996), lines 171–82.

11. William Shakespeare, attrib., "Shall I die?" MS. Rawlinson Poetry 160; printed with emendations in Stanley Wells and Gary Taylor, eds., *The New Complete Oxford Shakespeare* (Oxford: Clarendon Press, 1986), 883.

12. Herbert Mitgang, "Two U.S. Scholars [Samuel Schoenbaum and Robert Giroux] Excited by Find," *New York Times,* 24 November 1985.

13. Gary Taylor, "A New Shakespeare Poem" (n.p., December 1985).

14. Donald W. Foster, "A New 'Shakespeare' Poem," *New York Times Book Review,* 19 January 1986, 4; "Shall I Die?" *Times Literary Supplement (TLS),* 24 January 1986, 87; "Shall I Die?" *TLS,* 7 March 1986, 247: " 'Shall I Die' Post-Mortem: Defining Shakespeare," *Shakespeare Quarterly* 38.1 (1987): 58–77.

15. See Eric Sams, *Shakespeare's Lost Play: Edmund Ironside* (New York: St. Martin's, 1985). The manuscript hand, thought by Sams to be Shakespeare's, is that of a common theatrical scribe who elsewhere signs himself "W.P." (*not* William Peter); the play is probably by Robert Greene; Mark Dominik, *William Shakespeare and* The Birth of Merlin. (New York: Philosophical Library, 1985); Peter Levi, *A Private Commission: New Verses by Shakespeare* (London: Macmillan, 1988).

16. Stanley Wells and Gary Taylor, *William Shakespeare: A Textual Companion* (Oxford: Clarendon Press, 1987), 137.

17. Donald W. Foster, *Elegy by W.S.: A Study in Attribution* (Cranbury, N.J.: University of Delaware Press, 1989).

18. See Richard Abrams, "Breaching the Canon: Elegy by W.S.: The State of the Argument," *Shakespeare Newsletter (SNL)* 15.3 (Fall 1995): 51–54; Letter, *SNL* 46.2 (1996): 26; " 'Exercise in This Kind': Shakespeare and the 'Funeral Elegy' for William Peter," *Shakespeare Studies*, vol. 25 (1997): 141–70; "W[illiam] S[hakespeare]'s 'Funeral Elegy' and the Turn from the Theatrical," *Studies in English Literature* 36.2 (Spring 1996), 435–60. Repr. *Shakespearean Criticism*, vol. 41 (Detroit and London: Gale, 1998), 98–110.

19. " 'New' Shakespeare Elegy: Is It to Be or Not to Be?" *Chicago Tribune*, 30 December 1995.

20. Bill Honan, "A Sleuth Gets His Suspect: Shakespeare," *New York Times*, 14 January 1996.

21. Quentin Letts (NYC) and Russell Jenkins (London), " 'Lost' sonnet starts a war of words," London *Times*, 15 January 1996.

22. Brian Vickers, "Whose Thumbprints?" *TLS*, 8 March 1996, 16–18; Vickers, "The 'Funeral Elegy' for William Peter," *TLS*, 12 April 1996, 17; David Rennie, "Will? They Couldn't Be More Incorrect," London *Daily Telegraph*, 28 May 1996, 21.

23. Rennie (1996), 21.

24. Katherine Duncan-Jones, letter to *TLS*, 5 December 1997, 18–19; letter to *TLS*, 9 January 1998, 15.

25. Katherine Duncan-Jones, "Who Wrote 'A Funeral Elegie'?" *Shakespeare Studies*, vol. 25 (1997): 192–210; answered by Richard Abrams, "Exit Sclater," *Shakespeare Studies*, vol. 26 (1998): 302–14.

CHAPTER TWO: No, Really, He *Is* Anonymous

1. John Bunyan, *Pilgrim's Progress* (London: n.p., 1667; London: Penguin, 1987), 78.

2. *The French Connection*, dir. William Friedkin, screenplay by Robin Moore and Ernest Tidymann, Trimark, 1971.

3. Mark Miller, "Who Wrote the Book on Bill?" *Newsweek*, 26 January 1996, 29.

4. Anonymous, pseud. (Joe Klein), *Primary Colors* (New York: Random House, 1996). All quotations are from this edition. In the text archive supplied by *New York*'s editors, Joe Klein was chiefly represented by his contributions to *Newsweek*, 1993–1996.

5. Anonymous, *"No, Really, I Am Anonymous,"* *New York Times Book Review*, 19 May 1996, 43.

6. Cited words and quotations from Michael Kelly are taken from *Martyrs' Day* (New York: Random House, 1993).

7. Donald Foster, "Primary Culprit," *New York*, 26 February 1996 (released 15 February), 50–57.

8. "Wanted: Anonymous," *Washington Post*, 2 February 1996.

9. Bunyan, *Pilgrim's Progress*, 78.

10. "Exclusive: Prime Suspect," *Newsweek*, 19 February 1996, 6.

11. James Boswell, *Boswell's Life of Johnson*, ed. G. B. Hill, rev. C. F. Powell, vol. 4 (Oxford: Clarendon Press, 1934): 305–6.

12. William Shakespeare, *The Two Gentlemen of Verona* 4.4.27.

13. Anonymous, *"No, Really, I Am Anonymous,"* 43.

14. David Streitfeld, " 'Anonymous' Undone by His Own Hand?" *Washington Post*, 17 July 1996.

15. Ibid.

16. Miller, "Who Wrote the Book on Bill?" 29; "We're Sick of Hearing About . . . ," *Newsweek*, 12 February 1996, 12; "Exclusive: Prime Suspect," 6; "Perspectives," quoting Joe Klein, *Newsweek*, 26 February 1996, 21.

17. Joe Klein, "A Brush with Anonymity," *Newsweek*, 29 July 1996, 26.

18. Ibid.

CHAPTER THREE: A Professor's Whodunit

1. Theodore J. Kaczynski (TJK hereafter), "Autobiography," case doc. GX-182014C (1979), 164.

2. TJK to David Kaczynski (DK hereafter), in Spanish, case doc. T-65 (28 March 1989), trans. anon., FBI (1996).

3. TJK, "Autobiography," 60.

4. TJK, letter to DK, case doc. T-13 (25 January 1984).

5. Quin Denvir, John Balazas, Lauren J. Weil, and Judy Clarke, "Notice of Motion and Motion to Suppress Evidence," U.S. District Court for the Eastern District of California (3 March 1997), 3.

6. Terry D. Turchie, "Affidavit of Assistant Special Agent in Charge, Terry D. Turchie," and James Fitzgerald, "A Text Comparison of the 'T'

(Ted) Documents and the 'U' (Unabom) Documents," U.S. District of Montana (3 April 1996).

7. TJK, letter to DK, enclosing letter from "Hercules" to Louis de Branges, upon news that de Branges had proved Bieberbach's Conjecture, a 68-year-old problem, the most famous mathematical conundrum in geometric function theory, case doc. T-25 (4 September 1985).

8. Quin Denvir et al., eds., "Declarations and Appendices in Support of Defendant's Motion to Suppress," with Appendices (28 February–2 March 1997).

9. Robin T. Lakoff, "Declaration of Robin T. Lakoff, Ph.D." (2 March 1997), in Denvir et al., "Motion," Declaration 6, 3.

10. Denvir et al., "Motion," 62.

11. FC, letter to *New York Times,* case doc. U-7 (20 April 1995).

12. Apios Tuberosa, pseud., "How I Blew Up Harold Snilly," case doc. T-132 (1970). TJK supplies a factual account of the incident in his 1979 "Autobiography."

13. Lauren J. Weil, ed., "Critique of the FBI Analysis of the T-Documents and the U-Documents" (3 March 1997), in Denvir et al., "Motion," Appendix 1.

14. FC, "Industrial Society," case doc. U-14 (19 September 1995); TJK, letters to DK, case docs. T-80 (14 November 1994), T-24 (? June 1985), T-33 (15 March 1986), T-61 (16 November 1988).

15. Quin Denvir, Judy Clarke, et al., "Reply Memorandum" (4 May 1997), 40.

16. Denvir, Clarke, et al., "Reply Memorandum," 40–41.

17. Robin T. Lakoff, "Second Declaration of Robin T. Lakoff, Ph.D.," Denvir, Clarke, et al., "Reply Memorandum," exhibit 4, 4.

18. FC, letter to *New York Times,* case doc. U-7 (20 April 1995).

19. TJK, undated journal entry, case doc. GX-18-2014F, 3.

20. John Douglas, interview by Richard Cole, "Unabomber Will Kill Again," *Los Angeles Times,* 29 October 1995.

21. Richard Jewell was described to investigators as a police groupie, a wannabe detective in search of hero status. A former sheriff's deputy, he had unhappily resigned from the sheriff's department in August 1995 after a demotion. He next worked as a college security guard but was

asked to resign on account of alleged overzealous performance of his duties. Notably unsuccessful in a law enforcement career, Jewell had seeming grounds for resentment. He was unmarried, had no girlfriend, and lived with his mother. He had studied explosives.

22. John Douglas and Mark Olshaker, *Unabomber* (New York: Pocket Books, 1996), 18.

23. Ibid., 10–13.

24. James Brussel, *Casebook of a Crime Psychiatrist* (New York: Bernard Geis Associates, 1968).

25. Portions of the Brussel profile were released in *New York Journal American,* 4 December 1956, and *New York Times,* 4 December 1956.

26. FP, pseud., letter to *New York Journal American,* 26 December 1956, pub. 10 January 1957; publication was delayed while the New York Police Department investigated leads contained in the letter.

27. Juan Carlos Davalos (TJK, trans.), "The Fort of Tacuil," with letter to DK, case doc. T-28 (? Nov. 1985).

28. "Interview with John Douglas," American College of Forensic Examiners (7 June 1996), on-line, available at http://catalog.com/experts/acfe.html.

29. Tamara Fluehe, interview with Salt Lake City Police, 20 February 1987.

30. TJK to Stella Meister, cover letter for "The Adventures of H. Bascomb Thurgood," case doc. T-161 (n.d., ca. 1966–1967).

31. FC, letter to *New York Times,* case doc U-9 (24 June 1995).

32. TJK, "Autobiography," 179.

33. TJK, undated journal entry, case doc. GX-18-2014F, 4 (dup. journal entry, 169); case doc. GX-18-2014D, 102.

34. "Give 'Em Something to Cry About," New York *Daily News,* 26 August 1999.

35. Ted Kaczynski, "Ship of Fools," *Off!,* September 1999; on-line, available at http://www.contextbooks.com/TJK2255/TJKstory.html.

36. TJK, letter to DK, case doc. T-80 (14 November 1994).

37. Joseph Conrad, "Some Reflections on the Loss of the *Titanic,*" in *Notes on Life and Letters* (New York: Doubleday, 1921), 215, 218.

38. Edward John Smith, "Design of an Attitude Control System for a Large Space Vehicle," abstract, *Dissertation Abstracts International* (1966): 3521-B.

Ted Kaczynski's own abstract, for his 1967 University of Michigan dissertation on "Boundary Functions," appears in the 1967 *DAI*.

39. TJK, letter to DK, case doc. T-65 (28 March 1989).

40. "Foam cutter," "Fermat's Conjecture," Henri de Toulouse-Lautrec's personal cipher (which looks like "FC" in a print favored by Kaczynski), Conrad's "FP," and Ted's own dream of hooligans killing with "2 × 4s" and a "club" are among the possible textual influences on Ted's choice of "FC" as a logo. In a 1995 letter to *Penthouse* magazine, FC said that the acronym stands for "Freedom Club."

41. FC, letter to *New York Times*, case doc. U-7 (20 April 1995).

42. Elizabeth Gleick, "A Serial Bomber Strikes," *Time*, 26 December 1994, 129.

43. Kevin Goldman, "AIDS-Related Product Enters Mass Media," *Wall Street Journal*, 2 December 1994; see also Stuart Elliott, "New Managers at Three Agencies," *New York Times*, 5 December 1994.

44. "Environmentalism à la Burson-Marsteller," *Earth First! Journal*, February 1994, 9.

45. TJK, letter to DK, case doc. T-85 (19 January 1985).

46. Jacques Ellul, *The Technological Bluff*, trans. Geoffrey W. Bromiley (Grand Rapids, Mich.: Eerdmans, 1990), 54.

47. FC, case doc. U-14 (19 September 1995), par. 108, 113, 99, 66 n.13.

48. TJK quoted the same passage in a signed but unpublished letter to *Newsweek*, case doc. T-135 (? Feb. 1970); Aldous Huxley, *Brave New World Revisited* (New York: Harper, 1958), 128, 141, 144.

49. George F. Will, "Clinton Pops Up on Bush's Right," *Chicago Sun-Times*, 2 August 1992 (nationally syndicated column).

50. "Is It a Dream or Is It a Nightmare?," extracts from Jacques Ellul, *The Technological Society*, trans. John Wilkinson, *Saturday Review* 48 (6 February 1965): 58–59.

51. TJK, case doc. T-85 (19 January 1985).

52. *Saturday Review* 52 (5 April 1969): 40; *Saturday Review* 54 (29 May 1971): 19. The *Book Review Index* lists only six other periodicals to have reviewed *Chinese Political Thought*, all of them academic or library journals.

53. TJK, letter to *Saturday Review*, 28 February 1970, 33.

54. William Glaberson, "In Book, Unabomber Pleads His Case," *New York Times*, 1 March 1999.

CHAPTER FOUR: Starr-Crossed Lovers

1. William Shakespeare, *Much Ado About Nothing* 3.3.166–8, in *The Riverside Shakespeare*, eds. G. Blakemore Evans et al. (Boston: Houghton Mifflin, 1997), 366–98.

2. Peter Baker and Susan Schmidt, "FBI Taped Aide's Allegations," *Washington Post*, 22 January 1998.

3. Michael Isikoff, "A Twist in Jones v. Clinton," *Newsweek*, 11 August 1997, 30.

4. Kenneth W. Starr et al., eds., *Referral to the U.S. House of Representatives* (9 September 1998), section VIII, paragraph G, from transcript of FBI tape (13 January 1998).

5. Clifford Bernath, Second Deposition, Grand Jury (25 June 1998), 31, in Kenneth Starr et al., eds., *Supplemental Materials to the Referral to the U.S. House of Representatives*, 105th Congress, House Docs. 105–317 (9 September 1998), parts 1–3. On-line, http://icreport.access. gpo.gov/, 129.

6. Representative samples of Tripp's JCOC correspondence are included in "Tripp, Linda," Starr et al., *Supplemental Materials*, on-line, Supplement, 3859–99; handwritten notes on Lewinsky conversations, 3797–3843, 3905–60.

7. Linda Tripp, e-mail to Monica Lewinsky, Starr et al., *Supplemental Materials*, on-line, Supplement, 3845–56.

8. Linda Tripp, Deposition, Grand Jury (30 June 1998), Starr et al., *Supplemental Materials*, on-line, Supplement, 4048–49.

9. Monica Lewinsky, e-mail to Linda Tripp, Starr et al., *Supplemental Materials*, on-line, Supplement, 3845–56.

10. Starr et al., *Referral* (9 September 1998), n. 437.

11. Andrew Morton, *Monica's Story* (New York: St. Martin's Press, 1999), 65, 73–74, 148–51.

12. Quoted in Jim Dwyer, "The Unmaking of the President 1998," New York *Daily News*, 25 January 1998.

13. Psalms 91:3, 14; Morton, *Monica's Story*, 233.

14. Starr et al., *Referral* (9 September 1998), section XIII, paragraph J, from transcript of FBI tape (13 January 1998).

15. William Jefferson Clinton, Deposition, Jones v. Clinton (17 January 1998).

16. Bob Kerry, quoted in Martha Sherrill, "Grave Doubts," *Esquire,* January 1996, 91.

17. Morton, *Monica's Story,* 225.

18. Monica Lewinsky, "Handwritten Proffer" (1 February 1998), par. 1, 10–11, Starr et al., *Supplemental Materials,* part 4. Document Supplement, part B: Monica S. Lewinsky Statements, on-line, vol. 2, 709, 718.

19. In her Grand Jury testimony of August 6, 1998, Monica Lewinsky stated under oath that she typed the Talking Points text on her own computer.

20. Starr et al., *Referral* (9 September 1998), XIII.J. ("January 13–14: Lewinsky-Tripp Conversation and Talking Points"), Lewinsky ref. 8/6/98 Grand Jury, 223–37.

21. Linda R. Tripp, interview, *Today* (NBC), 12 February 1999.

22. Monica Lewinsky et al., "Points to Make in Affidavit" (a.k.a. Talking Points, 14 January 1998), Starr et al., *Supplemental Materials,* on-line, Supplement, 1241, 1242, 1243.

23. William Safire, "The Talking-Pointer," *New York Times,* 12 February 1998.

24. Morton, *Monica's Story,* 3.

25. M[onica Lewinsky], letter to "Sally" for job search (n.d., ca. Dec. 1997), Starr et al., *Supplemental Materials,* on-line, Supplement, 3968.

26. Monica Lewinsky: e-mail to Linda Tripp, 24 December 1997, Starr et al., *Supplemental Materials,* on-line, Supplement, 3858.

27. William Jefferson Clinton, Deposition, Grand Jury (17 August 1998). (Washington, D.C.: U.S. Government Federal Document Clearing House, 1998).

28. Monica Lewinsky, Deposition, Grand Jury (20 August 1998); "White House Considers Clinton's Response," CNN (23 January 1998).

29. Tripp-Lewinsky tape ([18] December 1997), partial transcription, Michael Isikoff, "Clinton and the Intern," *Newsweek,* 2 February 1998, 30.

30. William Jefferson Clinton, Deposition, Grand Jury (17 August 1998).

31. Steven G. Calabresi, "Some Normative Arguments for the Unitary Executive," *Arkansas Law Review* 48 (1995): 23–104. Calabresi observes, for example, that "*Presidents* have been *claiming* . . . *President* Nixon openly *claimed* . . . None of *President* Nixon's successors, however, *has claimed* . . . *President has claimed* . . . *President Reagan claimed*"—and he

asks, "*Is there anyone out there who really wants to disagree?*" Page 1 of the Talking Points warns Ms. Tripp that "the *President has claimed . . .*" and asks, "*Do you really want to contradict him?*"

32. Mike McCurry, White House Press Briefing, 16 September 1996, U.S. Newswire; George Stephanopoulos, quoted by Steven Heilbronner, "Clinton Soft Peddles Tax Hike," UPI, 25 January 1993. Available on-line through Lexis-Nexis.

33. Steven G. Calabresi, "Out of Order," *Journal of American Citizenship Policy Review* 79 (September–October 1996): 14.

34. Calabresi, "Some Normative Arguments," 82, 93–94.

35. Kathleen Willey, Deposition, United States v. Julie Hiatt Steele, U.S. District Court, Alexandria, Virginia (5 May 1999).

36. Leef Smith and Patricia Davis, "Willey Depicts Steele as Opportunist," *Washington Post*, 6 May 1999, A10.

37. Frank Carter had no knowledge of the Willey matter, no vested interest in it, and no writings that would put him in the bucket with other suspects.

38. Francis Carter, Deposition, Grand Jury (4 June 1998), Starr et al., *Supplemental Materials*, on-line, Supplement, 412–19.

39. Bruce R. Lindsey, Deposition, Grand Jury (18 February 1998), 131, 146. Starr et al., *Supplemental Materials*, on-line, Supplement, 2369, 2372.

40. Bruce R. Lindsey, Deposition, Grand Jury (18 February 1998), 2369.

41. *Newsweek* published a fake photo-facsimile of page 1, 27 January 1998 (issue dated February 2); on January 26 the *New York Times* scooped *Newsweek* with *Newsweek*'s own text. But the full three pages were subsequently carried by every major news organization, including the *Washington Post*.

42. Brian Blomquist, "Clinton Accuser Faced Threats," *New York Post*, 18 June 1998; "Kathleen Willey's Strange Encounter," ABC News, 17 June 1998, on-line, http://more.abcnews.go.com/sections/us/daily news/willey980617.html.

43. Linda Tripp, handwritten journal (14 January 1998), Starr et al., *Supplemental Materials*, on-line, Supplement, 3832–3.

44. Morton, *Monica's Story*, 210.

45. Kenneth W. Starr, "Civic Virtue (11 November 1996)," *Vital Speeches of the Day* 63 (1 January 1997): 169–71; see also Kenneth W.

Starr, "Christian Life in the Law," *Texas Law Review* 30 (1998); on-line, http://www.law.ttu.edu/lawrev/.

46. G. (Gershon) Legman, *The Limerick* (New York: Brandywine Press, 1970).

47. Michael Sneed, "The Starr Report," *Chicago Sun-Times,* 22 September 1998.

48. Kenneth Starr, interview with Diane Sawyer, *20/20* (ABC), 25 November 1998.

49. Harper Lee, *To Kill a Mockingbird* (New York: J. B. Lippincott, 1960), 247.

CHAPTER FIVE: Wanda, the Fort Bragg Bag Lady

1. Andrew Gordon, "Smoking Dope with Thomas Pynchon: A Sixties Memoir," in *The Vineland Papers: Critical Takes on Pynchon's Novel,* eds. Geoffrey Green, Donald J. Greiner, and Larry McCaffery (Normal, Ill: Dalkey Archive Press, 1994), 167–78.

2. Nancy Jo Sales, "Meet Your Neighbor, Thomas Pynchon," *New York,* 11 November 1996, 60–64 (photograph by Steve Macaulay).

3. James Bone, "Mystery Writer" London *Sunday Times Magazine,* 14 June 1997, 27–28.

4. Thomas Pynchon, *Mason & Dixon* (New York: Henry Holt, 1997), 9.

5. Wanda Tinasky, letter to *Anderson Valley News* (*AVA* hereafter), 12 June 1985.

6. ———, letter to *Mendocino Commentary,* 29 March 1984.

7. ———, letter to *Mendocino Commentary,* 26 April 1984.

8. ———, letter to *AVA,* 16 May 1984.

9. ———, letters to *AVA,* 9 January 1985, 13 March 1985.

10. ———, letter to *AVA,* 3 September 1984.

11. TR Factor, ed., *The Letters of Wanda Tinasky* (Portland, Ore.: Vers Libre Press, 1996), 10.

12. Wanda Tinasky, letter to *Mendocino Conmmentary,* 21 April 1983.

13. ———, letter to *New Settler Interview* (Summer 1986).

14. ———, letter to *AVA,* 28 May 1986. The Pynchon attribution was first suggested by Gaye Lebaron of the *Press Democrat,* letter to *AVA,* 24 January 1990.

15. Thomas Pynchon, "Proverbs for Paranoids," *Gravity's Rainbow* (New York: Viking, 1973), 251.

16. Scott McLemee, "Invisible, Inc.," *Lingua Franca* (September–October 1995), 39–74.

17. Wanda Tinasky, letter to *New Settler Interview*, January 1987.

18. ———, letter to *AVA*, 9 October 1985.

19. Thomas Pynchon, *The Crying of Lot 49* (orig. pub. 1966; New York: Harper, paperback, 1986), 94.

20. Charles Hollander, "Where's Wanda? The Case of Thomas Pynchon and the Bag Lady," *AVA*, 13 March 1996.

21. Pynchon, "Proverbs for Paranoids," *Gravity's Rainbow*, 237.

22. Melanie Jackson, letter to Fred Gardner, 14 June 1995.

23. TR Factor, "Earth to Bosk! Reality Check," *AVA* (photocopy, n.d., 1996?).

24. Ron Rosenbaum, "The Edgy Enthusiast: *The Letters of Wanda Tinasky*," *New York Observer*, 28 April 1997.

25. Pynchon, *Mason & Dixon*, 12.

26. Pynchon, *The Crying of Lot 49*, 180.

27. Tiger Tim Hawkins, pseud. (Thomas D. Hawkins), *Eve, The Common Muse of Henry Miller & Lawrence Durrell* (San Francisco: Ahab Press, 1963), 8.

28. Beaumont, Texas, *Sunday Enterprise*, 24 April 1955.

29. Thomas Hawkins, letter to jack green, 14 December 1962 (Fort Bragg, Calif.: Tenaya Middleton collection).

30. Wanda Tinasky, letter to *AVA*, 21 August 1985; letter to Beth Bosk, editor of *New Settler Interview*, summer 1986.

31. Pat McKay, "Husband Sought in Wife's Death," *Press Democrat*, 24 September 1988.

32. Gordon Leon Black, *Mendocino Commentary* (n.d., October 1986); repr. *Letters of Wanda Tinasky*, 73.

33. Black, ibid.

34. Pynchon, "Proverbs for Paranoids," *Gravity's Rainbow*, 262.

35. Karin Faulkner, "I Remember Wanda," *Letters of Wanda Tinasky*, 214–15.

36. Tiger Tim Hawkins, ed., *Freak's Literary Tertiary* 2.1 (1964).

37. Wanda Tinasky, letters to *AVA*, 16 May 1984, 18 September 1985; Gardner interview quoted in *Letters of Wanda Tinasky*, 23.

38. Wanda Tinasky, letter to *AVA,* 15 October 1986.

39. Lawrence Ferlinghetti, letter to Thomas D. "Tim" Hawkins, 17 December 1963 (Tenaya Middleton collection).

40. E.N. Tranas, pseud., letter to *AVA,* 2 January 1985; C.O. Jones, pseud., letter to *AVA,* 9 January 1985.

41. TR Factor, "From the Author: A NEW CONTROVERSY!" (review of TR Factor, ed., *The Letters of Wanda Tinasky*), on-line, http://www.amazon.com/exec/obidos/ts/book-reviews.

42. Hawkins, *Eve,* 25.

43. Steven Moore, Foreword, *The Letters of Wanda Tinasky* (1996), ix–xi.

CHAPTER SIX: Yes, Virginia, There *Was* a Santa Claus

1. Ogden Nash, "The Boy Who Laughed at Santa Claus" (Boston: Little, Brown, 1942).

2. Anon., *False Stories Corrected* (New York: S. Wood, 1813; repr. 1814)

3. Ibid.

4. Barnabe Googe, *The Popish Kingdom,* part 4 (London: 1570), lines 825–32 (ed. D. Foster).

5. Dr. Seuss, *How the Grinch Stole Christmas* (New York: Random House, 1957).

6. Joshua Sharp, *Citizens and Farmers Almanack for 1825* (Brunswick, N.Y.: Griggs, 1824), 25–26; David McClure, *United States Almanac for 1825* (Philadelphia: R. Desilver, 1824), 40; Sam Atkinson, ed., *Atkinson's Casket* (Philadelphia: n.p., 1826), n.p.

7. Henry Livingston, "Letter to my Brother Beekman; who then lived with Mr. Schenck at New Lebanon—1786," Henry Livingston, MS Poetry Book (1786–1791), 36, lines 1–10, ed. D. Foster, from transcript by W. Stephen Thomas (Arlington, Mass.: Thomas Collection).

8. Benson J. Lossing, correspondence, November–December 1886, Dutchess County Historical Society; Cornelia G. Goodrich, "Sketches of a Few Gentlemen of Ye Old Colonial Days," talk presented to Dutchess County Historical Society, typescript MS 316 (1921): 1–12; Henry Litchfield West, "Who Wrote ' 'Twas the Night Before Christmas'?," *The Bookman,* December 1920, Helen Wilkinson Reynolds, "Editorial Notes on the Writings of Henry Livingston," *Dutchess County Historical*

Society Yearbook 27 (1942): 85–104; Henry Noble MacCracken, "Humorists at Home," Blithe Dutchess (New York: Hastings House, 1958), 370–90.

9. Henry "Harry" Livingston, letter to Sarah "Sally" Welles, 30 December 1773 (Thomas collection).

10. Henry Livingston, "To Col. James Clinton, Little Britain," 19 August 1775, Poughkeepsie, N.Y.: Adriance Library. Printed in Kevin T. Gallagher, ed., "Livingston Family Correspondence," Dutchess County Historical Society Yearbook 65 (1980): 74.

11. Henry Livingston Jr., "Journal of Major Henry Livingston, of the Third New York Continental Line, August to December, 1775," ed. Gaillard Hunt, Pennsylvania Magazine 22 (1898): 22–24.

12. Livingston, "Letter to my Brother Beekman," lines 17–22.

13. Eliza Livingston Thomas, letter to Mrs. Annie Thomas, 1879 (Thomas collection). Not seen. Printed in MacCracken, Blithe Dutchess, 386.

14. Jeannie Livingston Denig, letter to William S. Thomas, 23 December 1918, from transcript in Thomas collection; printed also in MacCracken, Blithe Dutchess, 387–388.

15. The pertinent correspondence is summarized in Winthrop P. Tryon, " 'Twas the Night Before Christmas," Christian Science Monitor, 4 August 1920; MacCracken, Blithe Dutchess, 302–3; West, "Who Wrote," 370–90; and W. Stephen Thomas, "Does 'The Night Before Christmas' Belong to Dutchess County?" lecture delivered to Dutchess County Historical Society, 10 November 1977, typed transcript in Thomas collection.

16. Jane ("Jennie") Livingston Hubbard, letter to William S. Thomas (Thomas collection). Not seen. Quoted in Tryon, " 'Twas the Night," and Samuel White Patterson, The Poet of Christmas Eve: A Life of Clement Clarke Moore, 1779–1863 (New York: Morehouse-Gorham, 1956), 167.

17. Mrs. Edward Livingston Montgomery to William S. Thomas (Thomas collection). Not seen. Printed in West, Blithe Dutchess, 302–3.

18. Goodrich, "Sketches," 8–9; Goodrich paraphrases an original letter of 26 February 1917, headed 2015 East 40th Street, Cleveland (Thomas collection). Second sheet with signature is missing, but address and writing are those of Gertrude F. Thomas, granddaughter to Henry and Jane Livingston by their daughter Jane, and sister to William S. Thomas.

19. Benson J. Lossing, letter to Cornelia Goodrich, 25 November 1886, Dutchess County Historical Society MS 307.

20. Anon., "Sante Claus," *Poughkeepsie Journal*, 3 January 1821, lines 1–2, 4–10, 13–20; reprinted from *The Northern Whig*, 3 October 1820.

21. Orville Holley, ed., "A Visit from St. Nicholas," *Troy Sentinel*, 1 January 1829; quoted by Arthur Nicholas Hosking, *The Night Before Christmas: The True Story of "A Visit from St. Nicholas," with a Life of the Author, Clement Clarke Moore* (New York: Rudge, 1934), 26.

22. John Pintard, *Letters from John Pintard to His Daughter*, ed. Eliza Noel Pintard Davidson, vol. 4 (New York: New-York Historical Society, 1941), 106.

23. George Templeton Strong, *The Diary of George Templeton Strong*, ed. Allan Nevins and Milton H. Thomas, 4 vols. (New York: Macmillan, 1952), vol. 2, 240.

24. Strong, *Diary*, vol. 1, 140.

25. John Pintard, "Private Notebook," quoted by Charles W. Jones, "Knickerbocker Santa Claus," 357–83, *New-York Historical Society Quarterly* 38 (October 1954): 378.

26. Clement C. Moore, "A Trip to Saratoga," 4 parts, in *Poems* (New York: Bartlett & Welford, 1844), 15–65, part 2, lines 103–6.

27. ———, "To a Lady," *Poems*, 118–24, lines 13–15.

28. ———, "To the Fashionable Part of My Young Countrywomen," *Poems*, 69–73.

29. ———, "Lines Addressed to a Lady, as an Apology for Not Accepting Her Invitation to a Ball.—Written Many Years Ago," *Poems*, 105–8, lines 33–34, 43–48.

30. ———, letter to his mother, Charity Clarke Moore, 16 October 1813, New-York Historical Society (MSS Misc. Moore).

31. William Bard, "Answer to the Preceding," in Moore, *Poems*, 109–10, lines 1–2, 11, 20.

32. Philip Hone, "Answer to the Preceding," in Moore, *Poems*, 137–38, line 1.

33. Moore, *Poems*, 109–10, 137; Strong, *Diary*, vol. 2, 83.

34. Harry Livingston Jr., "Journal," 22.

35. "To the Editor of the European Magazine," by R, pseud. (Henry Livingston Jr.), *American Magazine* 5 (May 1788): 391–94.

36. "Astronomical Intelligence," by R, pseud. (Henry Livingston Jr.), *Poughkeepsie Journal,* 15 September 1789.

37. Henry Livingston, "To a gentleman on his leaving Pakepsy," Livingston MS Poetry Book (1786–1791), 32–33, lines 31–32, ed. D. Foster from transcript in Thomas collection.

38. Moore, "A Trip to Saratoga," *Poems,* 4:85–86; Moore, "Lines Addressed to the Young Ladies," *Poems,* 83–87, line 56.

39. Tobias George Smollett, *Roderick Random,* vol. 2 (1748), chap. 41; Literature Online, 1996.

40. Henry Livingston, "A Song," *Poughkeepsie Journal,* 15 January 1799; Clement Moore, "The Wine Drinker," *Poems,* 174–82, lines 69–72.

41. Proverbs 23:13–14.

42. Strong, *Diary,* vol. 1, 326.

43. "Original Documents from the Archives of the Society: The Autograph Copy of the 'Visit from St. Nicholas,'" *New-York Historical Society Quarterly Bulletin* 2 (January 1919): 111–15.

44. Elizabeth E. Kent, *A Century and a Half of Parish History, 1804–1854* (Troy, N.Y.: St. Paul's Episcopal Church, 1955), 17.

45. Casimir deR. Moore, letter to Henry Litchfield West, 28 December 1920, New-York Historical Society (MSS Misc. Moore). Quoted in MacCracken, *Blithe Dutchess,* 302.

46. Pintard, *Letters,* 126.

47. Neil H. Sonne, "'The Night Before Christmas': Who Wrote It?," *Historical Magazine of the Protestant Episcopal Church* (1971): 376–77.

48. T. W. C. Moore, letter to George H. Moore, 15 March 1862, New-York Historical Society (MSS Misc. Moore). Printed in *New-York Historical Society Quarterly Bulletin* 2 (4 January 1919): 111–15.

49. "Original Documents," *New-York Historical Society Quarterly Bulletin* (4 January 1919): 111.

50. Clement Clarke Moore, *A Lecture Introductory to the Course of Hebrew Instruction in the General Theological Seminary of the Protestant Episcopal Church . . . 14 November 1825* (New York: Swords, 1825), 6–7.

51. "L," pseud., "Letter from a Friend," in John Duer, *New Translation . . . of Juvenal (Miscellaneous Poems original and translated)* (New York: Sargeant, 1806), part 2, "Original Poems," xxi–xxiii.

52. Henry Livingston, "Translation of a letter from a tenant of Mrs. Van

Kleeck to that lady, dated January 9, 1787," Livingston MS poetry book, 50; ed. D. Foster from transcript in Thomas collection.

53. In his manuscript music book, compiled 1776–1784, Livingston has copied out the full text of Ramsay's "Oh Sawney" and "Lochabor": Henry Livingston, ed., Livingston MS Music book (1776–1784), 70, 94, 116 (Thomas collection).

54. Matthew Gregory Lewis, "The Wolf-King," *Tales of Terror* (London: n.p., 1801). Lewis's poem is derived from Charles Perrault's *Tales of Times Past*, first translated into English in 1739.

55. "Welcome to Literature Online," Literature Online (Lion). Online, http: //lion.chadwyck.com/home/. Lion reproduces the text of Moore's *Poems* (1844). Lion's second instance of "Happy Christmas" appears just four years later, in Richard Cobbold's "Christmas Day," and the third, in 1832, in a poem by Edward B. Lytton.

56. "A Visit from St. Nicholas," ed. C. F. Hoffman, *New York Mirror*, 6 January 1841 ("night before New-Year," line 1; "Happy New-Year to all," line 56).

57. The first instance of "Merry Christmas," line 56, appears in the *Rural Repository*, 1 January 1836, 126, where the poem is given the title "Christmas Times."

58. Moore, "The Pig and the Rooster," *Poems*, 165–69, lines 2, 10, 46.

59. Anon., *A New-Year's Present to the Little Ones from Five to Twelve (The Children's Friend; [no. 3])* (New York: William Gilley, 1821).

60. Charles W. Jones, "Knickerbocker Santa Claus," *New-York Historical Society Quarterly* (October 1954): 378.

61. Henry Livingston, "Of the Enormous Bones Found in America," *Poughkeepsie Journal*, 6 November 1790.

62. Paul Henri Mallet, *Northern Antiquities*, vol. 2 (London: 1770), 124. Livingston in various original and edited writings for the *Poughkeepsie Journal* and *New York Magazine and Literary Repository* references Erich Pontoppidan, *Natural History of Norway* (London: H. Linde, 1755); the Moravian Church, *Periodical accounts of the work of the Moravian missions* (London: Trust Society for the Furtherance of the Gospel, 1790); and a dictionary of mythology, not positively identified (several possibilities), referenced in his verse riddles ("rebuses"); possibly also Andrew Swinton, *Travels into Norway, Denmark, and Russia, in the years 1788 [–] 1791* (New York: Robinson, 1792).

63. Variants include "Donder and Blixim" (Miles Andrews, 1781), "Donder and Blixten" (John Collins, 1804), "Dunder and Blixum" (James Kirke, 1819).

64. Anon., "A Visit from St. Nicholas," *Troy Sentinel,* January 1829; Norman Tuttle, publisher of the *Sentinel,* issued several reprints as a single-sheet illustrated broadside, n.d., ca. 1829–1830.

65. Henry Livingston, "The Dance" (1787), Livingston MS Poetry book (1786–1791), 29–30, ed. D. Foster from transcript in Thomas collection. Printed in Helen Wilkinson, *Dutchess County Doorways* (New York: William Farquhar, 1931), 203.

66. Henry Livingston, letter of condolence to John P. Livingston of Boston, 12 October 1784 (New York Public Library MS; transcription, Thomas collection); Henry Livingston, letter to Dr. Charles Livingston, 25 August 1926 (transcription, Thomas collection).

67. Charles Fenno Hoffman., ed., *New York Poetry* (New York: G. Dearborn, 1837), with preface dated "Dec. 24, 1836"; reprinted in Hoffman, *New York Mirror,* 23 December 1837.

68. C. C. Moore, attrib., "Night Before Christmas–1823 Troy Sentinel," in *The Rover,* ed. Seba Smith (December 1843): 209.

69. Pattterson, *The Poet of Christmas Eve,* 150.

70. Moore, *Lecture,* 6–7.

71. Anon., "Old Santeclaus," *A New-Year's Present to the Little Ones from Five to Twelve.*

72. Moore's biographers (and Charles Jones, in "Knickerbocker Santa Claus") have demonstrated that Moore had dealings with the bookseller William Gilley, who was also publisher for the Protestant Episcopal Church of New York and a sometime neighbor to the Moore family. Gilley's list included, besides the Book of Common Prayer and the Episcopal psalter, Moore's favorite novelist, Sir Walter Scott, including *Guy Mannering,* plus works by all three of Moore's favorite poets: William Cowper, James Montgomery, and Robert Southey. Gilley also published the *State Triumvirate,* a political satire by Moore's colleague Gulian Verplanck, who in 1821 became one of four faculty members at the General Theological Seminary. Verplanck was also the uncle of Charles Fenno Hoffman, who a quarter-century later would attribute "The Night Before Christmas" to Clement Clarke Moore.

73. Casimir deR. Moore, letter to William S. Thomas, 13 December 1920, New-York Historical Society (MSS Misc. Thomas).

74. "Original Documents," *New-York Historical Society Quarterly Bulletin* (4 January 1919): 115.

75. Ibid., 114.

76. Norman Tuttle to Clement Clarke Moore, 26 February 1844 (from transcript made by Casimir deR. Moore, enclosed with letter to Henry Litchfield West, 28 December 1920), New-York Historical Society (MSS Misc. Moore).

77. Moore, *Poems,* v–vii.

78. Moore, "To My Dear Children," *Poems,* vii.

79. "L," pseud., "Letter from a Friend," vii–xxvi; "Lines Addressed to the Fashionable Part of My Young Countrywomen," 106–10; "Lines Addressed to the Young Ladies Who Attended Mr. Chilton's Lectures," 111–15; "Lines on Cowper The Poet," 116–18; "Verses Addressed to a Lady," 122–27; "Lines to Petrosa," 128–30; "Translation of . . . Aeschylus," 139–41, in Duer, *New Translation . . . of Juvenal.* Moore's pseudonyms elsewhere include "Hermes," "Florio," "A Lady of Fashion" (in 1805), "Columella," "Simplicius" (1806), "Philalethes" (1807), "A Citizen of New York" (1813), "A Landholder" (1818).

80. "L," pseud., "*Poems* of C. C. Moore, LL.D.," review dated "NY, Aug 26, 1844," *The Churchman,* 31 August 1844, 102.

81. Robert L. Livingston, *An Essay on Sheep . . . An Account of the Merinos of Spain* (with appended extracts from Tessier) (New York: Collins and Perkins, 1809; augmented, 1810, 1811).

82. Alexandre Henri Tessier, *A Complete Treatise on Merinos and Other Sheep*, Francis Durand, trans. (New York: Economical School Office, 1811) (from Alexandre Henri Tessier, *Instruction sur les bêtes à laine* [Paris: n.p., 1810]).

83. "New Year's Carrier's Address," *Poughkeepsie Journal* (1819), Adriance Memorial Library (Poughkeepsie) Special Collections, with ms. attrib. to Henry Livingston; Amy Pearce Ver Nooy, ed., "The Carrier's Address: A New Year's Greeting," *Dutchess County Historical Society Yearbook* 29 (1944): 44–50.

84. Henry Livingston, "Scots Wha Hae Wie Wallace Bled" (n.d. [1826/7]) (Thomas collection).

85. ———, "God is Love (for my beloved daughter Jane)" (n.d. [1826/7]) (Thomas collection).

86. Henry Livingston and Susan Livingston, letter to Charles and Eliza Livingston, 21 December 1827 (Thomas collection).

87. Henry Livingston, Obituary, *Poughkeepsie Journal,* 5 March 1828.

EPILOGUE: After Words

1. John Keats, "Two Sonnets on Fame," *Poetical Works* (1906); Albert Jay Nock, *Our Enemy, the State* (Caldwell, Idaho: Caxton, 1935); Theodore J. Kaczynski, letter to *Saturday Review,* case doc. T-137 (1971); FC, pseud., "Industrial Society and Its Future," case doc. U-14 (1996), par. 185.

A C K N O W L E D G M E N T S

With hearty and sincere thanks:

To Professors Jack Haeger and Scott Hymas, who first pointed me in this direction and gave me a shove. To the literature faculty at UC Santa Barbara who nursed me through graduate school, most especially to Garrett Stewart, who taught me style, and has it. To Michael Best, Stephen Booth, Richard Helgerson, Arthur Kinney, Ian Lancashire, Steven Urkowitz, and the many others in professional literary studies whose originality, intelligence, and courage have kept my ideals intact. And to the faculty and administrators of Vassar College for their collegiality and unflagging generosity.

To Kurt Andersen and Larry Doyle, for making me sharpen my points. To my mentor, Peter Tauber, who got me started in more ways than one, and Richard Abrams, a friend and scholar whose criticism and editorial advice were invaluable, especially during that last crucial week when I didn't think I would make deadline.

To the servants of justice—officers and agents, defenders and prosecutors, FBI and ATF agents—whom I have come to know during the past four years. To Stephen Freccero, Jim Fitzgerald, and Michael Kane, for teaching me the ropes. And with a special regard for Steve Thomas, one of the finest men I've known in any walk of life.

To the friends I've made in the media, especially Phil Weiss, Susan Grobman, and Shelley Ross, for their tips and support.

To the countless librarians and archivists who have helped me each step of the way, not only with documentation for the stories that made it into this book but for the stories that didn't; and to the librarians of Vassar College most of all. To the many folks across North America and the United Kingdom who have assisted me with correspondence, family records, literary manuscripts, or technical assistance; especially to Tenaya Middleton and Ed Sander of Fort Bragg for their hospitality and shared documents, and to Bruce Anderson for more; to Stephen Livingston Thomas, for original manuscripts and artwork by Henry Livingston Jr. Most especially to Mary Van Deusen, for her invaluable and inexhaustible assistance with the Santa Claus chapter.

To John Sterling and Liz Stein at Henry Holt, for their generosity and advice, and for giving me the extra time I needed to finish. To Chris Calhoun, my friend and literary representative, who cannot be thanked enough.

For love and support during four turbulent years: my parents and my three brothers. Kate and Marty, friends for life. Above all, my wife, Gwen, who's also my best, most critical reader, and my two boys, Blake and Eric, of whom I am more proud than of anything I could ever hope to write.

INDEX

Don Foster was born in Chicago in 1950. Since 1986 he has taught at Vassar College, where he is a professor of English literature on the Jean Webster Chair. He has assisted with dozens of criminal investigations and civil suits involving anonymous or pseudonymous writings, including Unabom, the "Army of God" bombings, and the JonBenét Ramsey homicide investigation. He lives in Poughkeepsie, New York, with his wife and two sons.

Edward R. Hamilton
Bookseller
Falls Village, CT
Mon 10 Mar 2003
$3.95 + .50 pstg & hndlg